W9-BFM-280

SUPERB ™

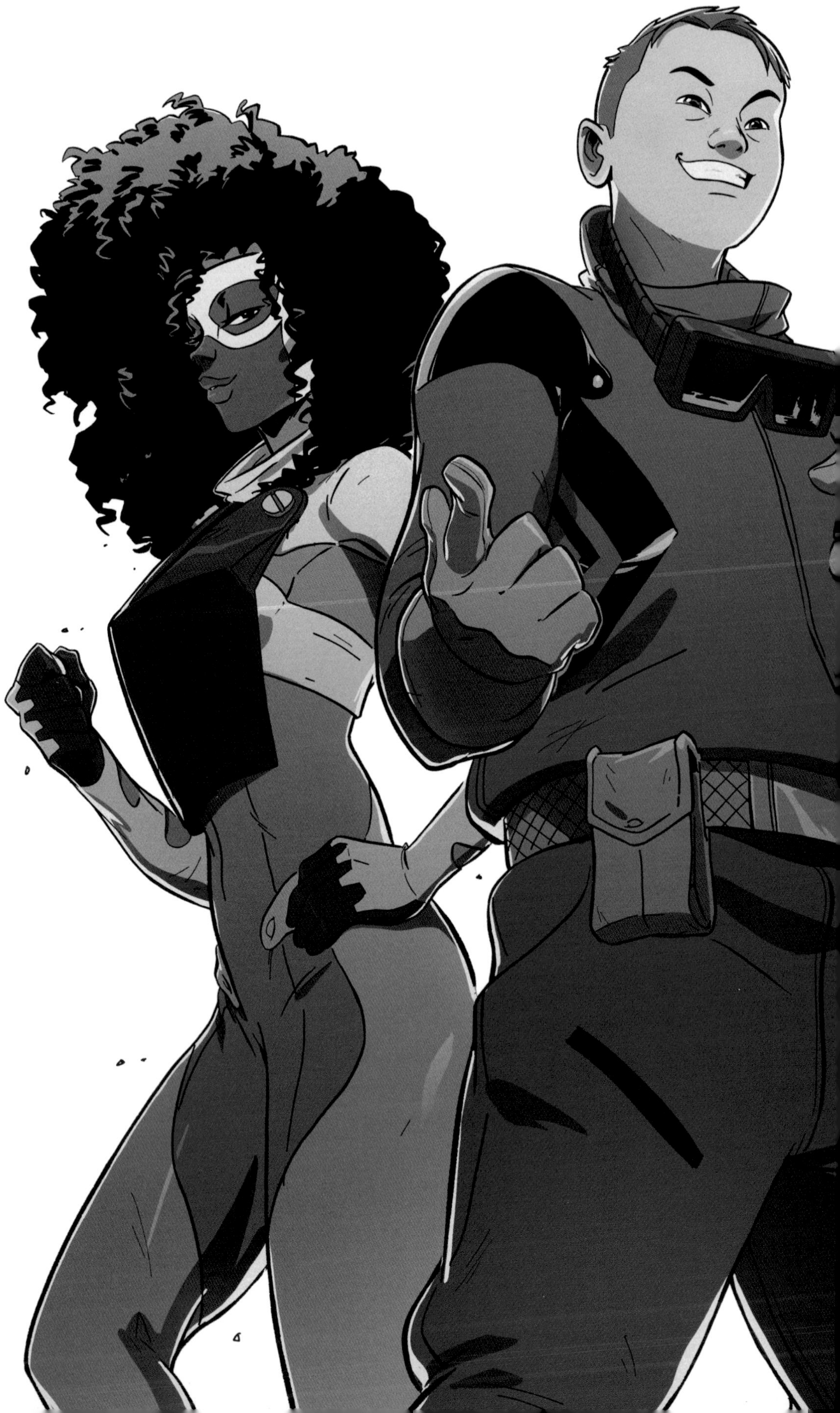

CATALYST PRIME

SUPERB™

GENERATION WARS

Written by **SHEENA C. HOWARD** and **DAVID F. WALKER**
Penciled by **ALITHA MARTINEZ** and **RAY-ANTHONY HEIGHT**
Inked by **LEBEAU L. UNDERWOOD, ALITHA MARTINEZ,** and **RAY-ANTHONY HEIGHT**
Lettered by **AW'S TOM NAPOLITANO**
Colored by **VERONICA GANDINI** and **SOTOCOLOR**

JOSEPH ILLIDGE • Senior Editor
DESIREE RODRIGUEZ • Editorial Assistant

Cover by **RAY-ANTHONY HEIGHT, LEBEAU L. UNDERWOOD,** and **VERONICA GANDINI**

LION FORGE

ISBN: 978-1-941302-85-9

Library of Congress Control Number: 2018937459

10 9 8 7 6 5 4 3 2 1

CHAPTER ONE

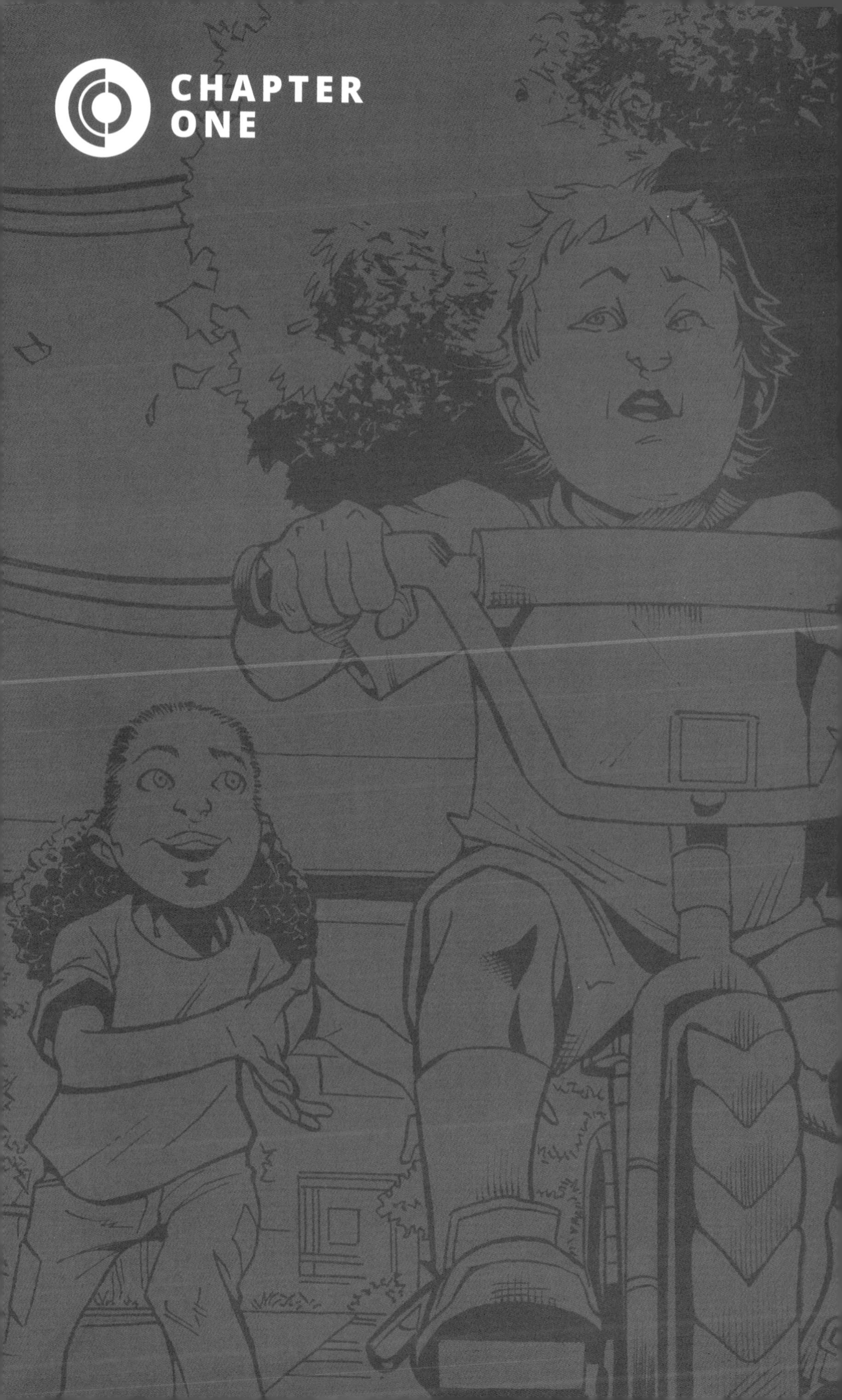

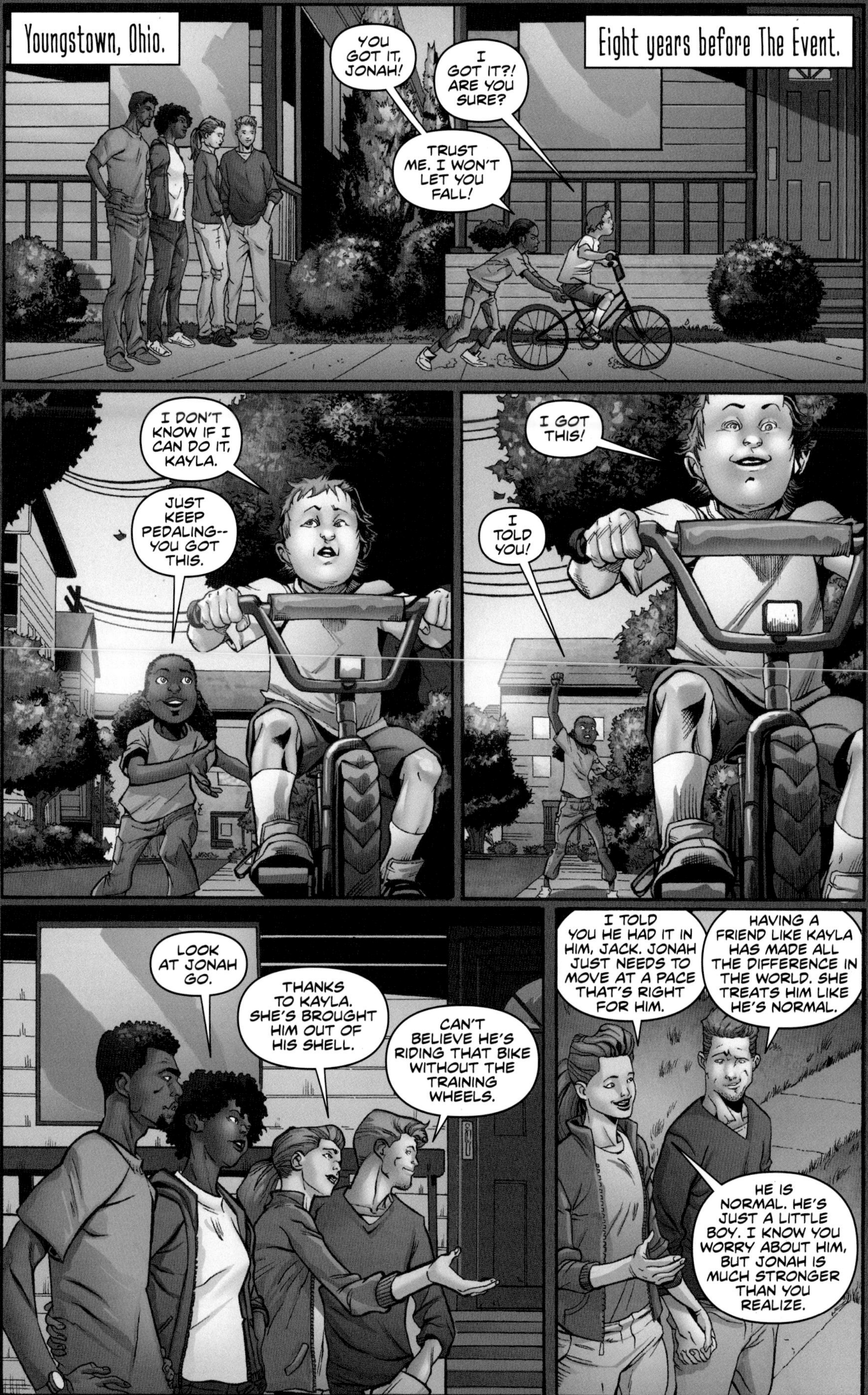
Youngstown, Ohio.
Eight years before The Event.
YOU GOT IT, JONAH!
I GOT IT?! ARE YOU SURE?
TRUST ME. I WON'T LET YOU FALL!
I DON'T KNOW IF I CAN DO IT, KAYLA.
JUST KEEP PEDALING-- YOU GOT THIS.
I GOT THIS!
I TOLD YOU!
LOOK AT JONAH GO.
THANKS TO KAYLA. SHE'S BROUGHT HIM OUT OF HIS SHELL.
CAN'T BELIEVE HE'S RIDING THAT BIKE WITHOUT THE TRAINING WHEELS.
I TOLD YOU HE HAD IT IN HIM, JACK. JONAH JUST NEEDS TO MOVE AT A PACE THAT'S RIGHT FOR HIM.
HAVING A FRIEND LIKE KAYLA HAS MADE ALL THE DIFFERENCE IN THE WORLD. SHE TREATS HIM LIKE HE'S NORMAL.
HE IS NORMAL. HE'S JUST A LITTLE BOY. I KNOW YOU WORRY ABOUT HIM, BUT JONAH IS MUCH STRONGER THAN YOU REALIZE.

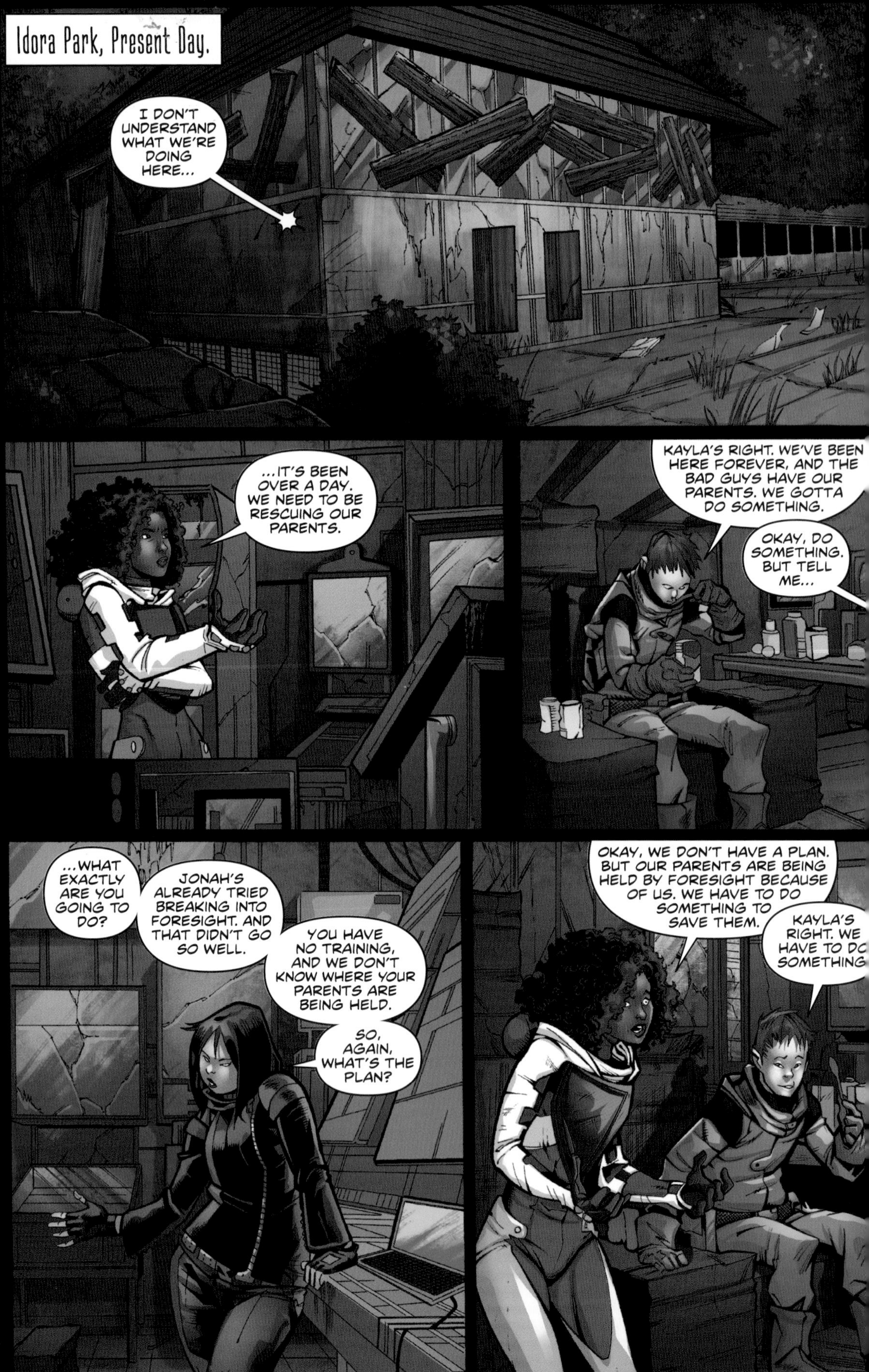
Idora Park, Present Day.
I DON'T UNDERSTAND WHAT WE'RE DOING HERE...
...IT'S BEEN OVER A DAY. WE NEED TO BE RESCUING OUR PARENTS.
KAYLA'S RIGHT. WE'VE BEEN HERE FOREVER, AND THE BAD GUYS HAVE OUR PARENTS. WE GOTTA DO SOMETHING.
OKAY, DO SOMETHING. BUT TELL ME...
...WHAT EXACTLY ARE YOU GOING TO DO?
JONAH'S ALREADY TRIED BREAKING INTO FORESIGHT. AND THAT DIDN'T GO SO WELL.
YOU HAVE NO TRAINING, AND WE DON'T KNOW WHERE YOUR PARENTS ARE BEING HELD.
SO, AGAIN, WHAT'S THE PLAN?
OKAY, WE DON'T HAVE A PLAN. BUT OUR PARENTS ARE BEING HELD BY FORESIGHT BECAUSE OF US. WE HAVE TO DO SOMETHING TO SAVE THEM.
KAYLA'S RIGHT. WE HAVE TO DO SOMETHING

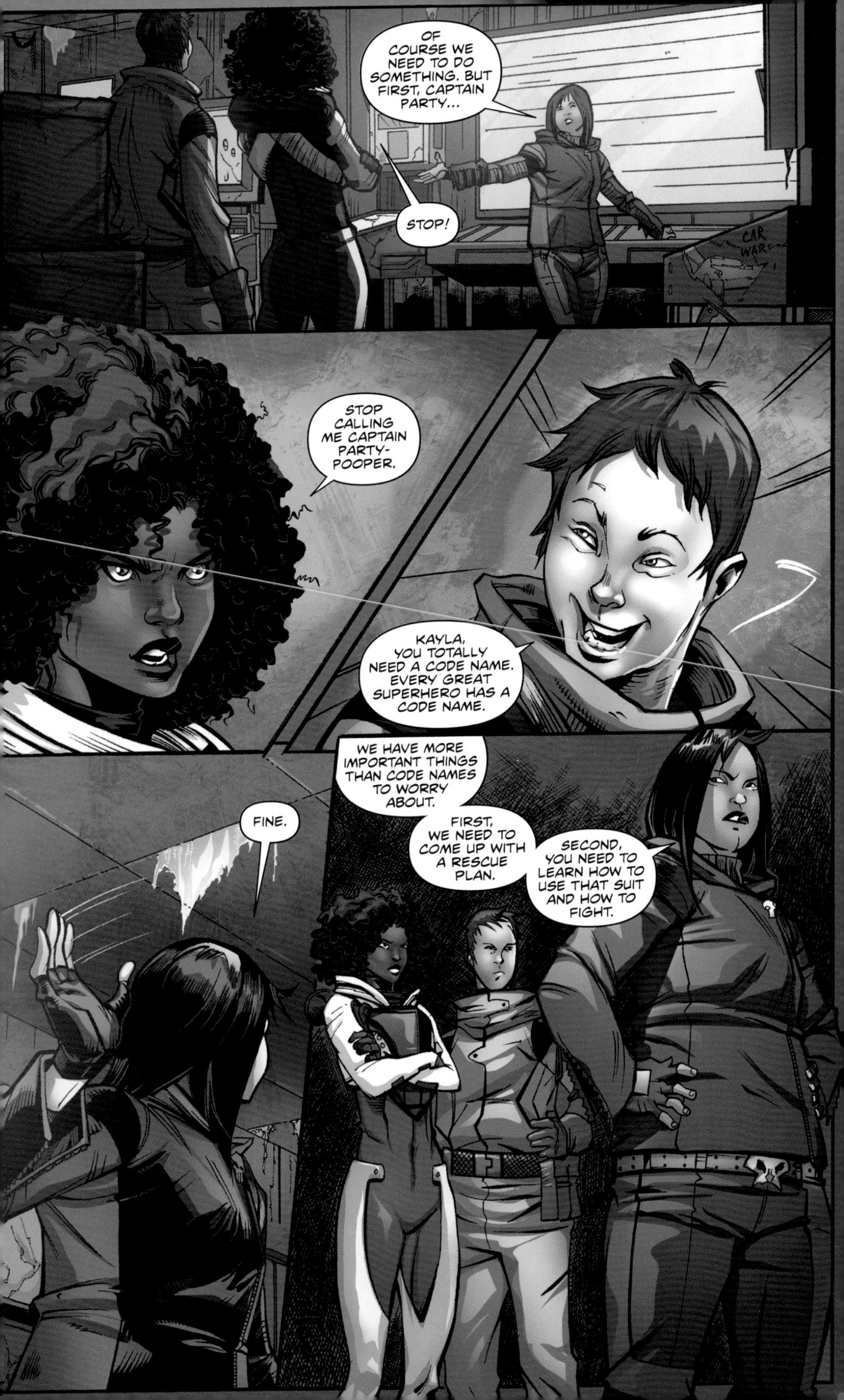
OF COURSE WE NEED TO DO SOMETHING. BUT FIRST, CAPTAIN PARTY...
STOP!
STOP CALLING ME CAPTAIN PARTY-POOPER.
KAYLA, YOU TOTALLY NEED A CODE NAME. EVERY GREAT SUPERHERO HAS A CODE NAME.
WE HAVE MORE IMPORTANT THINGS THAN CODE NAMES TO WORRY ABOUT.
FINE.
FIRST, WE NEED TO COME UP WITH A RESCUE PLAN.
SECOND, YOU NEED TO LEARN HOW TO USE THAT SUIT AND HOW TO FIGHT.

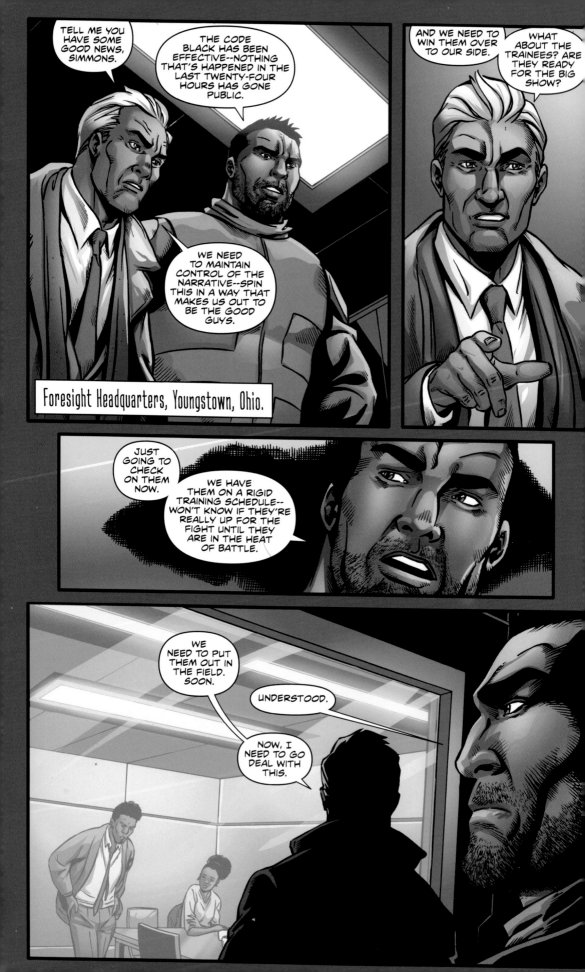

TELL ME YOU HAVE SOME GOOD NEWS, SIMMONS.

THE CODE BLACK HAS BEEN EFFECTIVE--NOTHING THAT'S HAPPENED IN THE LAST TWENTY-FOUR HOURS HAS GONE PUBLIC.

WE NEED TO MAINTAIN CONTROL OF THE NARRATIVE--SPIN THIS IN A WAY THAT MAKES US OUT TO BE THE GOOD GUYS.

AND WE NEED TO WIN THEM OVER TO OUR SIDE.

WHAT ABOUT THE TRAINEES? ARE THEY READY FOR THE BIG SHOW?

Foresight Headquarters, Youngstown, Ohio.

JUST GOING TO CHECK ON THEM NOW.

WE HAVE THEM ON A RIGID TRAINING SCHEDULE-- WON'T KNOW IF THEY'RE REALLY UP FOR THE FIGHT UNTIL THEY ARE IN THE HEAT OF BATTLE.

WE NEED TO PUT THEM IN THE FIELD. SOON.

UNDERSTOOD.

NOW, I NEED TO GO DEAL WITH THIS.

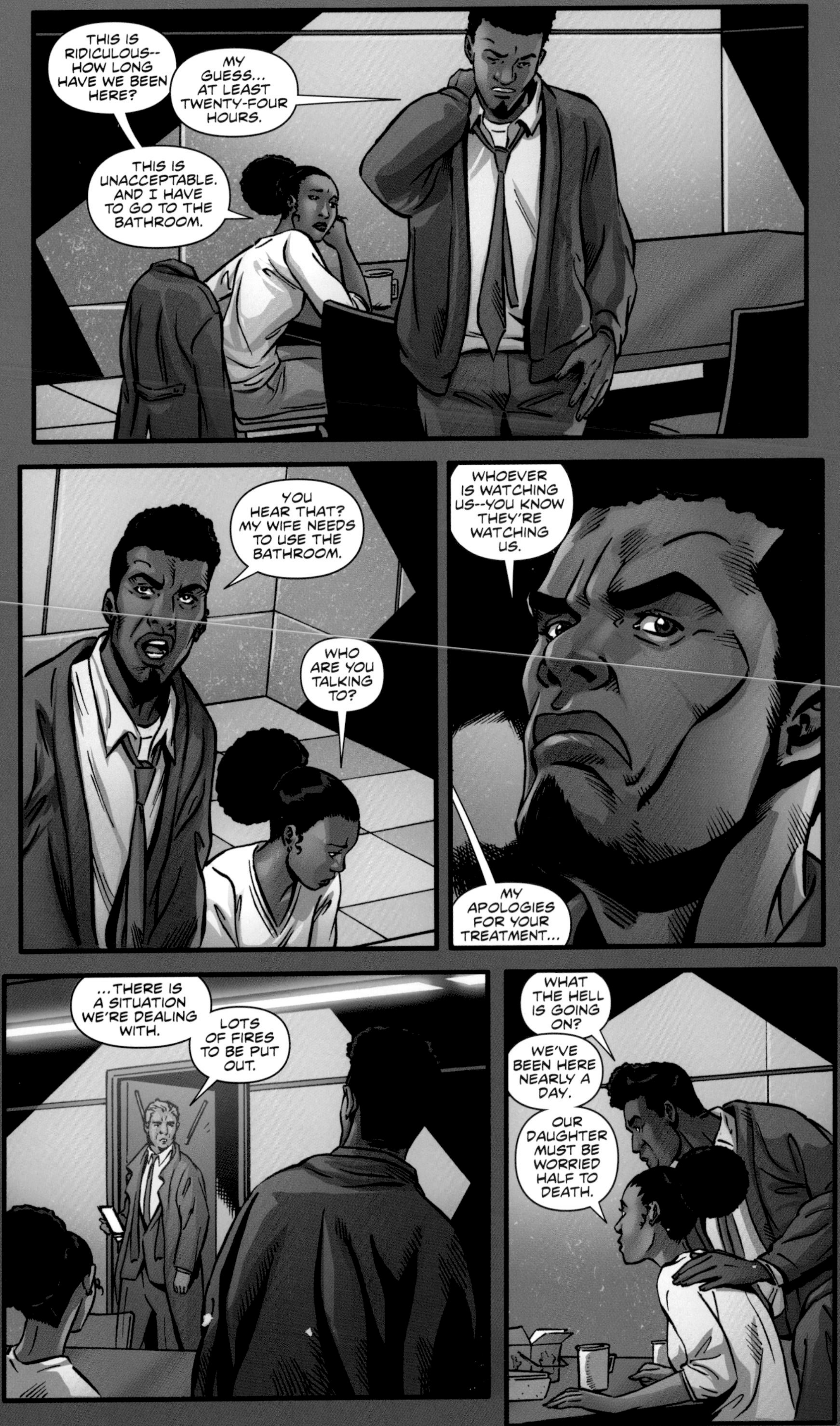
THIS IS RIDICULOUS-- HOW LONG HAVE WE BEEN HERE?
MY GUESS... AT LEAST TWENTY-FOUR HOURS.
THIS IS UNACCEPTABLE. AND I HAVE TO GO TO THE BATHROOM.
YOU HEAR THAT? MY WIFE NEEDS TO USE THE BATHROOM.
WHO ARE YOU TALKING TO?
WHOEVER IS WATCHING US--YOU KNOW THEY'RE WATCHING US.
MY APOLOGIES FOR YOUR TREATMENT...
...THERE IS A SITUATION WE'RE DEALING WITH.
LOTS OF FIRES TO BE PUT OUT.
WHAT THE HELL IS GOING ON?
WE'VE BEEN HERE NEARLY A DAY.
OUR DAUGHTER MUST BE WORRIED HALF TO DEATH.

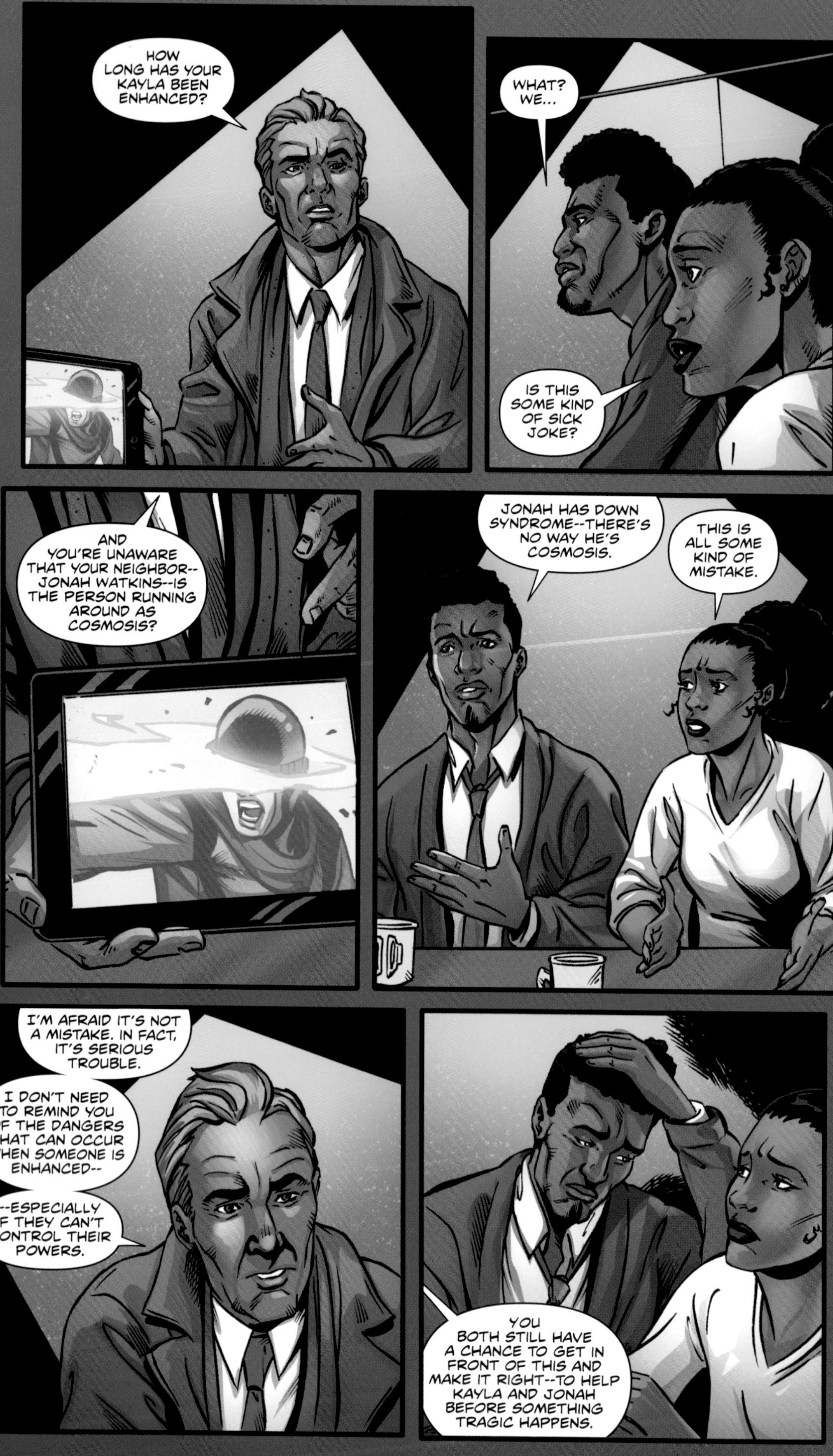
HOW LONG HAS YOUR KAYLA BEEN ENHANCED?
WHAT? WE...
IS THIS SOME KIND OF SICK JOKE?
AND YOU'RE UNAWARE THAT YOUR NEIGHBOR--JONAH WATKINS--IS THE PERSON RUNNING AROUND AS COSMOSIS?
JONAH HAS DOWN SYNDROME--THERE'S NO WAY HE'S COSMOSIS.
THIS IS ALL SOME KIND OF MISTAKE.
I'M AFRAID IT'S NOT A MISTAKE. IN FACT, IT'S SERIOUS TROUBLE.
I DON'T NEED TO REMIND YOU OF THE DANGERS THAT CAN OCCUR WHEN SOMEONE IS ENHANCED--
--ESPECIALLY IF THEY CAN'T CONTROL THEIR POWERS.
YOU BOTH STILL HAVE A CHANCE TO GET IN FRONT OF THIS AND MAKE IT RIGHT--TO HELP KAYLA AND JONAH BEFORE SOMETHING TRAGIC HAPPENS.

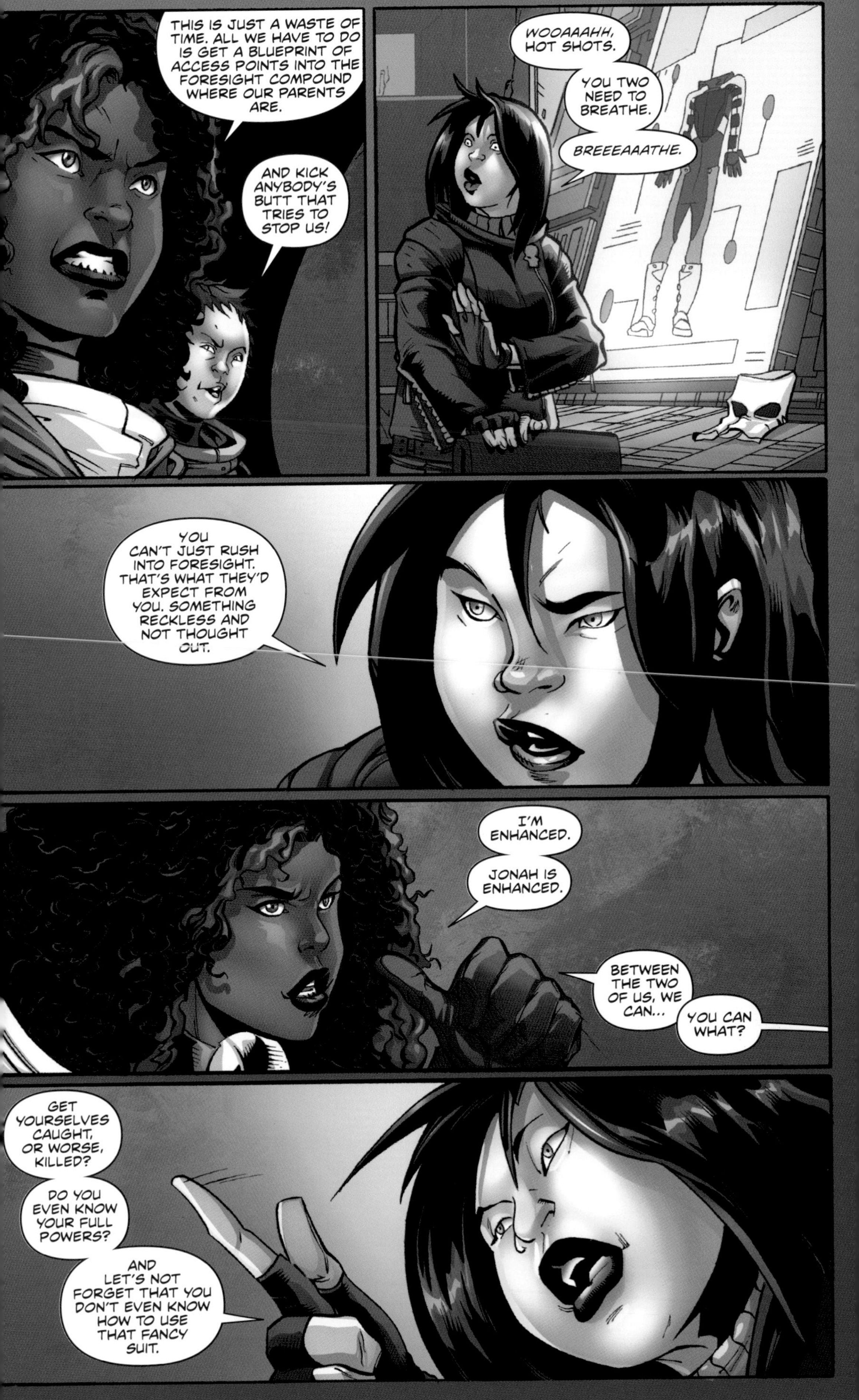

THIS IS JUST A WASTE OF TIME. ALL WE HAVE TO DO IS GET A BLUEPRINT OF ACCESS POINTS INTO THE FORESIGHT COMPOUND WHERE OUR PARENTS ARE.
AND KICK ANYBODY'S BUTT THAT TRIES TO STOP US!
WOOAAAHH, HOT SHOTS.
YOU TWO NEED TO BREATHE.
BREEEAAATHE.
YOU CAN'T JUST RUSH INTO FORESIGHT. THAT'S WHAT THEY'D EXPECT FROM YOU. SOMETHING RECKLESS AND NOT THOUGHT OUT.
I'M ENHANCED.
JONAH IS ENHANCED.
BETWEEN THE TWO OF US, WE CAN...
YOU CAN WHAT?
GET YOURSELVES CAUGHT, OR WORSE, KILLED?
DO YOU EVEN KNOW YOUR FULL POWERS?
AND LET'S NOT FORGET THAT YOU DON'T EVEN KNOW HOW TO USE THAT FANCY SUIT.

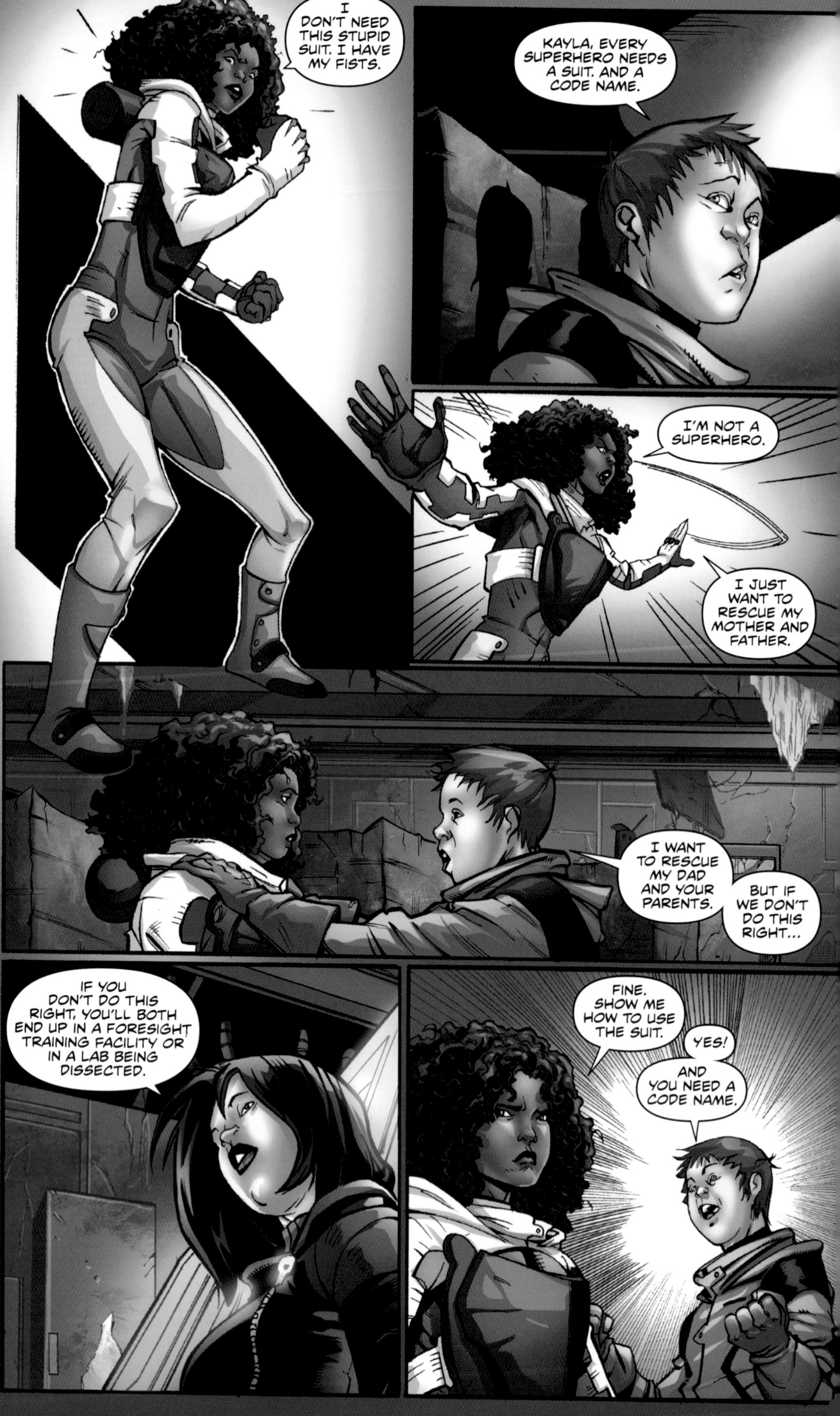
I DON'T NEED THIS STUPID SUIT. I HAVE MY FISTS.
KAYLA, EVERY SUPERHERO NEEDS A SUIT. AND A CODE NAME.
I'M NOT A SUPERHERO.
I JUST WANT TO RESCUE MY MOTHER AND FATHER.
I WANT TO RESCUE MY DAD AND YOUR PARENTS.
BUT IF WE DON'T DO THIS RIGHT...
IF YOU DON'T DO THIS RIGHT, YOU'LL BOTH END UP IN A FORESIGHT TRAINING FACILITY OR IN A LAB BEING DISSECTED.
FINE. SHOW ME HOW TO USE THE SUIT.
YES!
AND YOU NEED A CODE NAME.

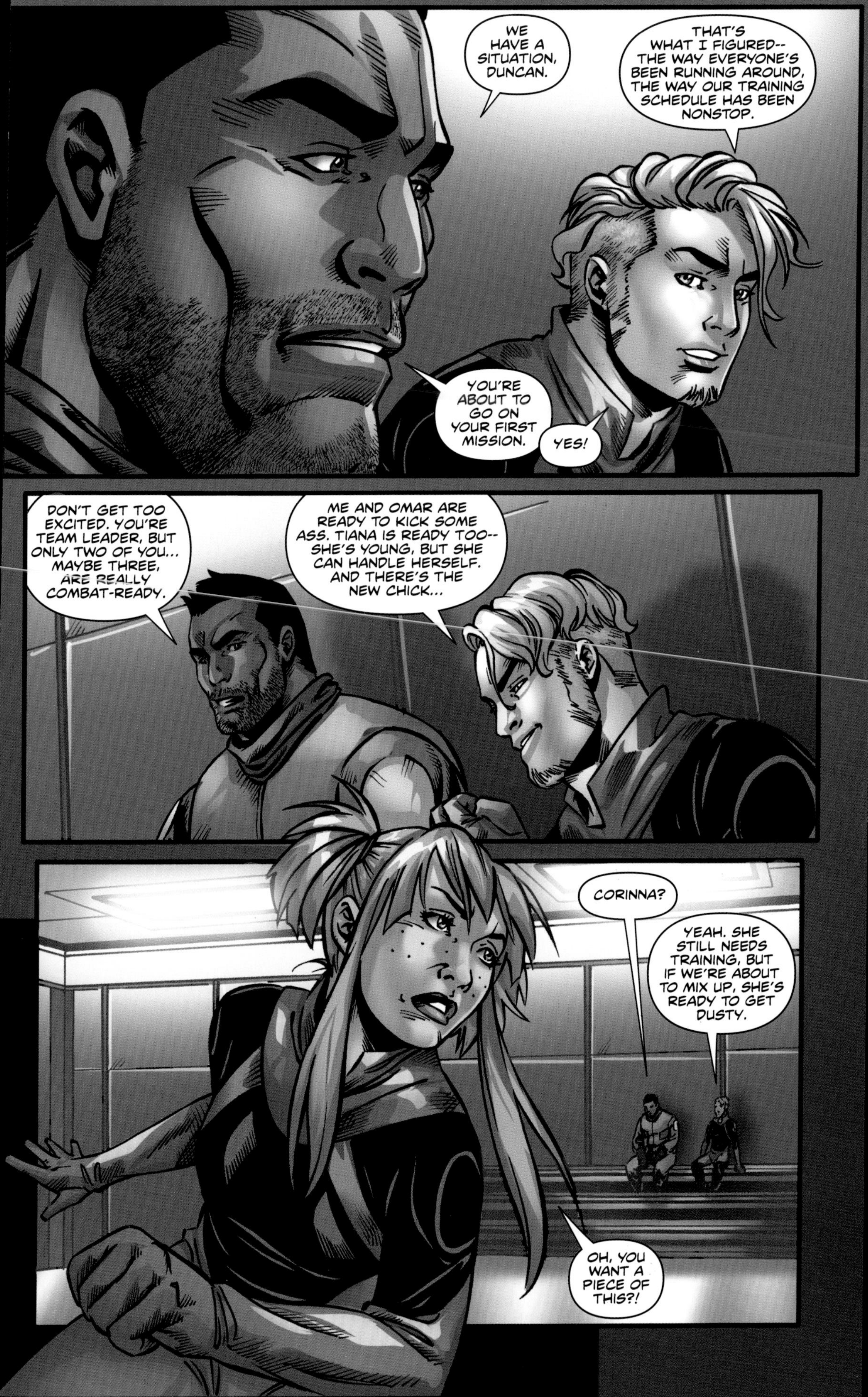
WE HAVE A SITUATION, DUNCAN.
THAT'S WHAT I FIGURED-- THE WAY EVERYONE'S BEEN RUNNING AROUND, THE WAY OUR TRAINING SCHEDULE HAS BEEN NONSTOP.
YOU'RE ABOUT TO GO ON YOUR FIRST MISSION.
YES!
DON'T GET TOO EXCITED. YOU'RE TEAM LEADER, BUT ONLY TWO OF YOU... MAYBE THREE, ARE REALLY COMBAT-READY.
ME AND OMAR ARE READY TO KICK SOME ASS. TIANA IS READY TOO-- SHE'S YOUNG, BUT SHE CAN HANDLE HERSELF. AND THERE'S THE NEW CHICK...
CORINNA?
YEAH. SHE STILL NEEDS TRAINING, BUT IF WE'RE ABOUT TO MIX UP, SHE'S READY TO GET DUSTY.
OH, YOU WANT A PIECE OF THIS?!

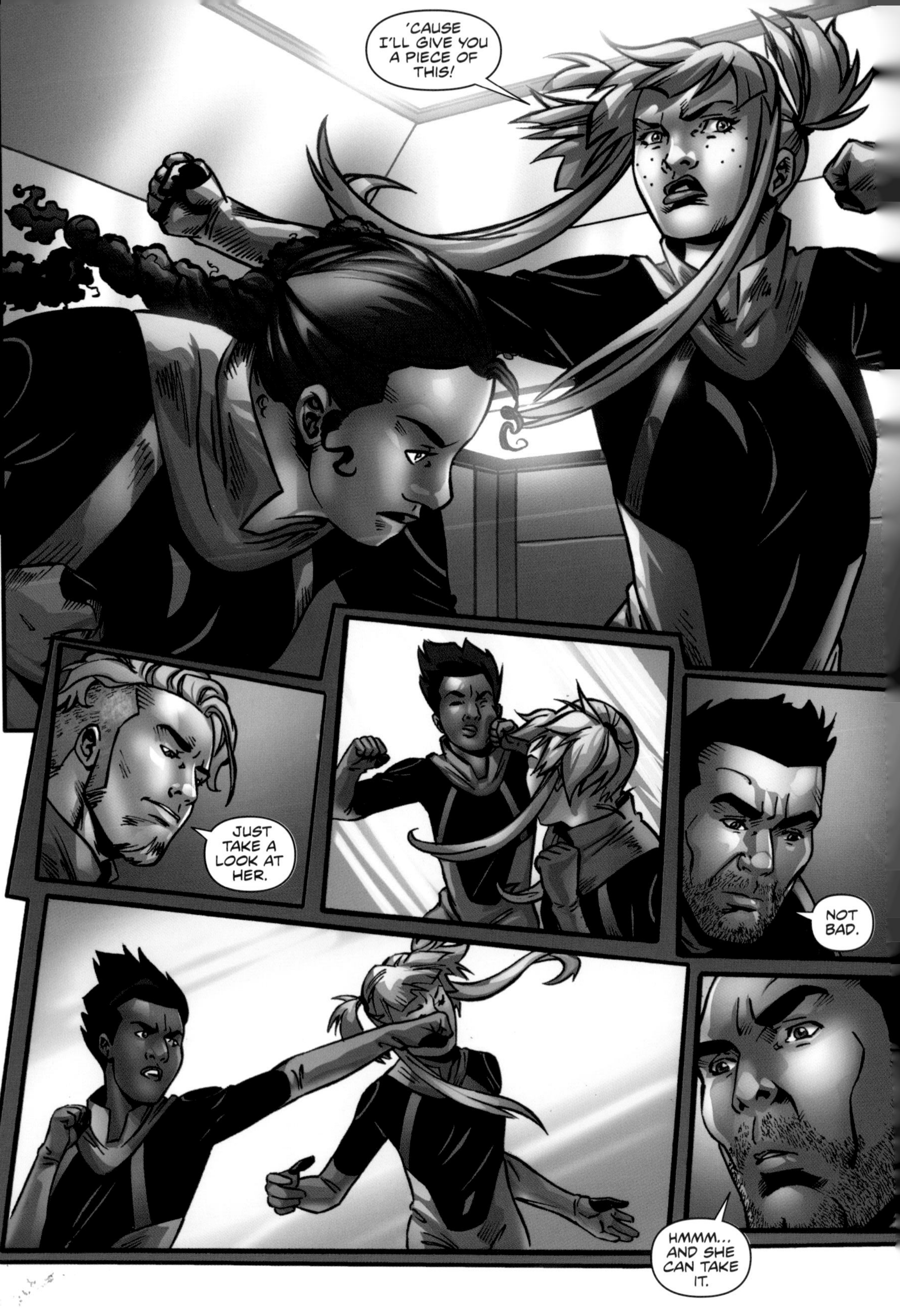
'CAUSE I'LL GIVE YOU A PIECE OF THIS!
JUST TAKE A LOOK AT HER.
NOT BAD.
HMMM... AND SHE CAN TAKE IT.

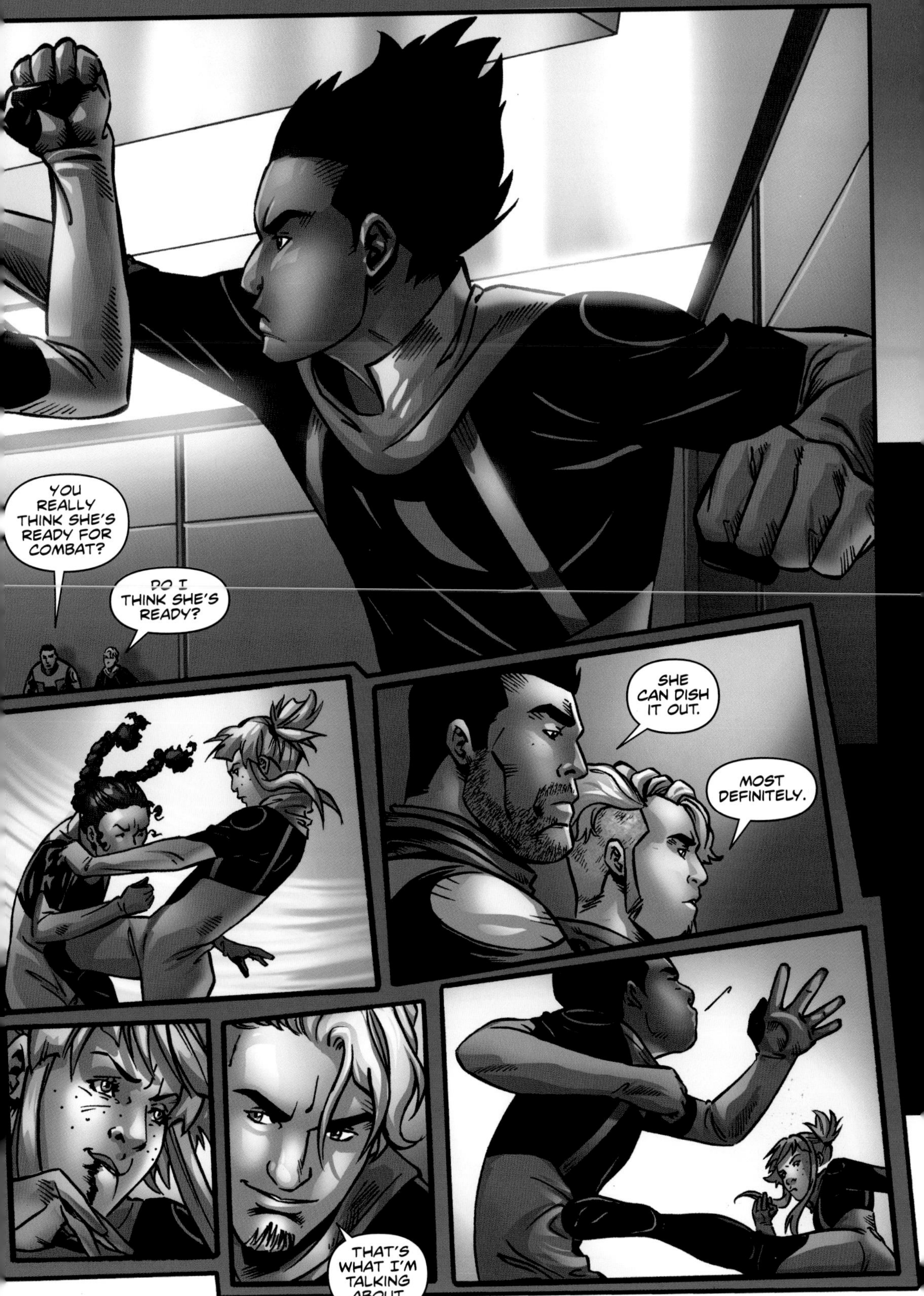
YOU REALLY THINK SHE'S READY FOR COMBAT?
DO I THINK SHE'S READY?
SHE CAN DISH IT OUT.
MOST DEFINITELY.
THAT'S WHAT I'M TALKING ABOUT.

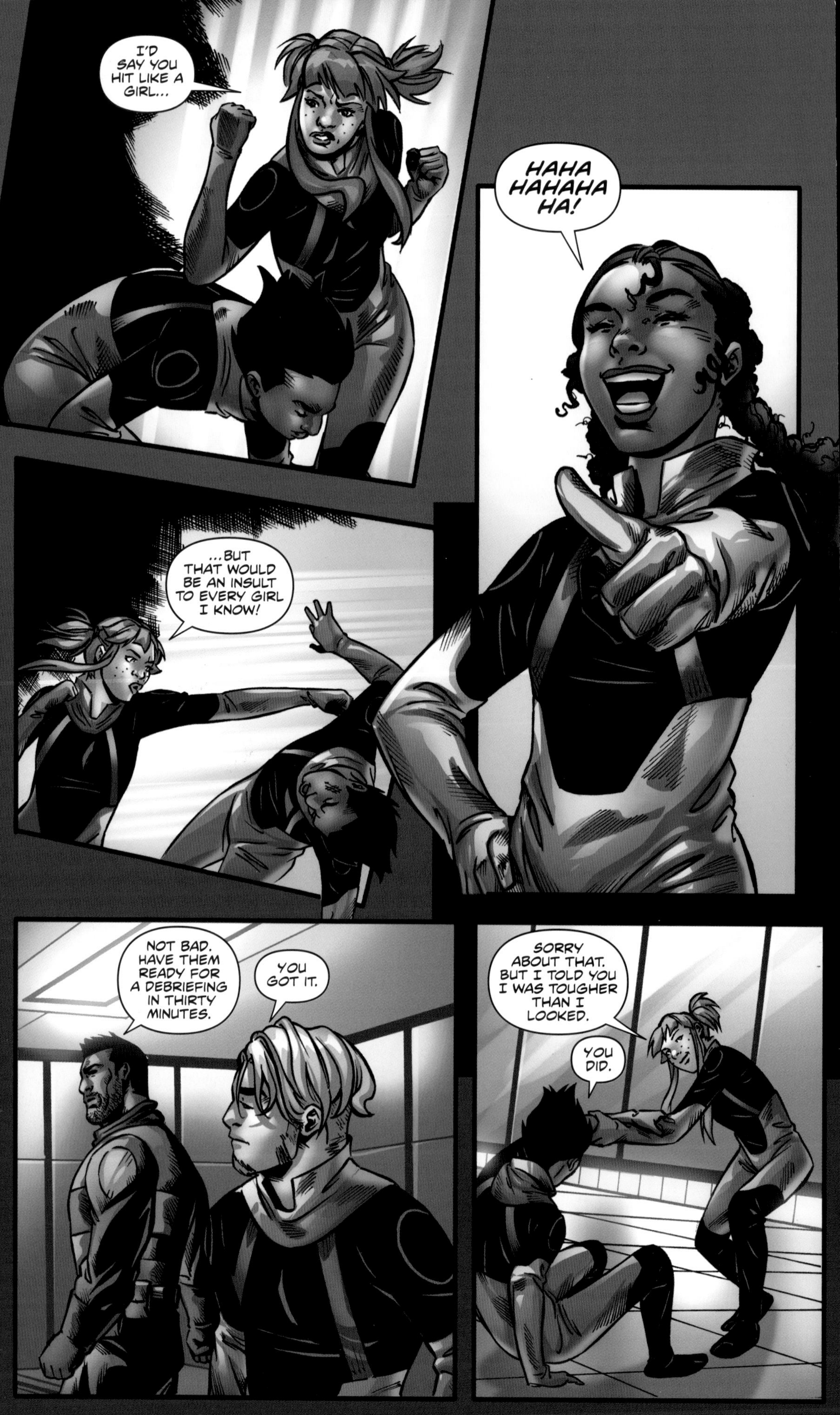
I'D SAY YOU HIT LIKE A GIRL...
HAHA HAHAHA HA!
...BUT THAT WOULD BE AN INSULT TO EVERY GIRL I KNOW!
NOT BAD. HAVE THEM READY FOR A DEBRIEFING IN THIRTY MINUTES.
YOU GOT IT.
SORRY ABOUT THAT. BUT I TOLD YOU I WAS TOUGHER THAN I LOOKED.
YOU DID.

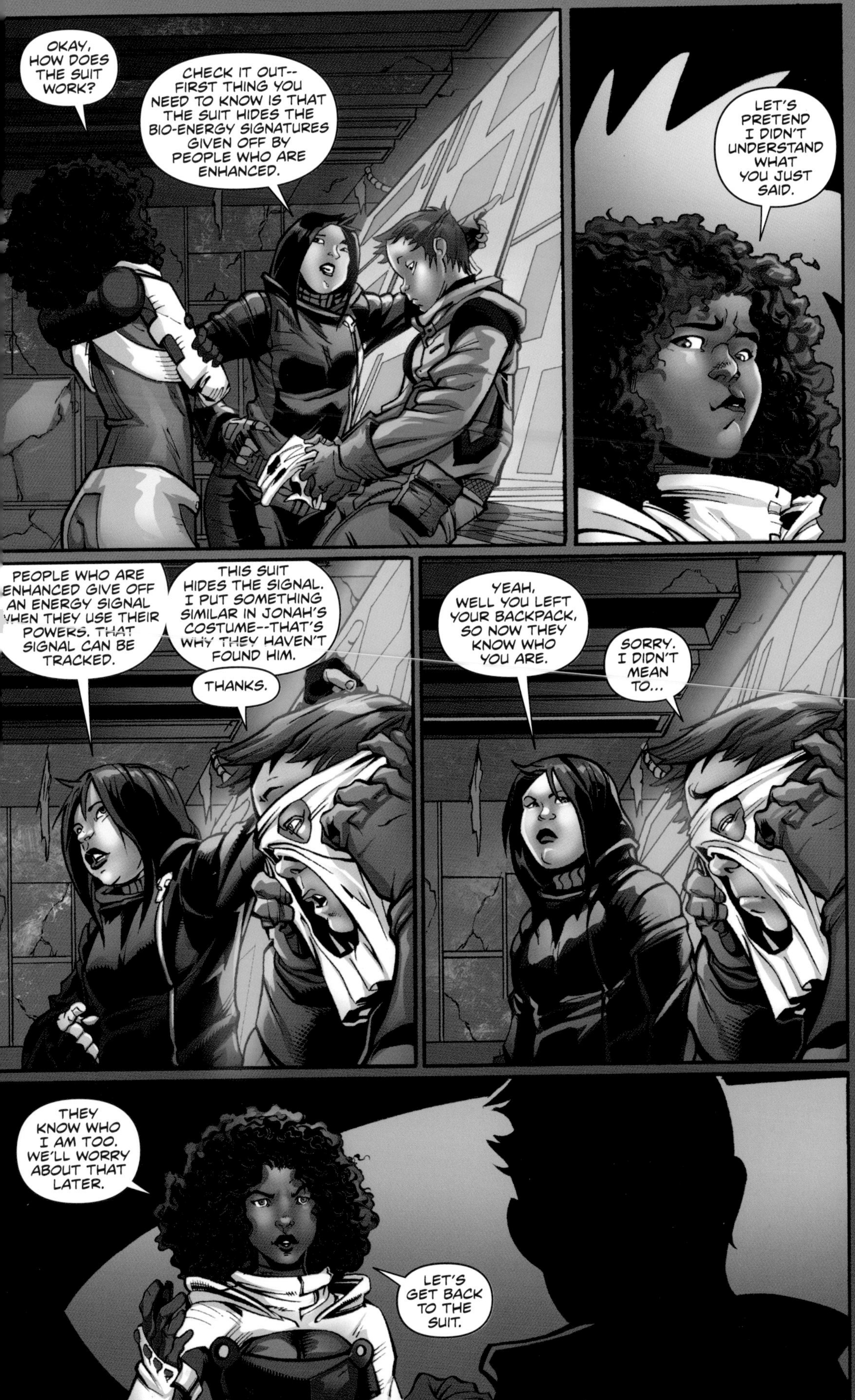
OKAY, HOW DOES THE SUIT WORK?
CHECK IT OUT-- FIRST THING YOU NEED TO KNOW IS THAT THE SUIT HIDES THE BIO-ENERGY SIGNATURES GIVEN OFF BY PEOPLE WHO ARE ENHANCED.
LET'S PRETEND I DIDN'T UNDERSTAND WHAT YOU JUST SAID.
PEOPLE WHO ARE ENHANCED GIVE OFF AN ENERGY SIGNAL WHEN THEY USE THEIR POWERS. THAT SIGNAL CAN BE TRACKED.
THIS SUIT HIDES THE SIGNAL. I PUT SOMETHING SIMILAR IN JONAH'S COSTUME--THAT'S WHY THEY HAVEN'T FOUND HIM.
THANKS.
YEAH, WELL YOU LEFT YOUR BACKPACK, SO NOW THEY KNOW WHO YOU ARE.
SORRY. I DIDN'T MEAN TO...
THEY KNOW WHO I AM TOO. WE'LL WORRY ABOUT THAT LATER.
LET'S GET BACK TO THE SUIT.

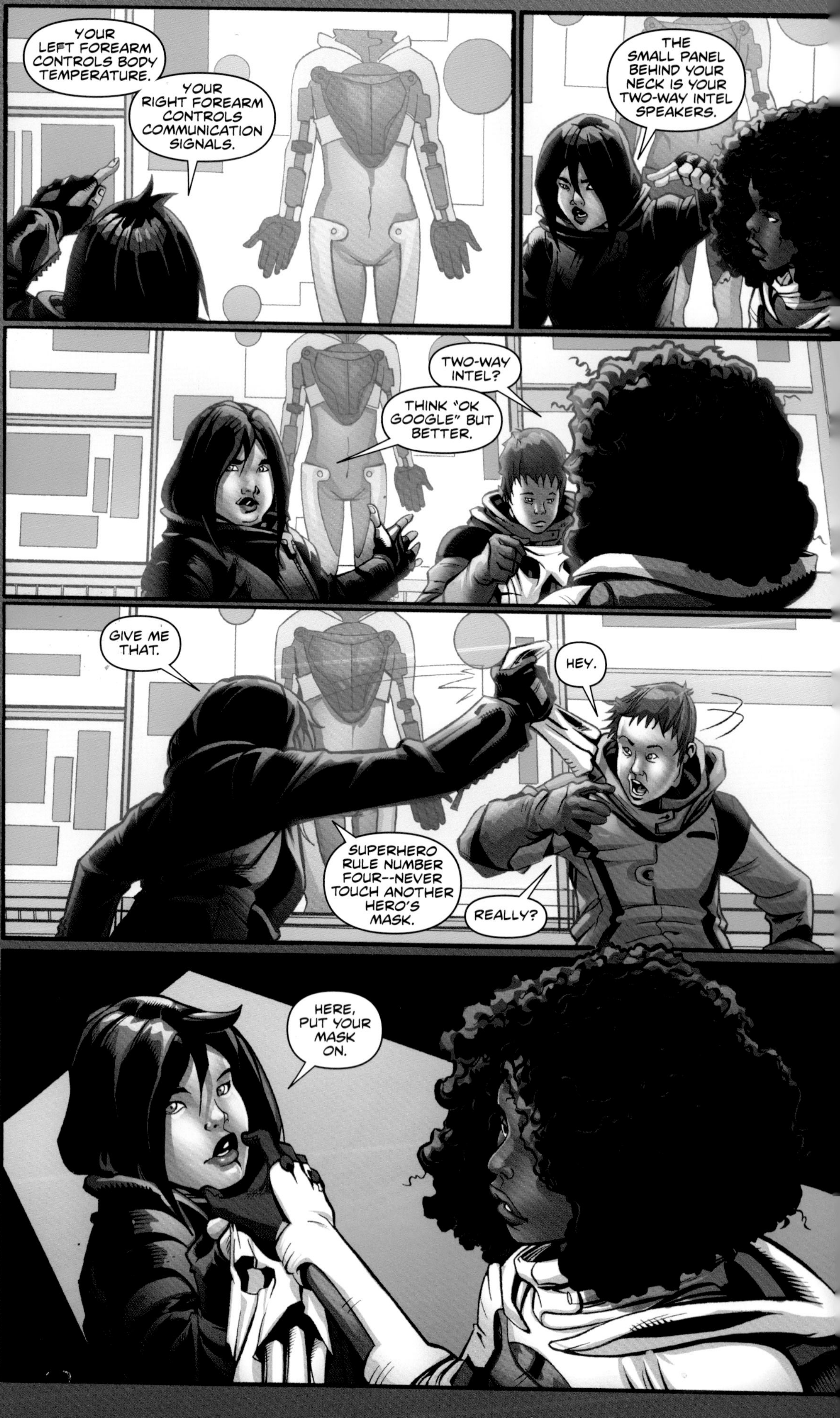
YOUR LEFT FOREARM CONTROLS BODY TEMPERATURE.
YOUR RIGHT FOREARM CONTROLS COMMUNICATION SIGNALS.
THE SMALL PANEL BEHIND YOUR NECK IS YOUR TWO-WAY INTEL SPEAKERS.
TWO-WAY INTEL?
THINK "OK GOOGLE" BUT BETTER.
GIVE ME THAT.
HEY.
SUPERHERO RULE NUMBER FOUR--NEVER TOUCH ANOTHER HERO'S MASK.
REALLY?
HERE, PUT YOUR MASK ON.

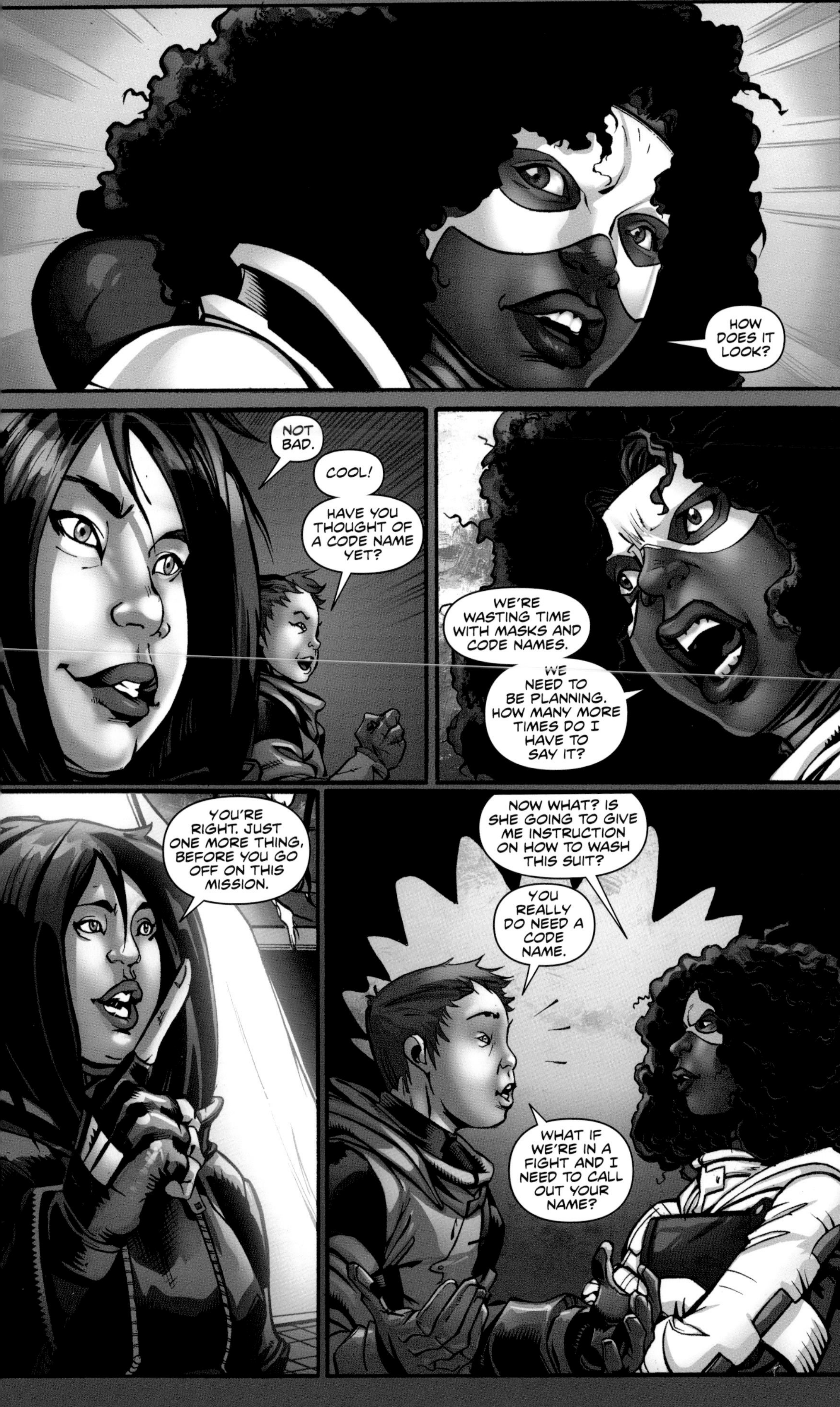
HOW DOES IT LOOK?
NOT BAD.
COOL!
HAVE YOU THOUGHT OF A CODE NAME YET?
WE'RE WASTING TIME WITH MASKS AND CODE NAMES.
WE NEED TO BE PLANNING. HOW MANY MORE TIMES DO I HAVE TO SAY IT?
YOU'RE RIGHT. JUST ONE MORE THING, BEFORE YOU GO OFF ON THIS MISSION.
NOW WHAT? IS SHE GOING TO GIVE ME INSTRUCTION ON HOW TO WASH THIS SUIT?
YOU REALLY DO NEED A CODE NAME.
WHAT IF WE'RE IN A FIGHT AND I NEED TO CALL OUT YOUR NAME?

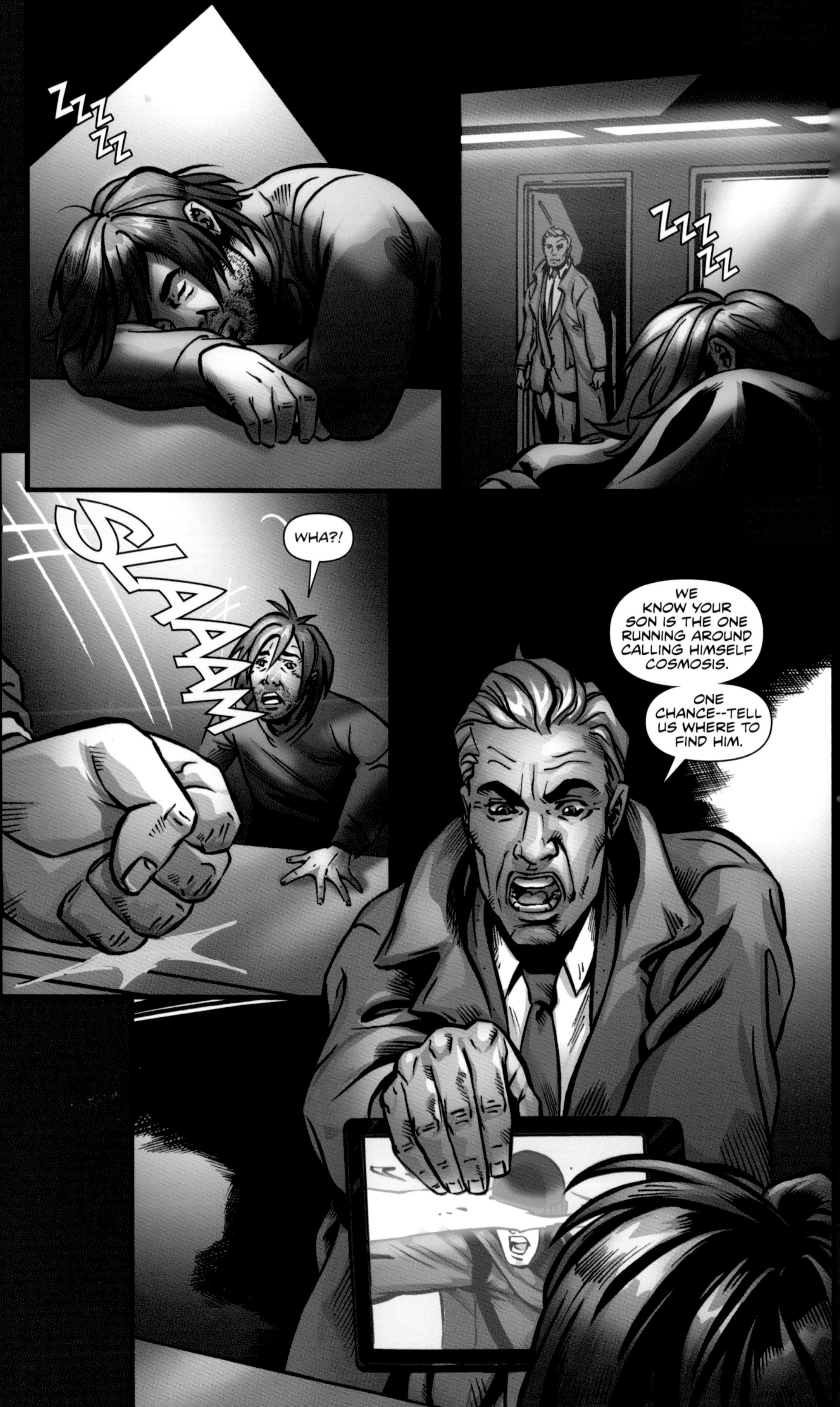
ZZZZZ
ZZZZZ
SLAAAM
WHA?!
WE KNOW YOUR SON IS THE ONE RUNNING AROUND CALLING HIMSELF COSMOSIS.
ONE CHANCE--TELL US WHERE TO FIND HIM.

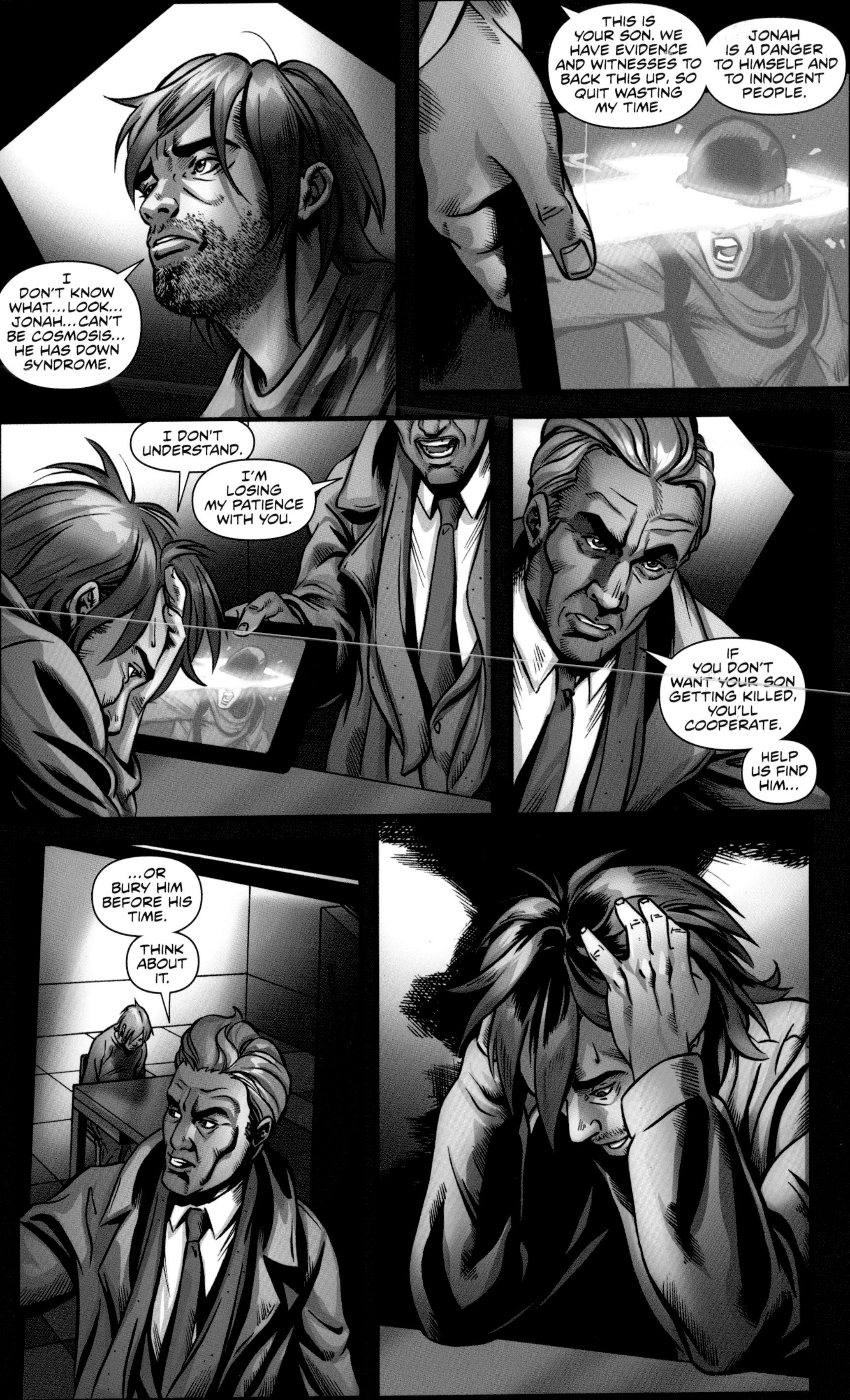
I DON'T KNOW WHAT...LOOK... JONAH...CAN'T BE COSMOSIS... HE HAS DOWN SYNDROME.
THIS IS YOUR SON. WE HAVE EVIDENCE AND WITNESSES TO BACK THIS UP, SO QUIT WASTING MY TIME.
JONAH IS A DANGER TO HIMSELF AND TO INNOCENT PEOPLE.
I DON'T UNDERSTAND.
I'M LOSING MY PATIENCE WITH YOU.
IF YOU DON'T WANT YOUR SON GETTING KILLED, YOU'LL COOPERATE.
HELP US FIND HIM...
...OR BURY HIM BEFORE HIS TIME.
THINK ABOUT IT.

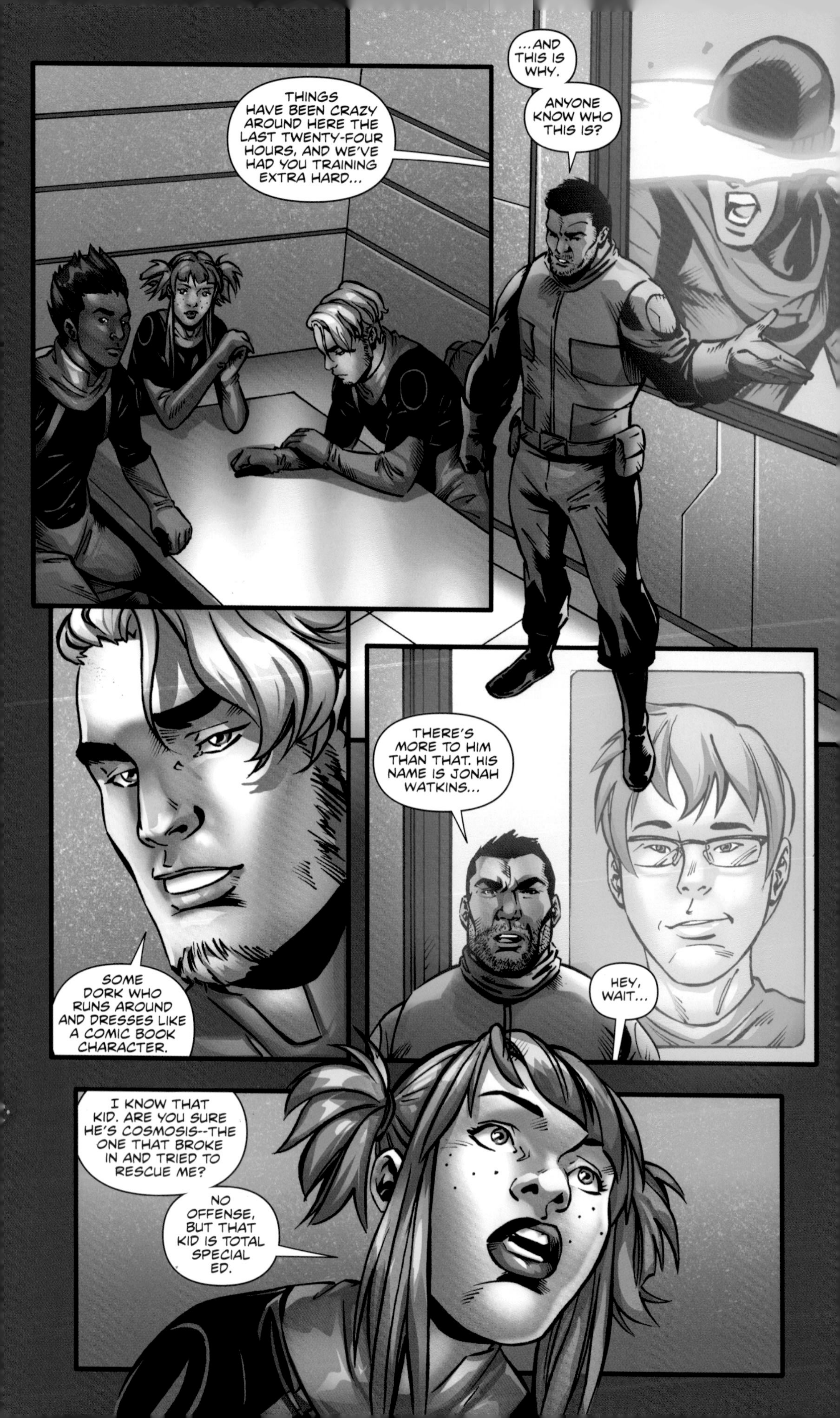
THINGS HAVE BEEN CRAZY AROUND HERE THE LAST TWENTY-FOUR HOURS, AND WE'VE HAD YOU TRAINING EXTRA HARD...
...AND THIS IS WHY.
ANYONE KNOW WHO THIS IS?
SOME DORK WHO RUNS AROUND AND DRESSES LIKE A COMIC BOOK CHARACTER.
THERE'S MORE TO HIM THAN THAT. HIS NAME IS JONAH WATKINS...
HEY, WAIT...
I KNOW THAT KID. ARE YOU SURE HE'S COSMOSIS--THE ONE THAT BROKE IN AND TRIED TO RESCUE ME?
NO OFFENSE, BUT THAT KID IS TOTAL SPECIAL ED.

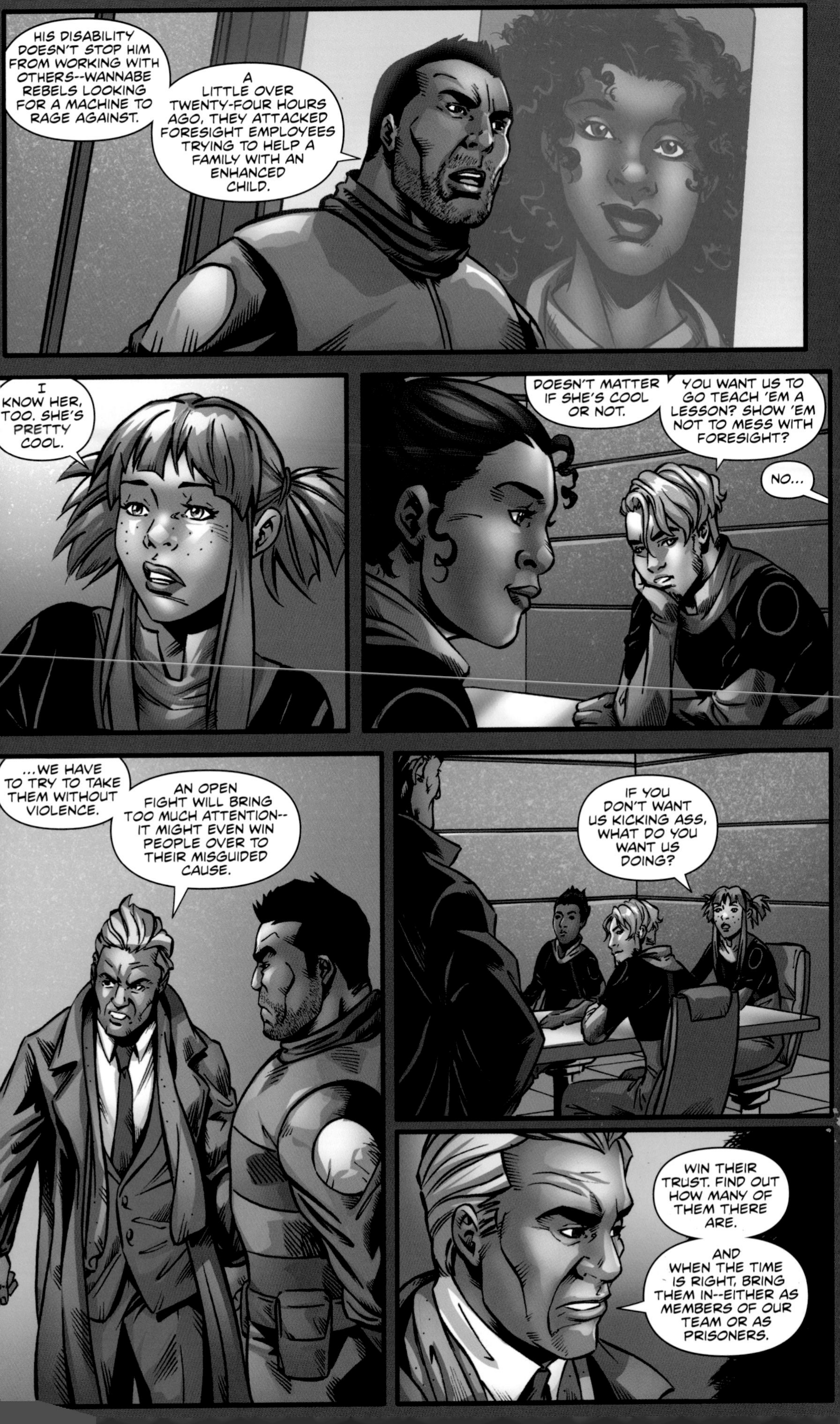
HIS DISABILITY DOESN'T STOP HIM FROM WORKING WITH OTHERS--WANNABE REBELS LOOKING FOR A MACHINE TO RAGE AGAINST.
A LITTLE OVER TWENTY-FOUR HOURS AGO, THEY ATTACKED FORESIGHT EMPLOYEES TRYING TO HELP A FAMILY WITH AN ENHANCED CHILD.
I KNOW HER, TOO. SHE'S PRETTY COOL.
DOESN'T MATTER IF SHE'S COOL OR NOT.
YOU WANT US TO GO TEACH 'EM A LESSON? SHOW 'EM NOT TO MESS WITH FORESIGHT?
NO...
...WE HAVE TO TRY TO TAKE THEM WITHOUT VIOLENCE.
AN OPEN FIGHT WILL BRING TOO MUCH ATTENTION--IT MIGHT EVEN WIN PEOPLE OVER TO THEIR MISGUIDED CAUSE.
IF YOU DON'T WANT US KICKING ASS, WHAT DO YOU WANT US DOING?
WIN THEIR TRUST. FIND OUT HOW MANY OF THEM THERE ARE.
AND WHEN THE TIME IS RIGHT, BRING THEM IN--EITHER AS MEMBERS OF OUR TEAM OR AS PRISONERS.

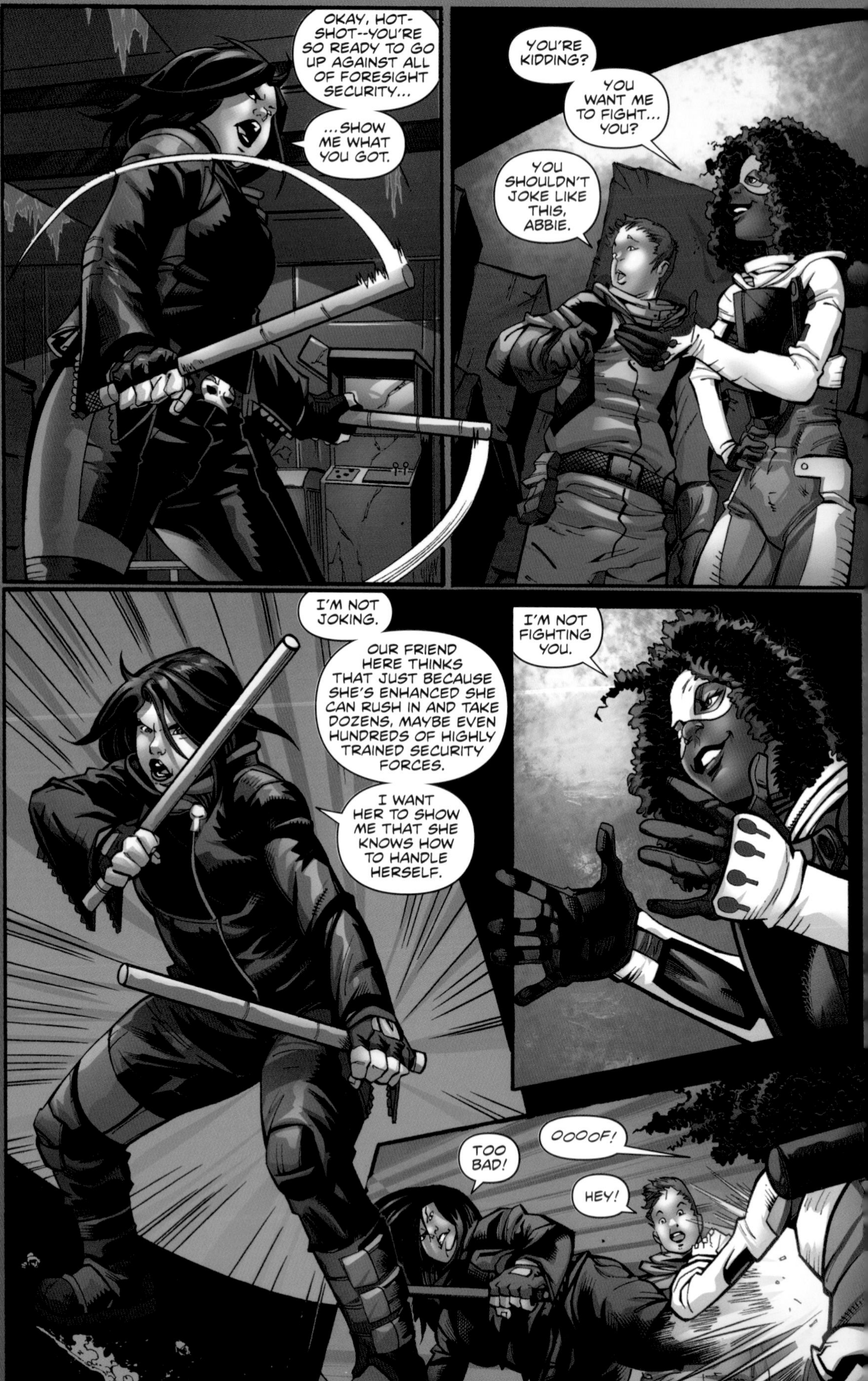
OKAY, HOT-SHOT--YOU'RE SO READY TO GO UP AGAINST ALL OF FORESIGHT SECURITY...
...SHOW ME WHAT YOU GOT.
YOU'RE KIDDING?
YOU WANT ME TO FIGHT... YOU?
YOU SHOULDN'T JOKE LIKE THIS, ABBIE.
I'M NOT JOKING.
OUR FRIEND HERE THINKS THAT JUST BECAUSE SHE'S ENHANCED SHE CAN RUSH IN AND TAKE DOZENS, MAYBE EVEN HUNDREDS OF HIGHLY TRAINED SECURITY FORCES.
I WANT HER TO SHOW ME THAT SHE KNOWS HOW TO HANDLE HERSELF.
I'M NOT FIGHTING YOU.
TOO BAD!
OOOOF!
HEY!

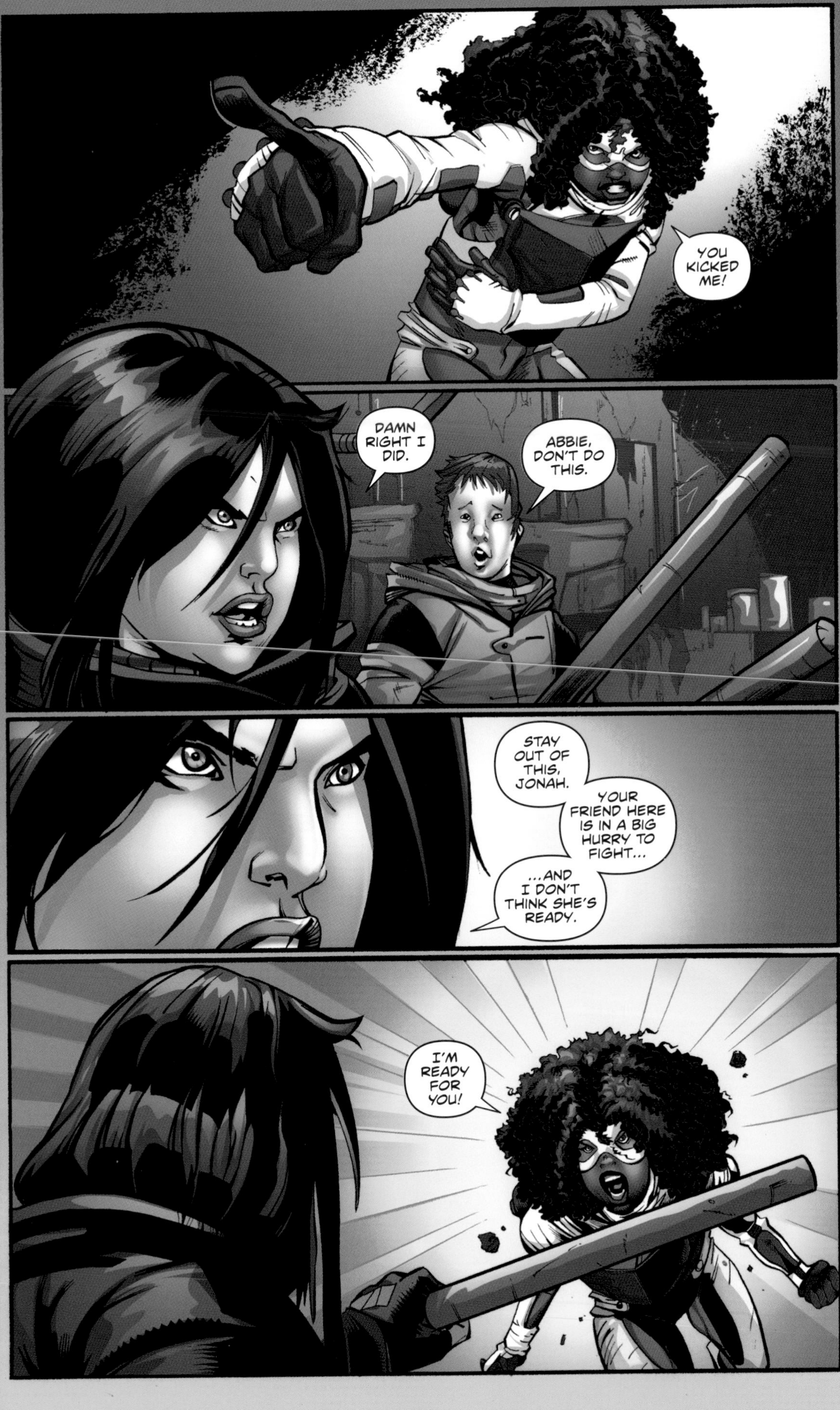
YOU KICKED ME!
DAMN RIGHT I DID.
ABBIE, DON'T DO THIS.
STAY OUT OF THIS, JONAH.
YOUR FRIEND HERE IS IN A BIG HURRY TO FIGHT...
...AND I DON'T THINK SHE'S READY.
I'M READY FOR YOU!

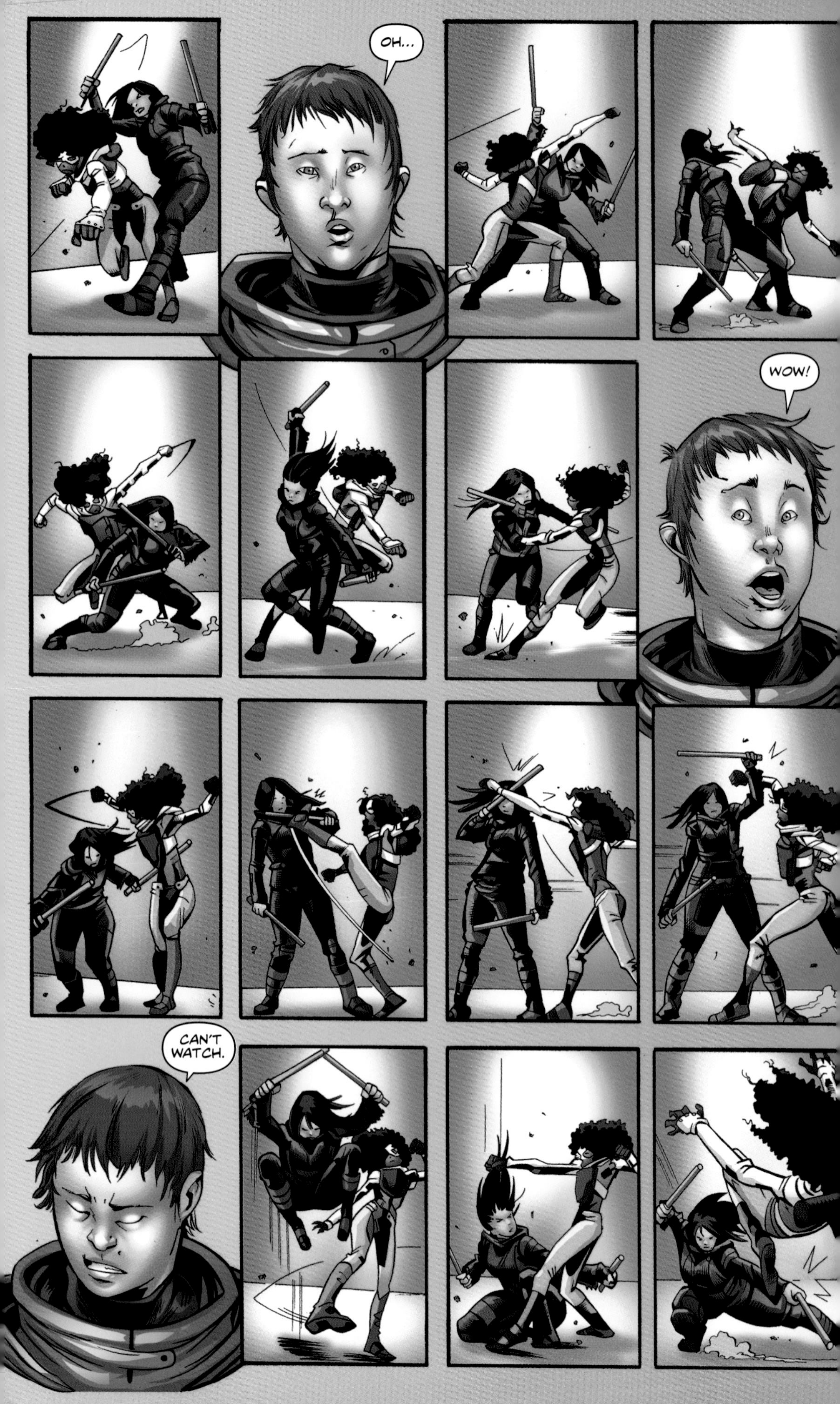
OH...
WOW!
CAN'T WATCH.

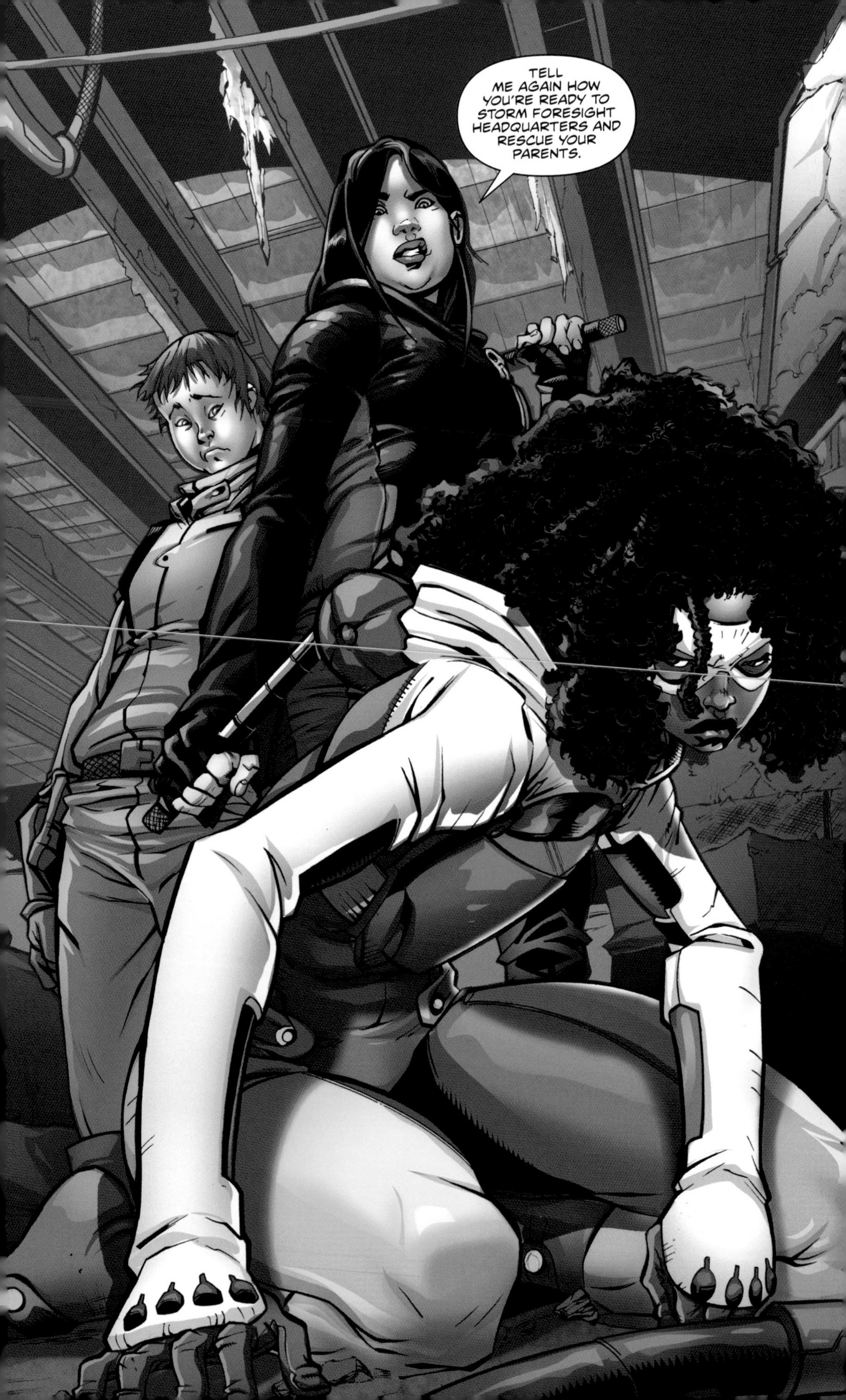
TELL ME AGAIN HOW YOU'RE READY TO STORM FORESIGHT HEADQUARTERS AND RESCUE YOUR PARENTS.

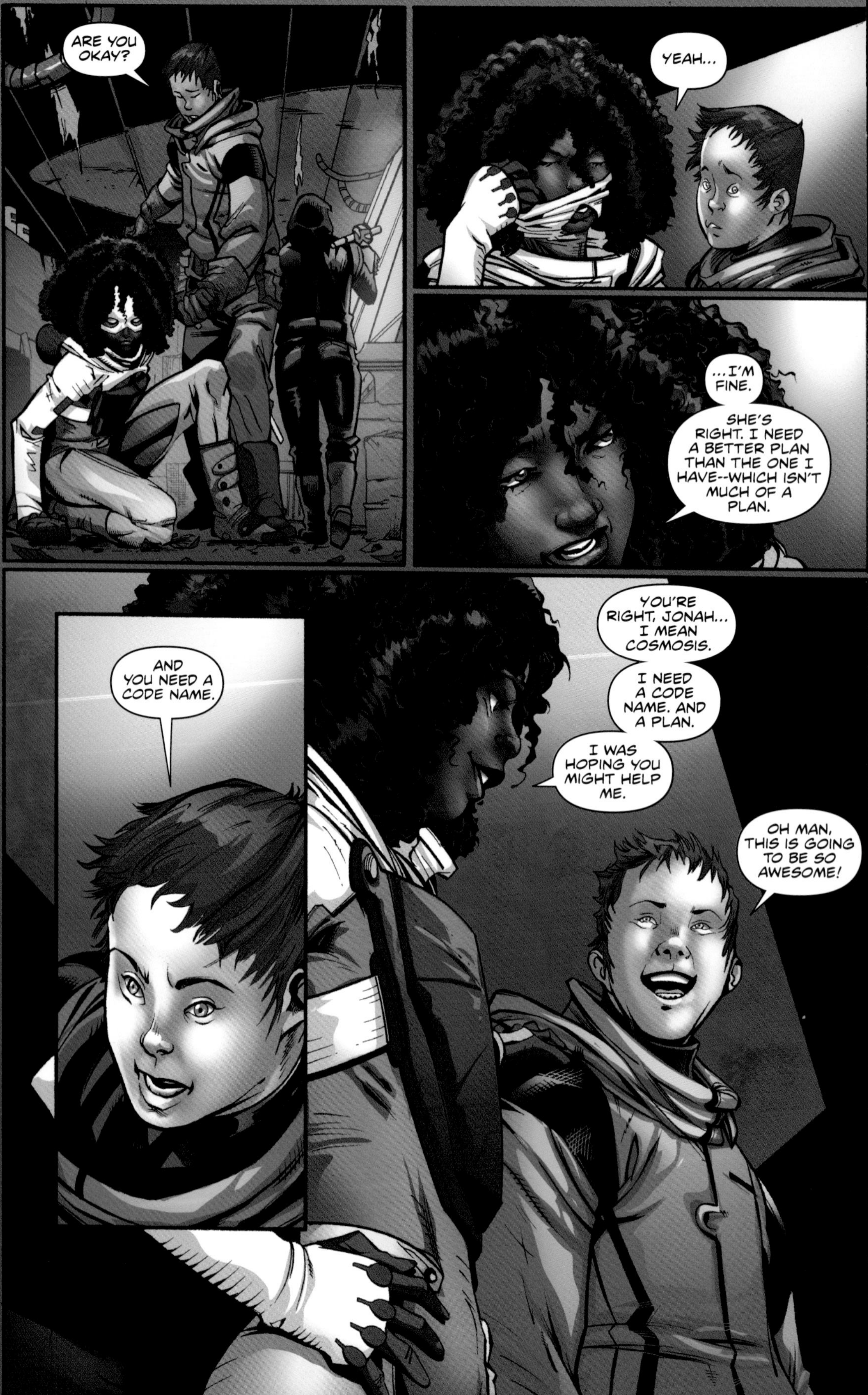
ARE YOU OKAY?
YEAH...
...I'M FINE.
SHE'S RIGHT. I NEED A BETTER PLAN THAN THE ONE I HAVE--WHICH ISN'T MUCH OF A PLAN.
AND YOU NEED A CODE NAME.
YOU'RE RIGHT, JONAH... I MEAN COSMOSIS.
I NEED A CODE NAME. AND A PLAN.
I WAS HOPING YOU MIGHT HELP ME.
OH MAN, THIS IS GOING TO BE SO AWESOME!

CHAPTER TWO

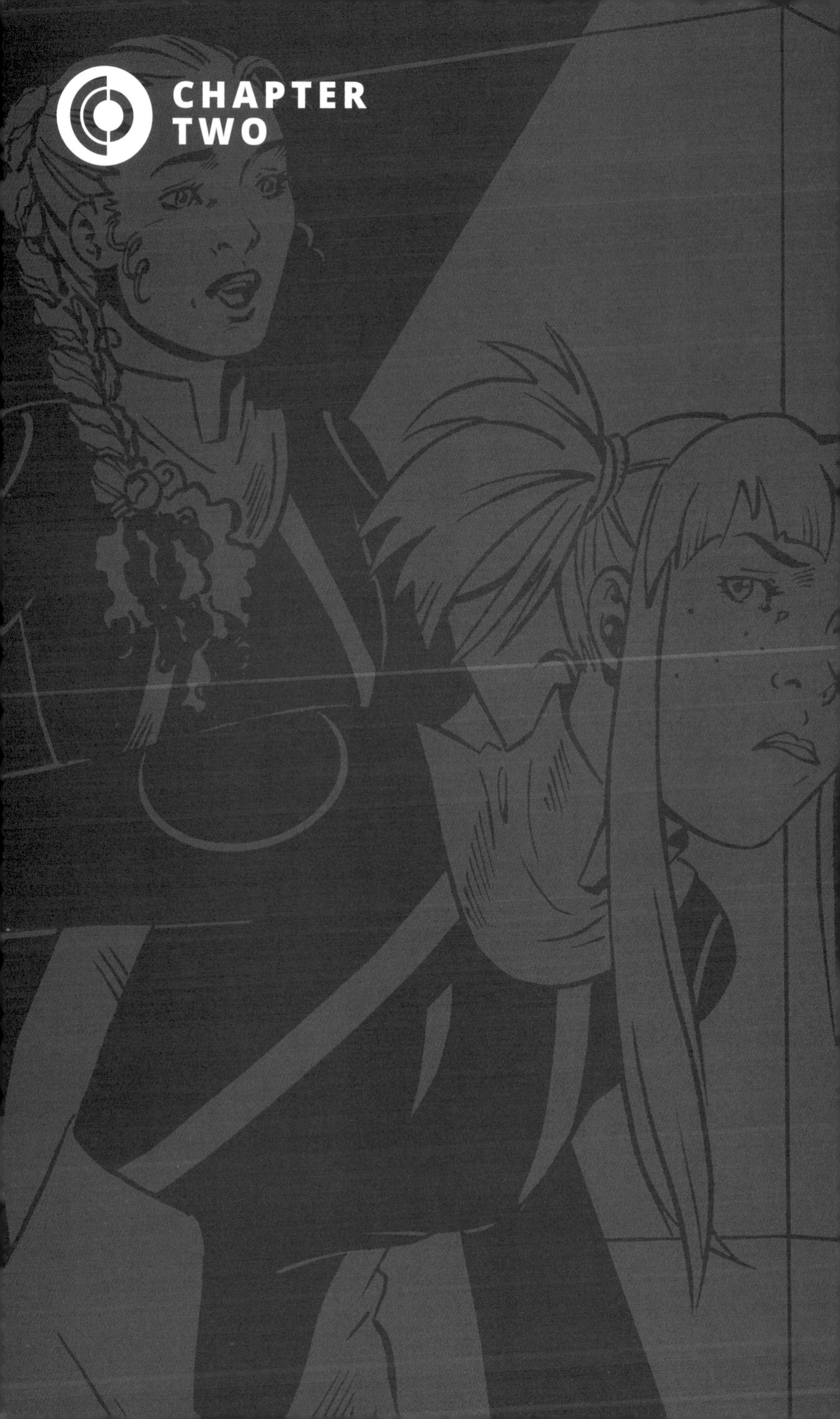

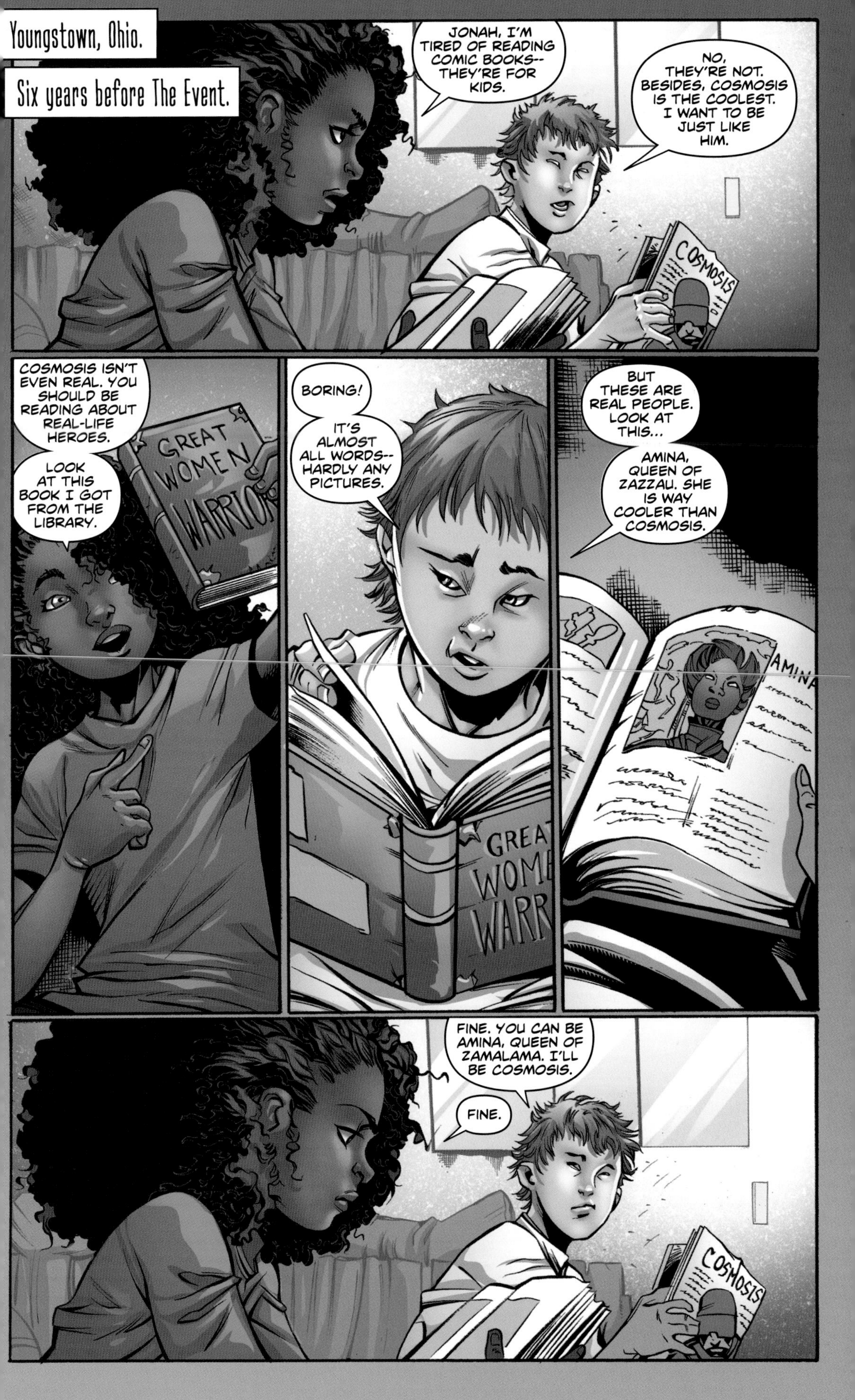
Youngstown, Ohio.
Six years before The Event.
JONAH, I'M TIRED OF READING COMIC BOOKS--THEY'RE FOR KIDS.
NO, THEY'RE NOT. BESIDES, COSMOSIS IS THE COOLEST. I WANT TO BE JUST LIKE HIM.
COSMOSIS
COSMOSIS ISN'T EVEN REAL. YOU SHOULD BE READING ABOUT REAL-LIFE HEROES.
LOOK AT THIS BOOK I GOT FROM THE LIBRARY.
GREAT WOMEN WARRIO
BORING!
IT'S ALMOST ALL WORDS--HARDLY ANY PICTURES.
GREAT WOME WARR
BUT THESE ARE REAL PEOPLE. LOOK AT THIS...
AMINA, QUEEN OF ZAZZAU. SHE IS WAY COOLER THAN COSMOSIS.
AMINA
FINE. YOU CAN BE AMINA, QUEEN OF ZAMALAMA. I'LL BE COSMOSIS.
FINE.
COSMOSIS

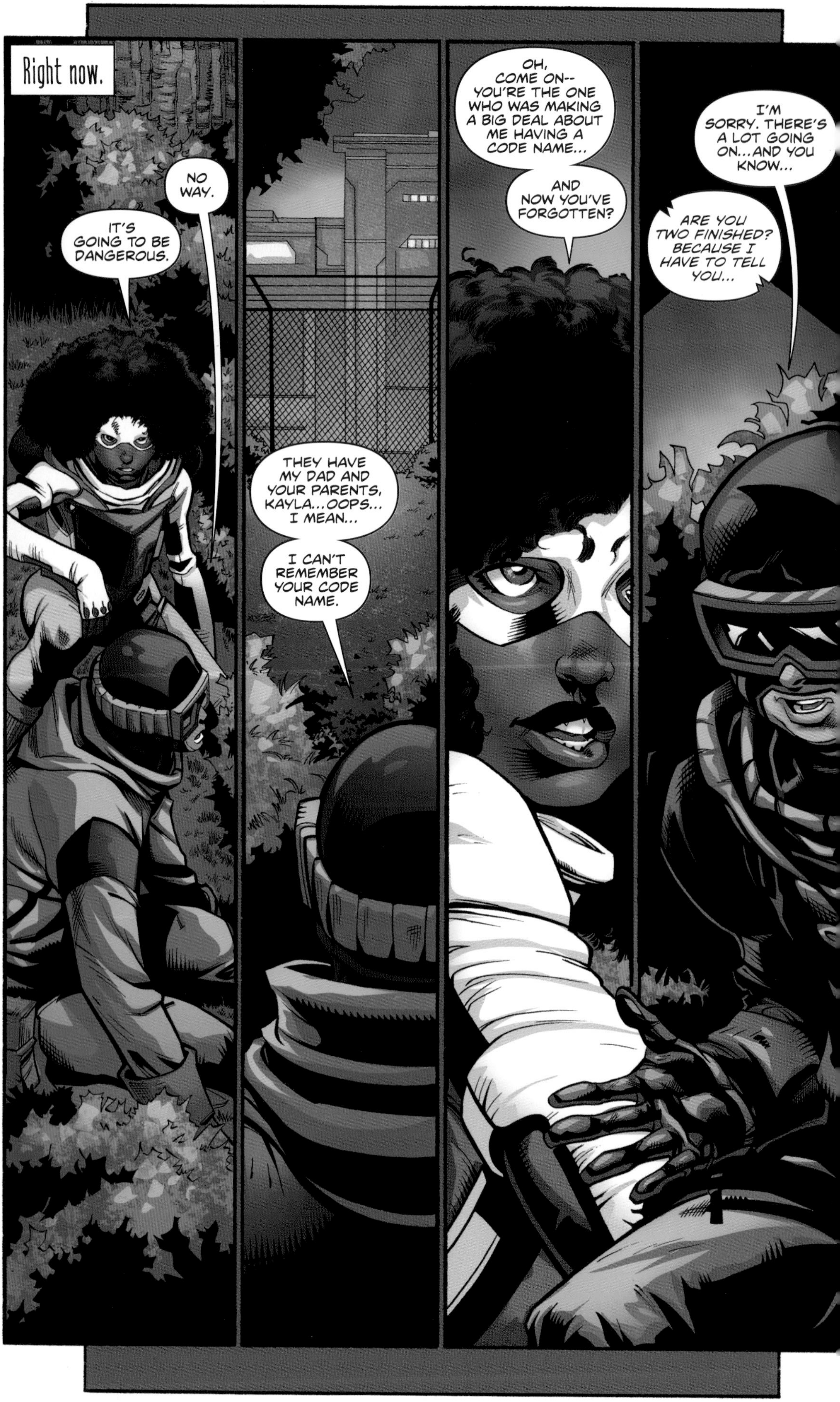
Right now.
IT'S GOING TO BE DANGEROUS.
NO WAY.
THEY HAVE MY DAD AND YOUR PARENTS, KAYLA...OOPS... I MEAN...
I CAN'T REMEMBER YOUR CODE NAME.
OH, COME ON-- YOU'RE THE ONE WHO WAS MAKING A BIG DEAL ABOUT ME HAVING A CODE NAME...
AND NOW YOU'VE FORGOTTEN?
I'M SORRY. THERE'S A LOT GOING ON...AND YOU KNOW...
ARE YOU TWO FINISHED? BECAUSE I HAVE TO TELL YOU...

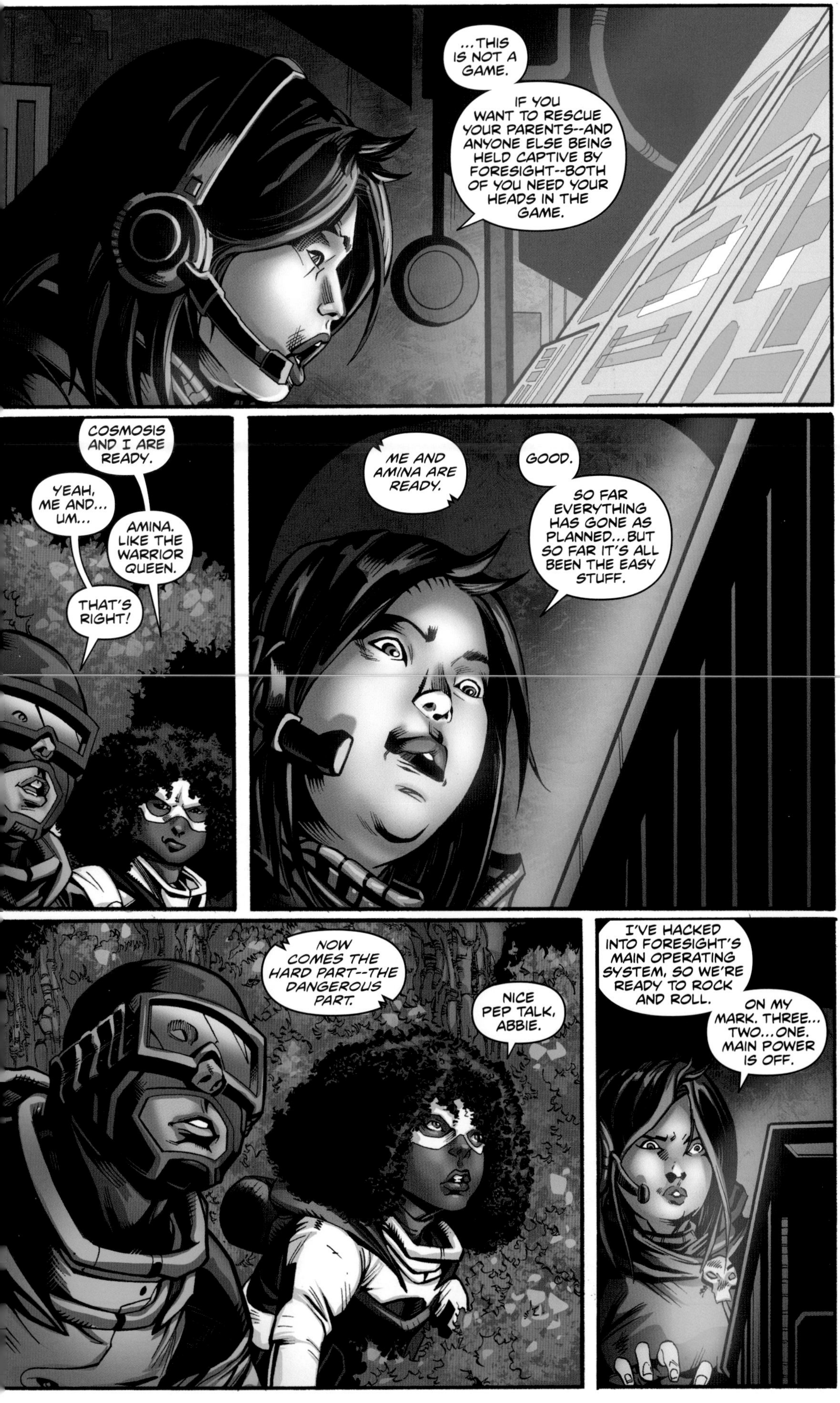
...THIS IS NOT A GAME.
IF YOU WANT TO RESCUE YOUR PARENTS--AND ANYONE ELSE BEING HELD CAPTIVE BY FORESIGHT--BOTH OF YOU NEED YOUR HEADS IN THE GAME.
COSMOSIS AND I ARE READY.
YEAH, ME AND... UM...
AMINA. LIKE THE WARRIOR QUEEN.
THAT'S RIGHT!
ME AND AMINA ARE READY.
GOOD.
SO FAR EVERYTHING HAS GONE AS PLANNED...BUT SO FAR IT'S ALL BEEN THE EASY STUFF.
NOW COMES THE HARD PART--THE DANGEROUS PART.
NICE PEP TALK, ABBIE.
I'VE HACKED INTO FORESIGHT'S MAIN OPERATING SYSTEM, SO WE'RE READY TO ROCK AND ROLL.
ON MY MARK. THREE... TWO...ONE. MAIN POWER IS OFF.

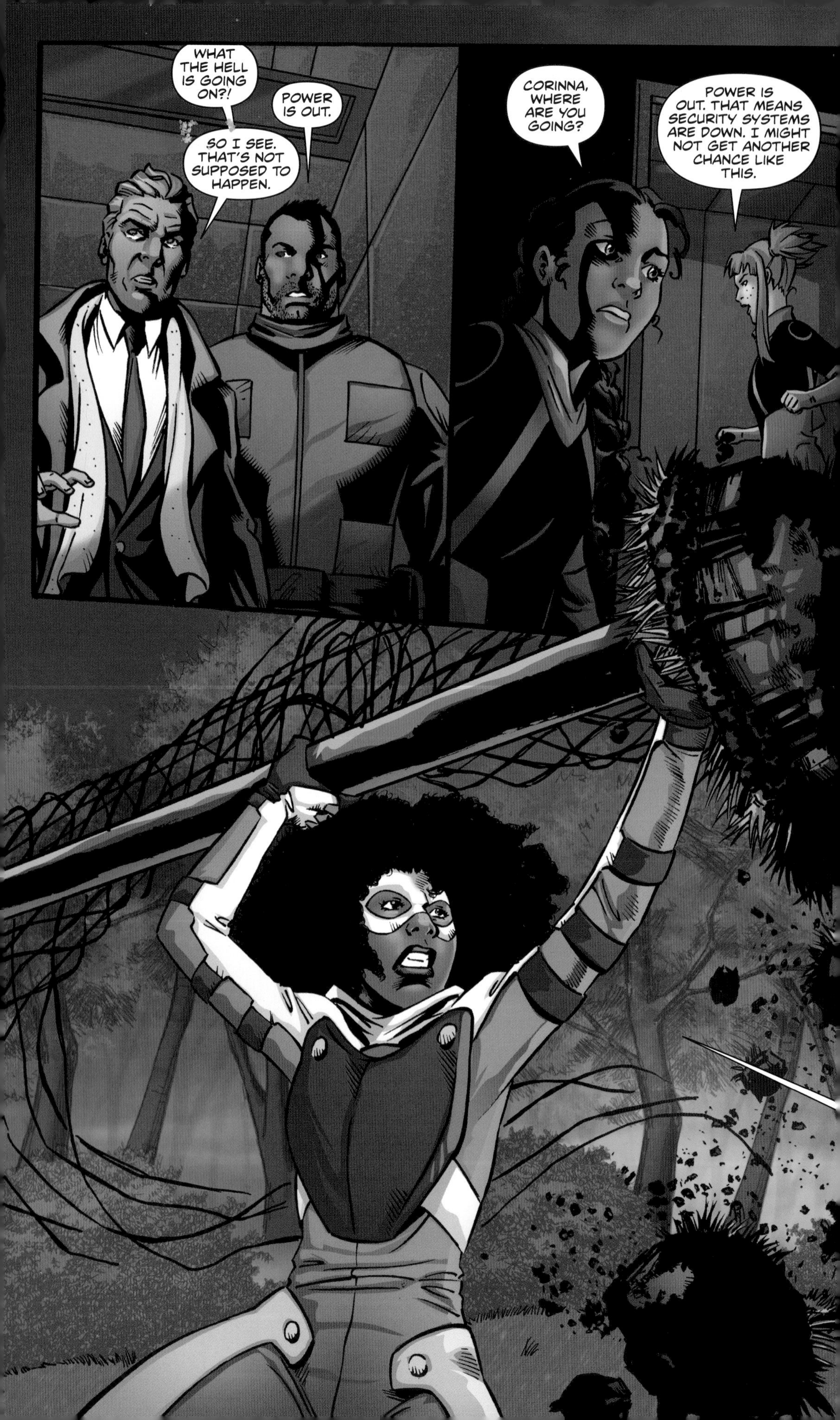
WHAT THE HELL IS GOING ON?!
POWER IS OUT.
SO I SEE. THAT'S NOT SUPPOSED TO HAPPEN.
CORINNA, WHERE ARE YOU GOING?
POWER IS OUT. THAT MEANS SECURITY SYSTEMS ARE DOWN. I MIGHT NOT GET ANOTHER CHANCE LIKE THIS.

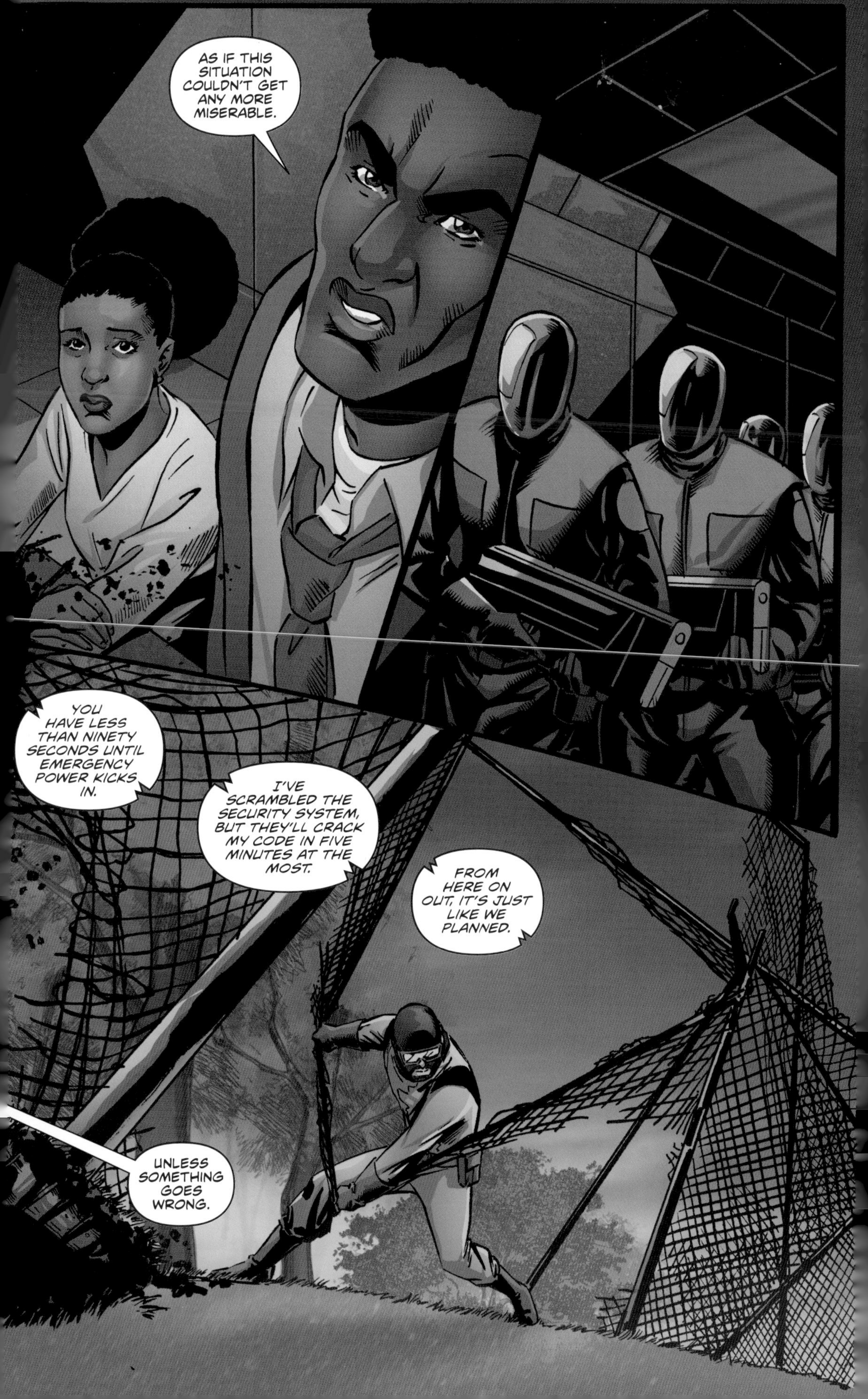
AS IF THIS SITUATION COULDN'T GET ANY MORE MISERABLE.
YOU HAVE LESS THAN NINETY SECONDS UNTIL EMERGENCY POWER KICKS IN.
I'VE SCRAMBLED THE SECURITY SYSTEM, BUT THEY'LL CRACK MY CODE IN FIVE MINUTES AT THE MOST.
FROM HERE ON OUT, IT'S JUST LIKE WE PLANNED.
UNLESS SOMETHING GOES WRONG.

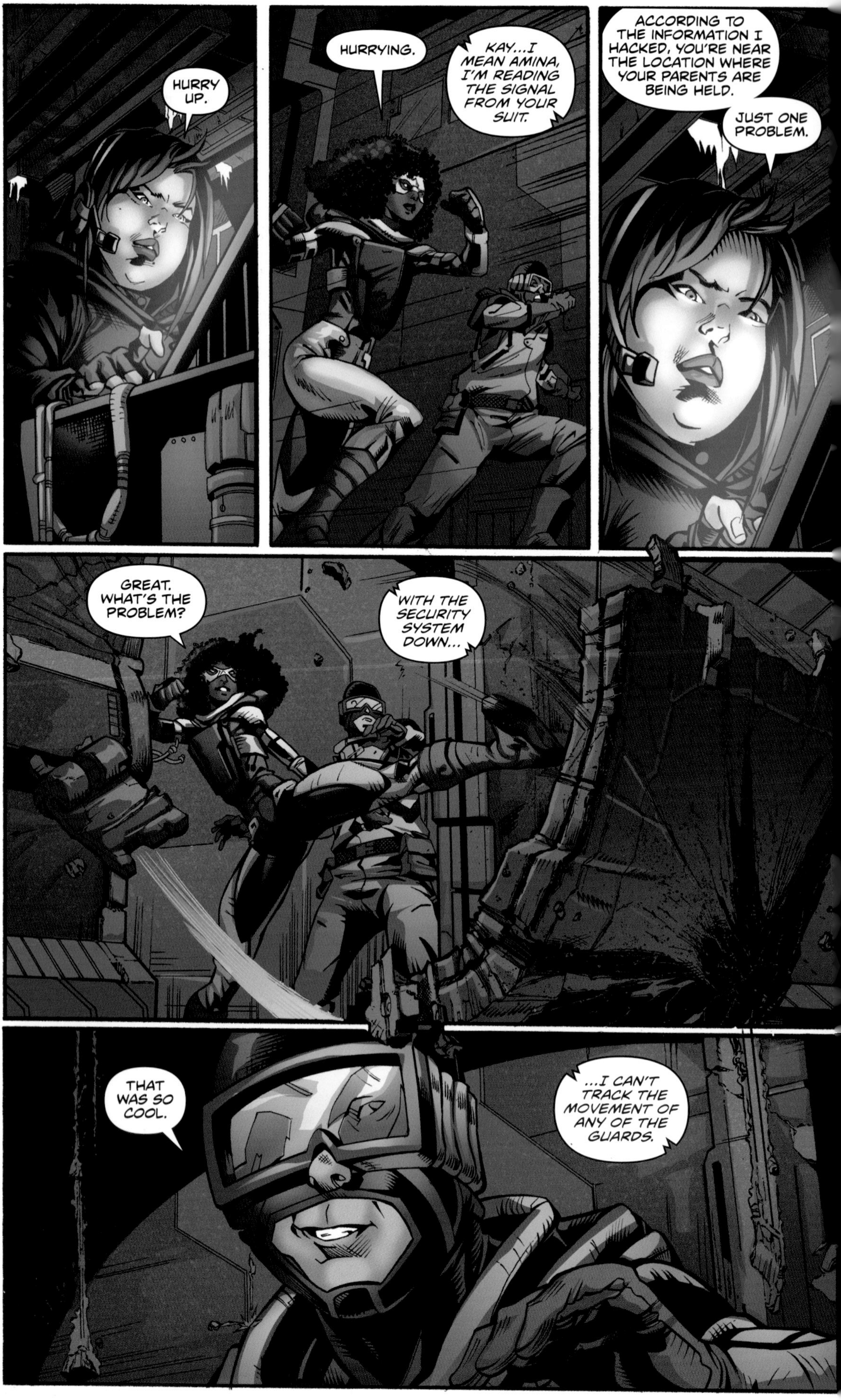
HURRY UP.
HURRYING.
KAY...I MEAN AMINA, I'M READING THE SIGNAL FROM YOUR SUIT.
ACCORDING TO THE INFORMATION I HACKED, YOU'RE NEAR THE LOCATION WHERE YOUR PARENTS ARE BEING HELD.
JUST ONE PROBLEM.
GREAT. WHAT'S THE PROBLEM?
WITH THE SECURITY SYSTEM DOWN...
THAT WAS SO COOL.
...I CAN'T TRACK THE MOVEMENT OF ANY OF THE GUARDS.

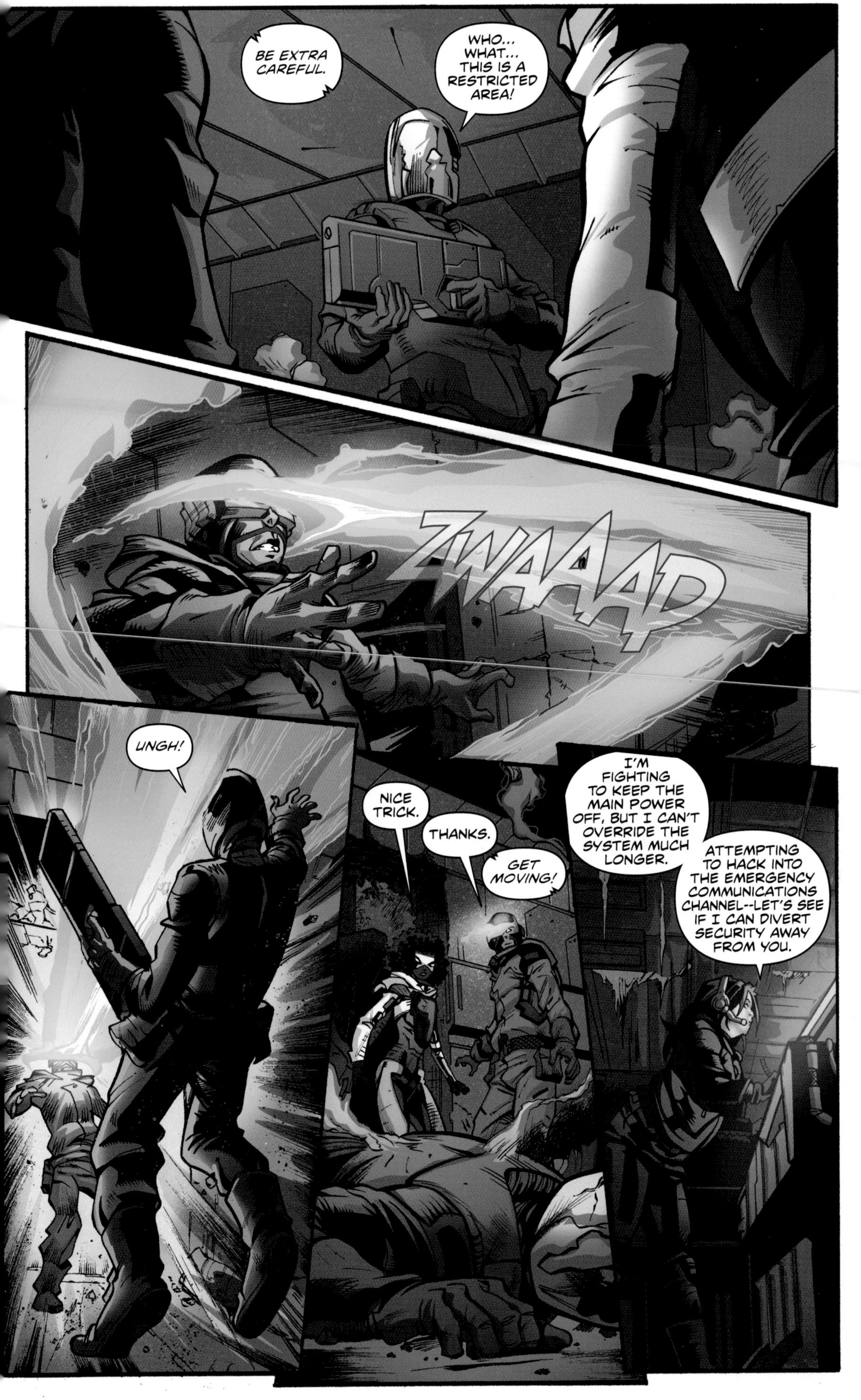
BE EXTRA CAREFUL.
WHO... WHAT... THIS IS A RESTRICTED AREA!
ZWAAAD
UNGH!
NICE TRICK.
THANKS.
GET MOVING!
I'M FIGHTING TO KEEP THE MAIN POWER OFF, BUT I CAN'T OVERRIDE THE SYSTEM MUCH LONGER.
ATTEMPTING TO HACK INTO THE EMERGENCY COMMUNICATIONS CHANNEL--LET'S SEE IF I CAN DIVERT SECURITY AWAY FROM YOU.

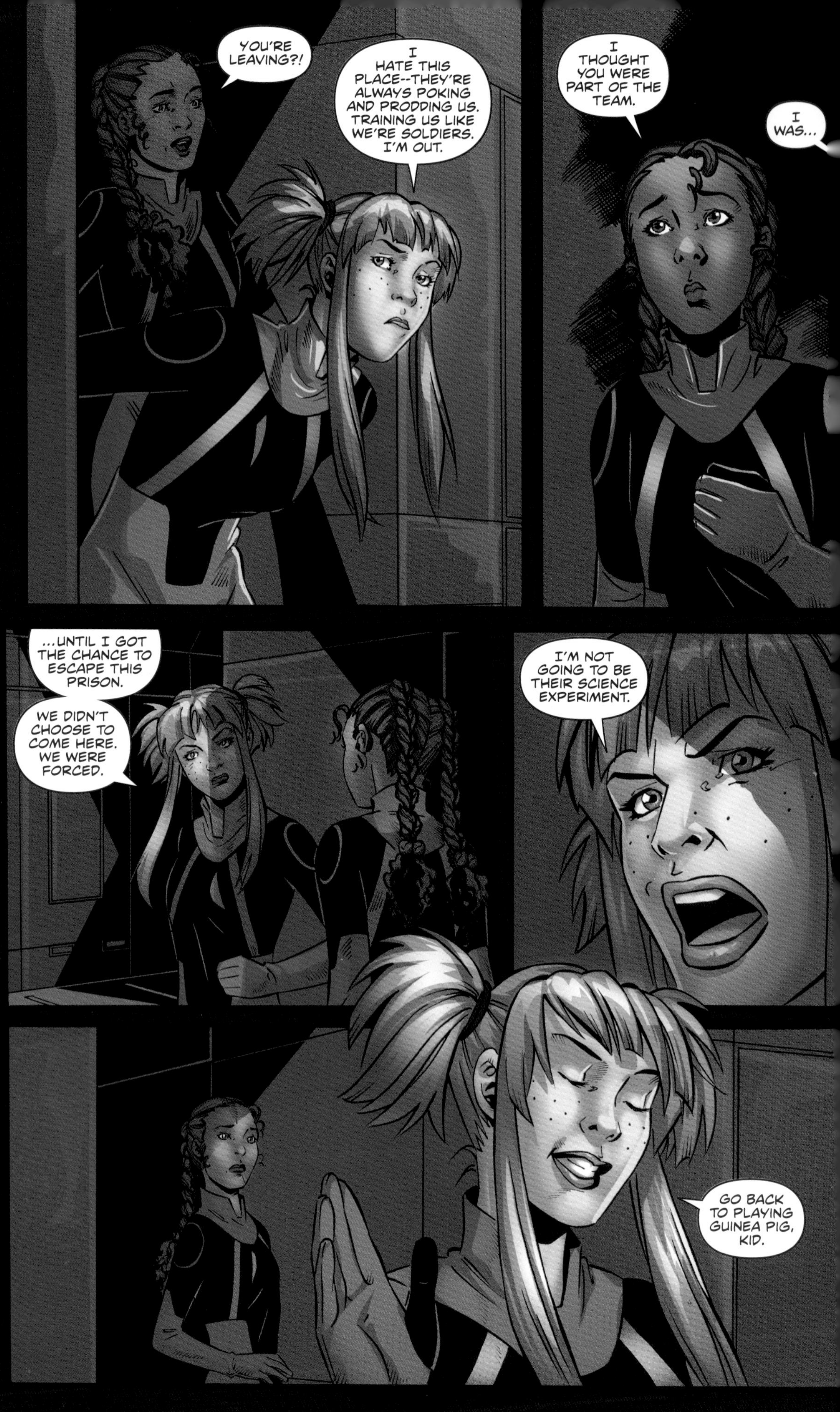
YOU'RE LEAVING?!
I HATE THIS PLACE--THEY'RE ALWAYS POKING AND PRODDING US. TRAINING US LIKE WE'RE SOLDIERS. I'M OUT.
I THOUGHT YOU WERE PART OF THE TEAM.
I WAS...
...UNTIL I GOT THE CHANCE TO ESCAPE THIS PRISON.
WE DIDN'T CHOOSE TO COME HERE. WE WERE FORCED.
I'M NOT GOING TO BE THEIR SCIENCE EXPERIMENT.
GO BACK TO PLAYING GUINEA PIG, KID.

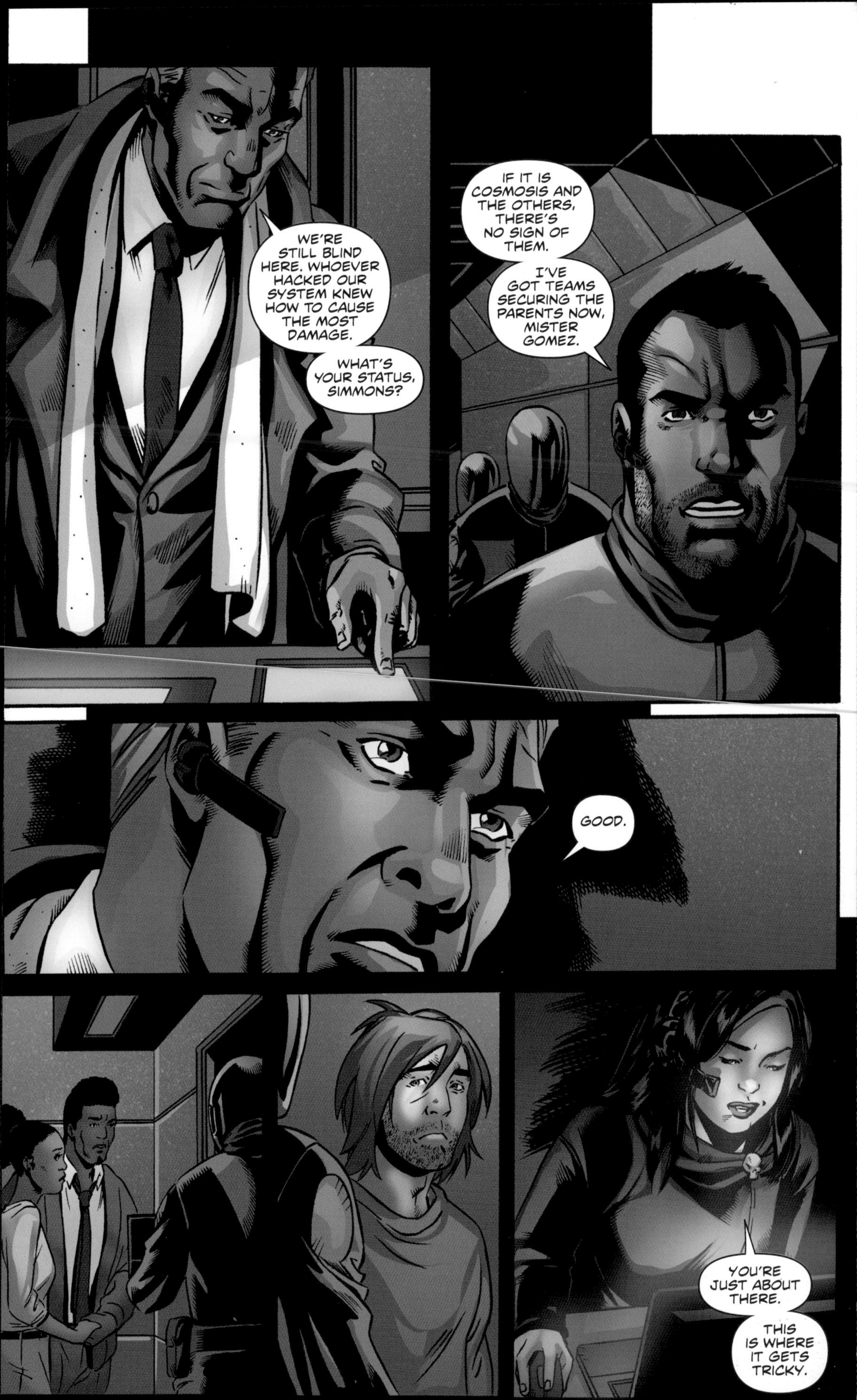
WE'RE STILL BLIND HERE. WHOEVER HACKED OUR SYSTEM KNEW HOW TO CAUSE THE MOST DAMAGE.
WHAT'S YOUR STATUS, SIMMONS?
IF IT IS COSMOSIS AND THE OTHERS, THERE'S NO SIGN OF THEM.
I'VE GOT TEAMS SECURING THE PARENTS NOW, MISTER GOMEZ.
GOOD.
YOU'RE JUST ABOUT THERE.
THIS IS WHERE IT GETS TRICKY.

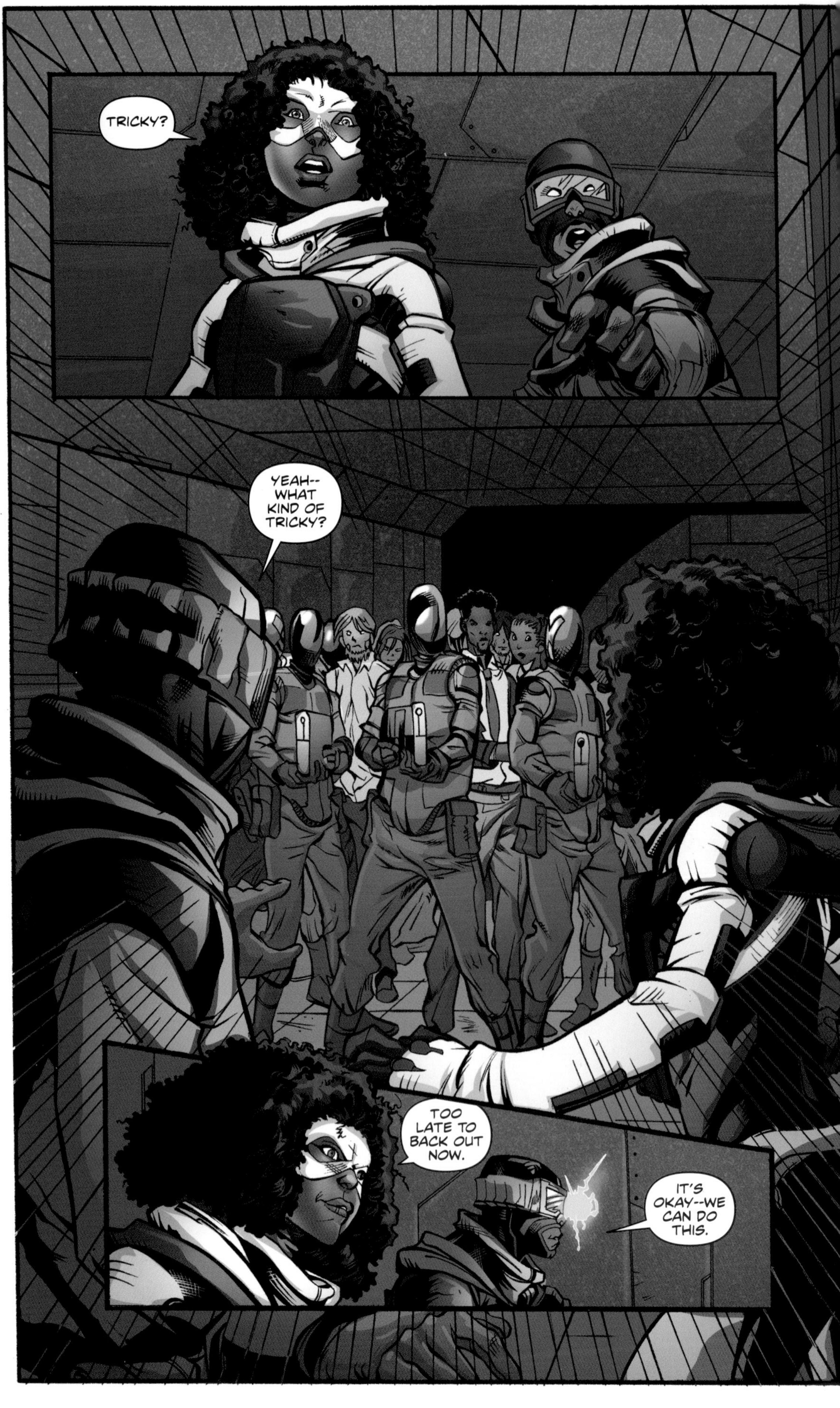
TRICKY?
YEAH-- WHAT KIND OF TRICKY?
TOO LATE TO BACK OUT NOW.
IT'S OKAY--WE CAN DO THIS.

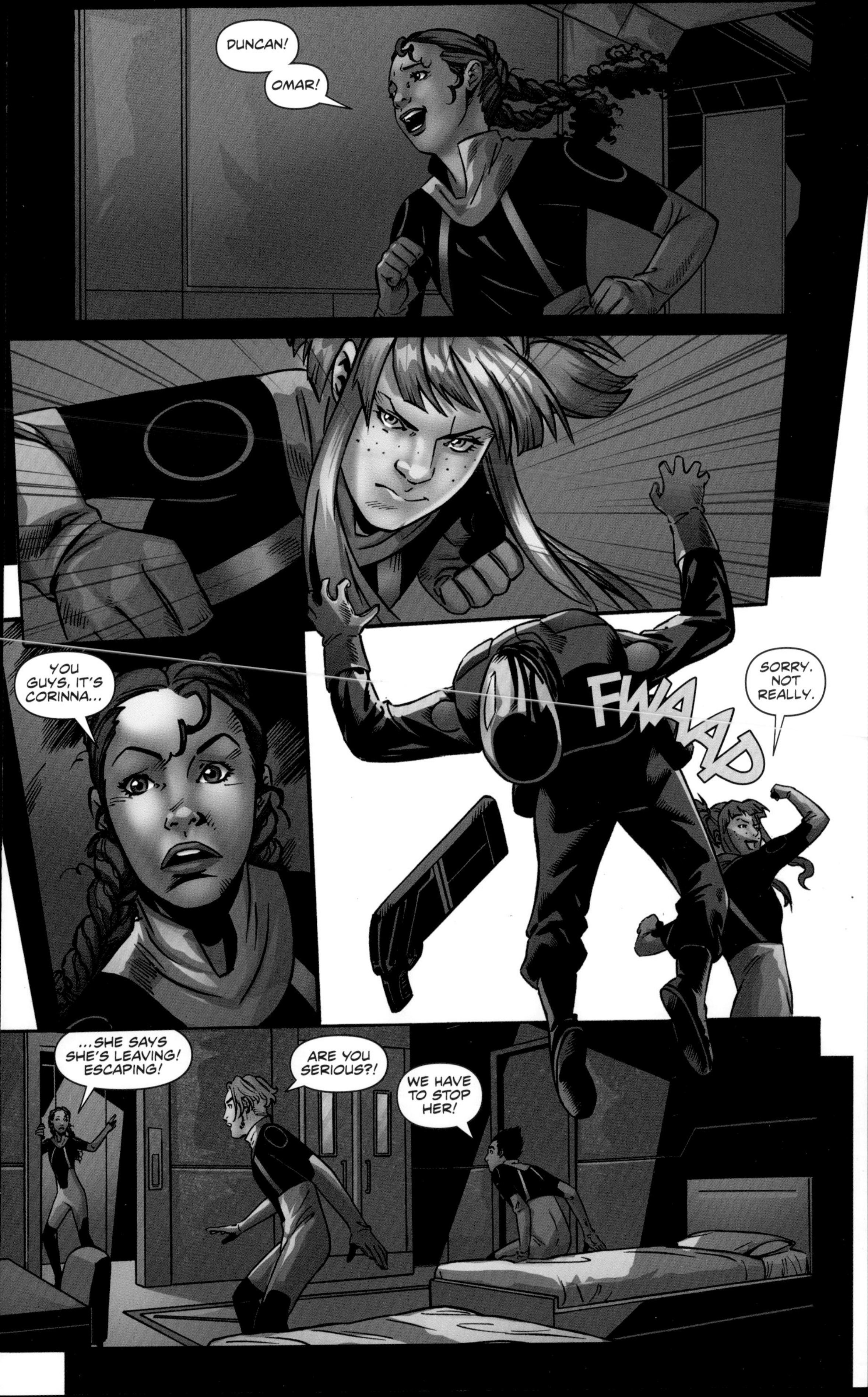
DUNCAN!
OMAR!
YOU GUYS, IT'S CORINNA...
FWAAAP
SORRY. NOT REALLY.
...SHE SAYS SHE'S LEAVING! ESCAPING!
ARE YOU SERIOUS?!
WE HAVE TO STOP HER!

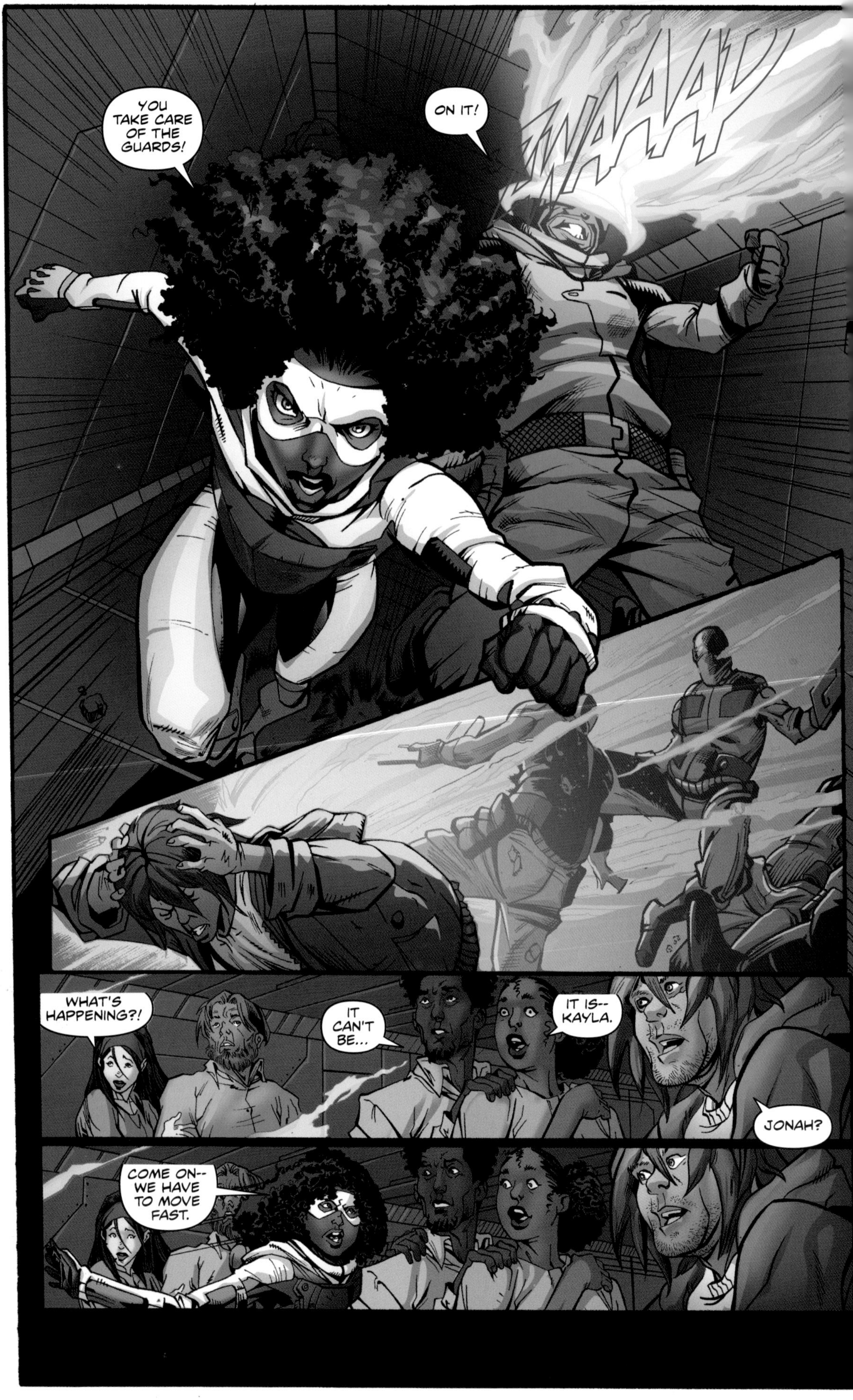
YOU TAKE CARE OF THE GUARDS!
ON IT!
WHAT'S HAPPENING?!
IT CAN'T BE...
IT IS-- KAYLA.
JONAH?
COME ON-- WE HAVE TO MOVE FAST.

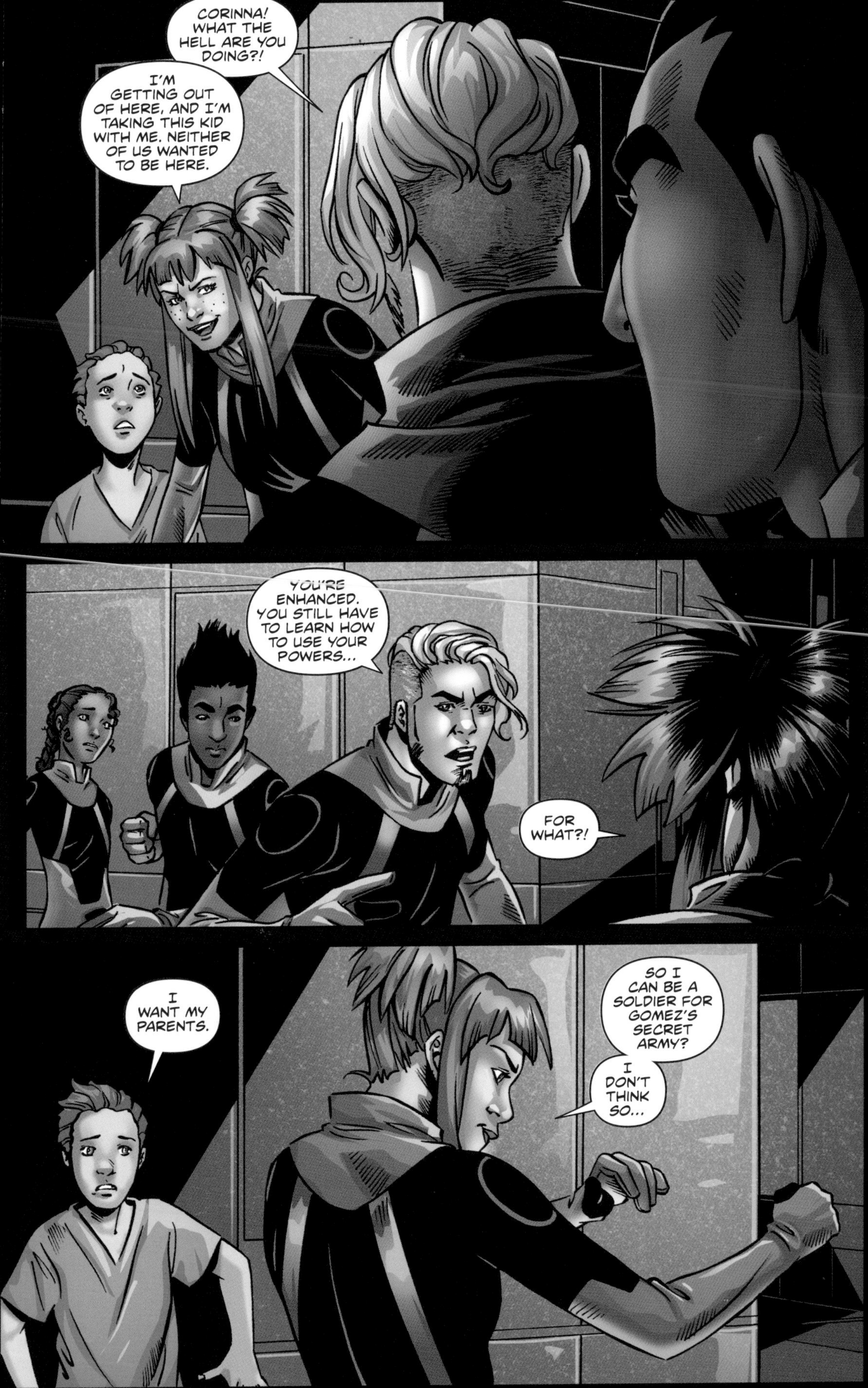
CORINNA! WHAT THE HELL ARE YOU DOING?!
I'M GETTING OUT OF HERE, AND I'M TAKING THIS KID WITH ME. NEITHER OF US WANTED TO BE HERE.
YOU'RE ENHANCED. YOU STILL HAVE TO LEARN HOW TO USE YOUR POWERS...
FOR WHAT?!
I WANT MY PARENTS.
SO I CAN BE A SOLDIER FOR GOMEZ'S SECRET ARMY?
I DON'T THINK SO...

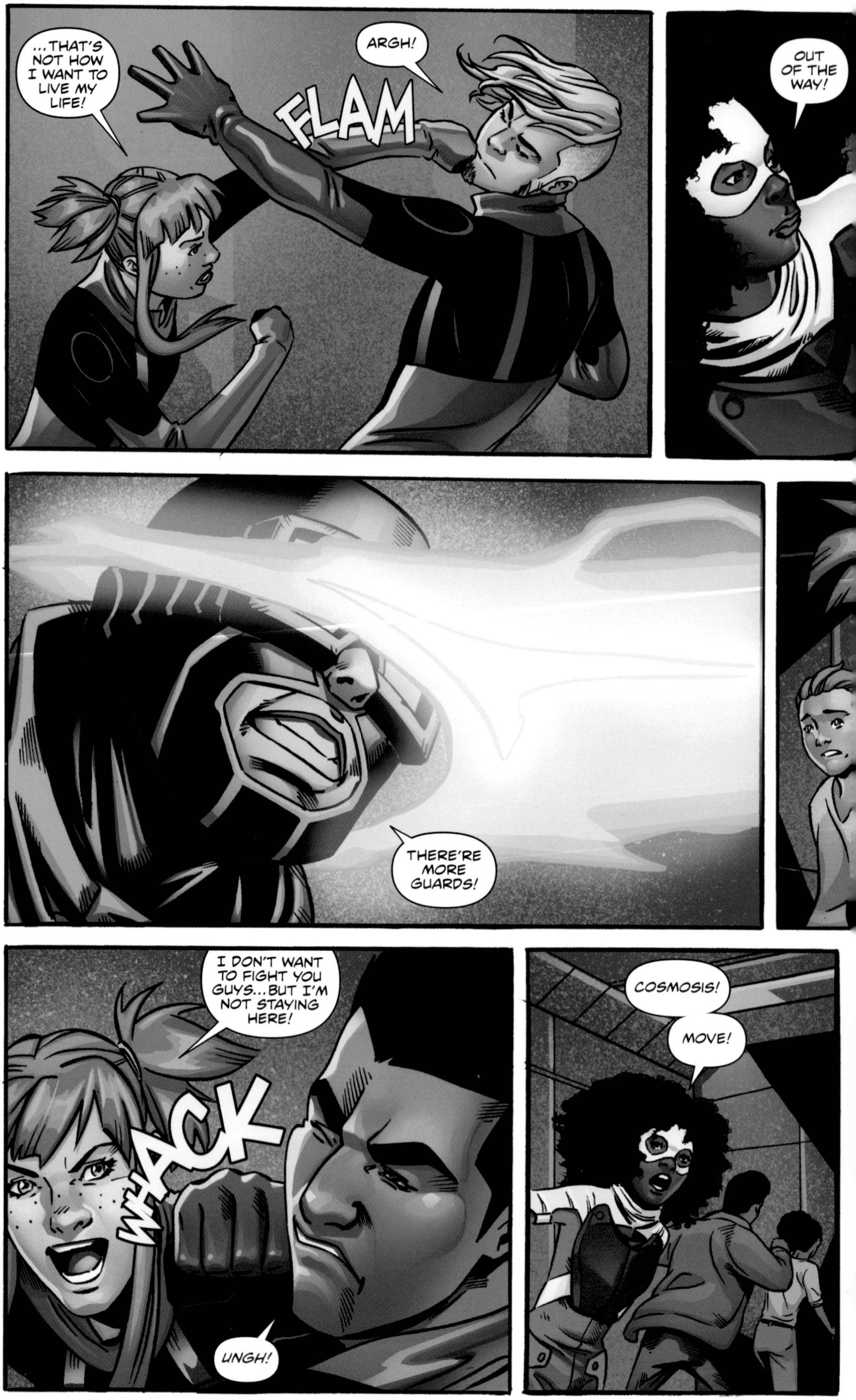

...THAT'S NOT HOW I WANT TO LIVE MY LIFE!
ARGH!
FLAM
OUT OF THE WAY!
THERE'RE MORE GUARDS!
I DON'T WANT TO FIGHT YOU GUYS...BUT I'M NOT STAYING HERE!
WHACK
UNGH!
COSMOSIS!
MOVE!

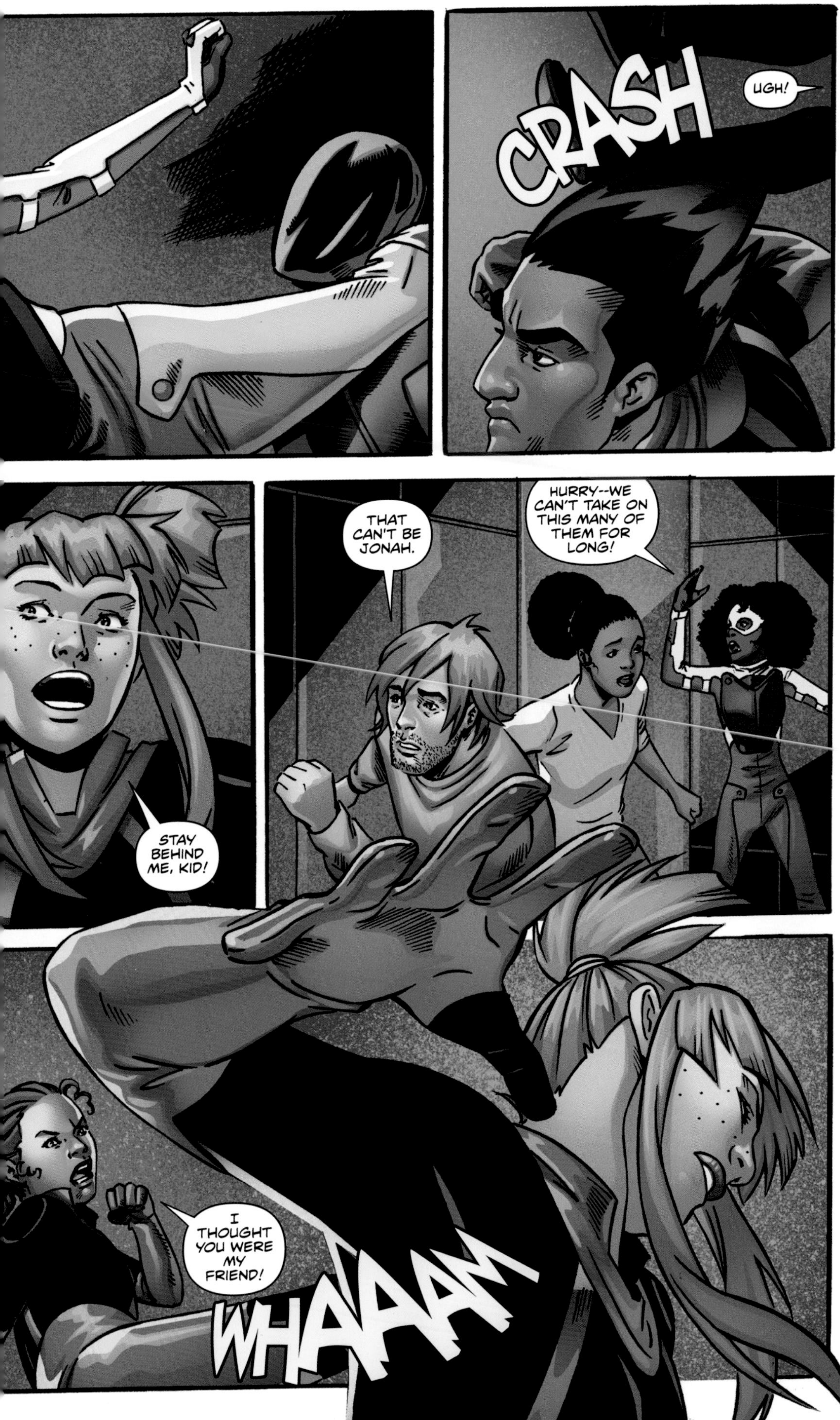
CRASH
UGH!
STAY BEHIND ME, KID!
THAT CAN'T BE JONAH.
HURRY--WE CAN'T TAKE ON THIS MANY OF THEM FOR LONG!
I THOUGHT YOU WERE MY FRIEND!
WHAAAM

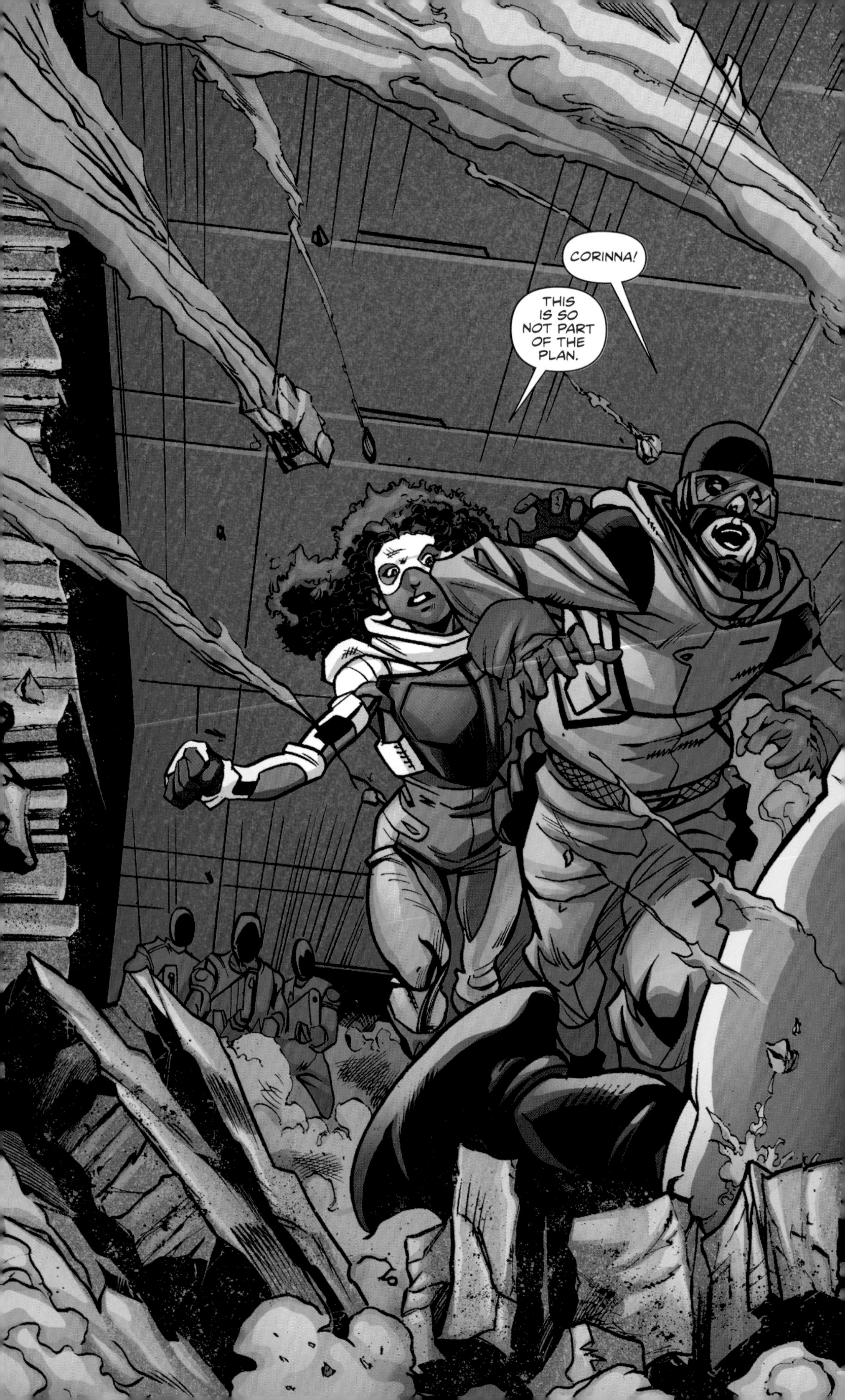
CORINNA!
THIS IS SO NOT PART OF THE PLAN.

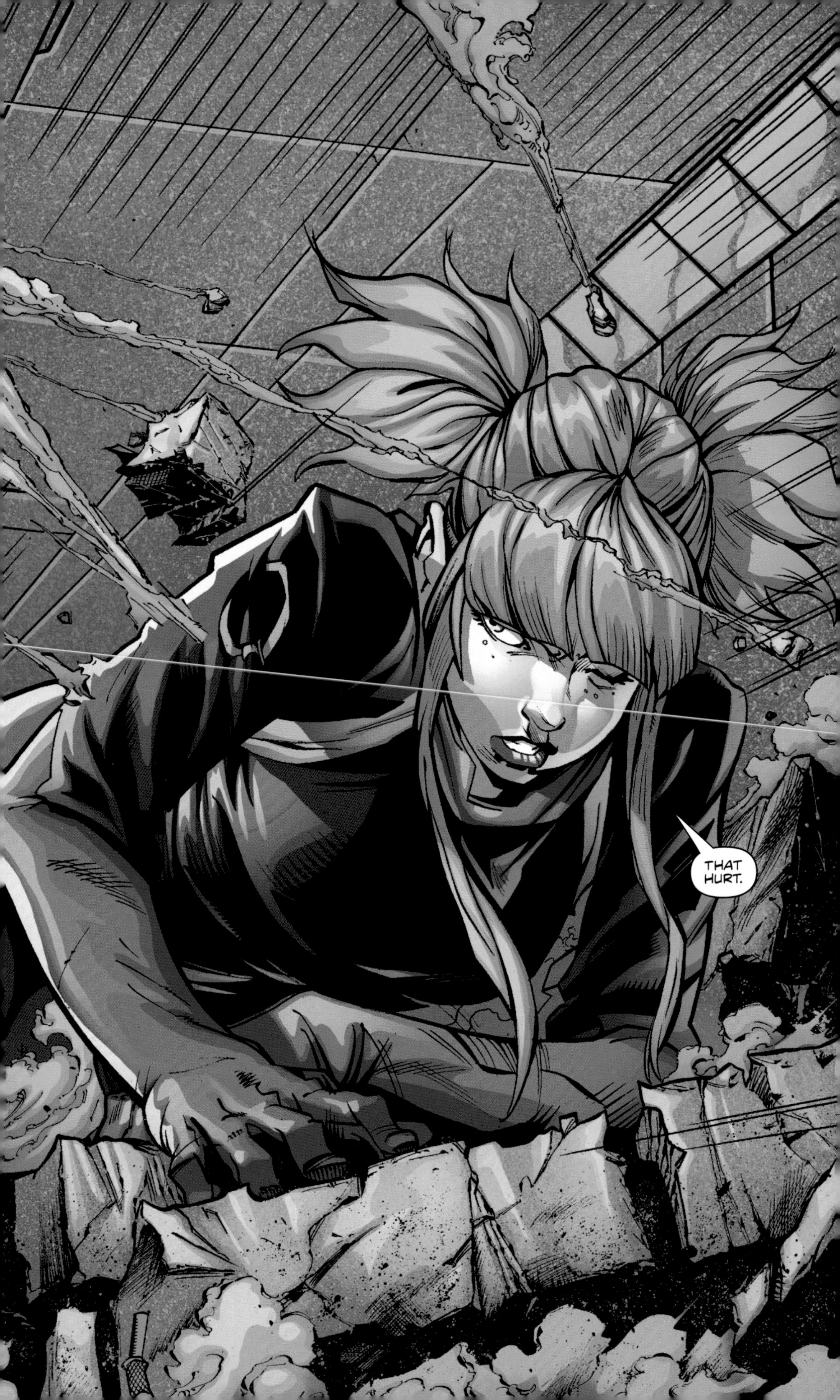
THAT HURT.

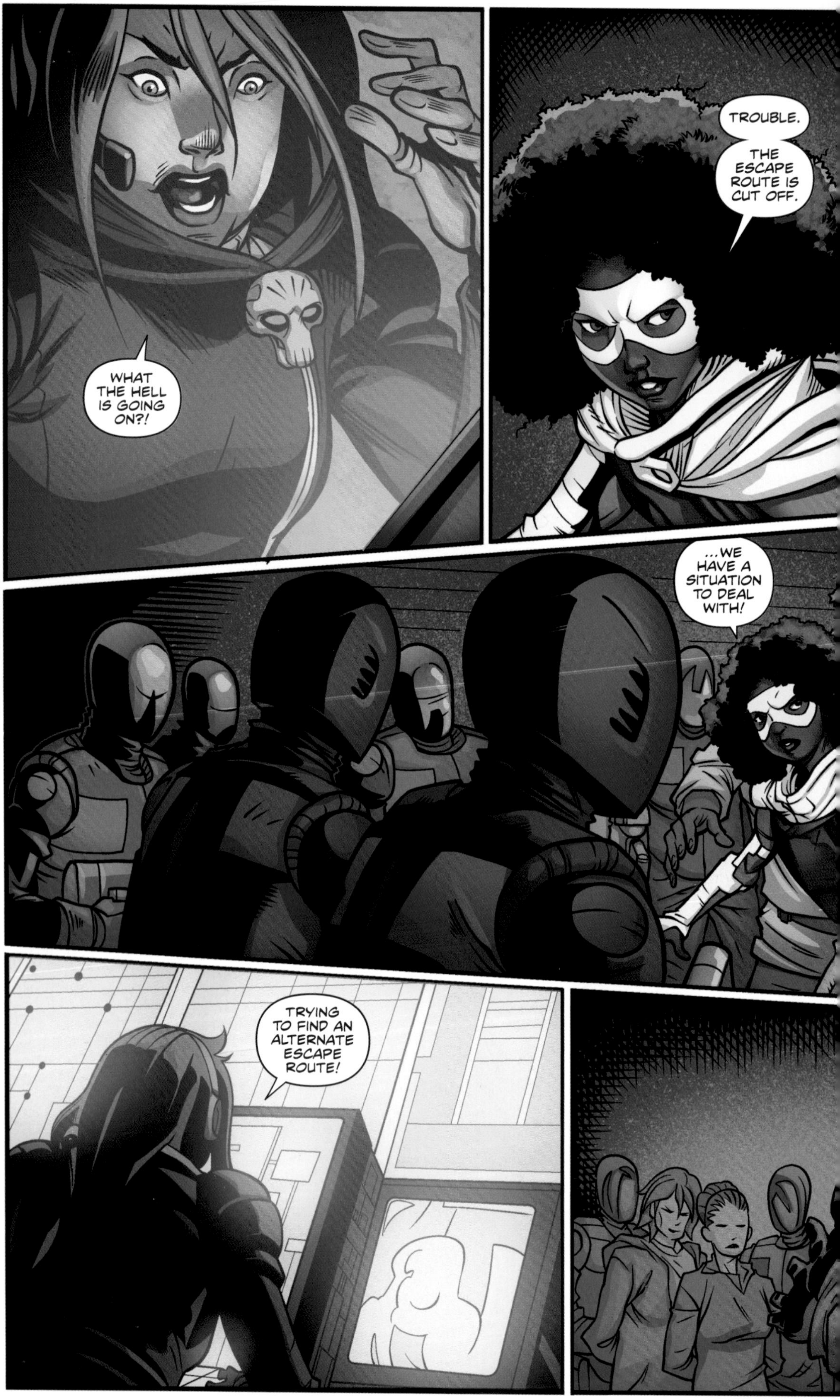

WHAT THE HELL IS GOING ON?!
TROUBLE.
THE ESCAPE ROUTE IS CUT OFF.
...WE HAVE A SITUATION TO DEAL WITH!
TRYING TO FIND AN ALTERNATE ESCAPE ROUTE!

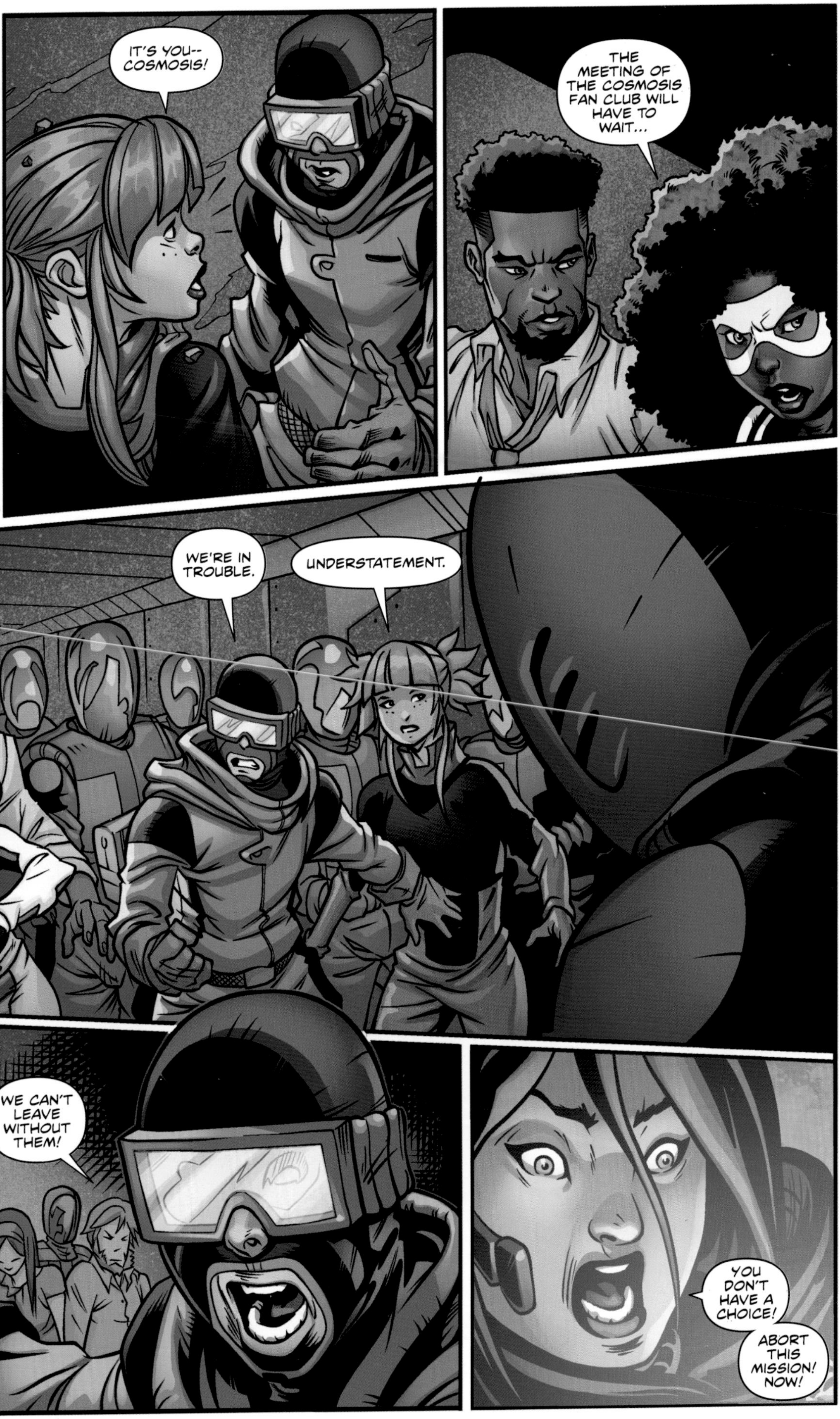
IT'S YOU-- COSMOSIS!
THE MEETING OF THE COSMOSIS FAN CLUB WILL HAVE TO WAIT...
WE'RE IN TROUBLE.
UNDERSTATEMENT.
WE CAN'T LEAVE WITHOUT THEM!
YOU DON'T HAVE A CHOICE!
ABORT THIS MISSION! NOW!

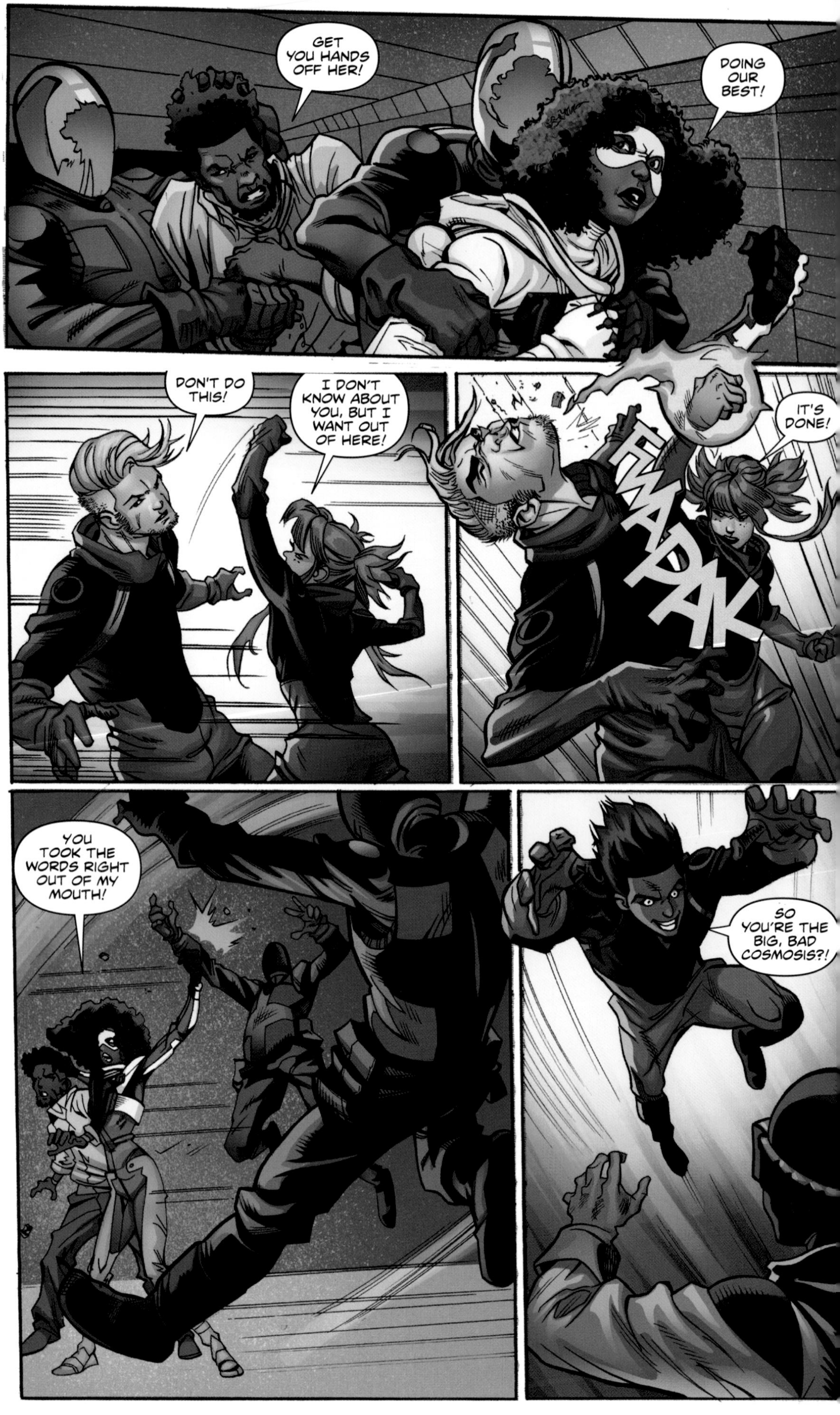
GET YOU HANDS OFF HER!
DOING OUR BEST!
DON'T DO THIS!
I DON'T KNOW ABOUT YOU, BUT I WANT OUT OF HERE!
FWAPAK
IT'S DONE!
YOU TOOK THE WORDS RIGHT OUT OF MY MOUTH!
SO YOU'RE THE BIG, BAD COSMOSIS?!

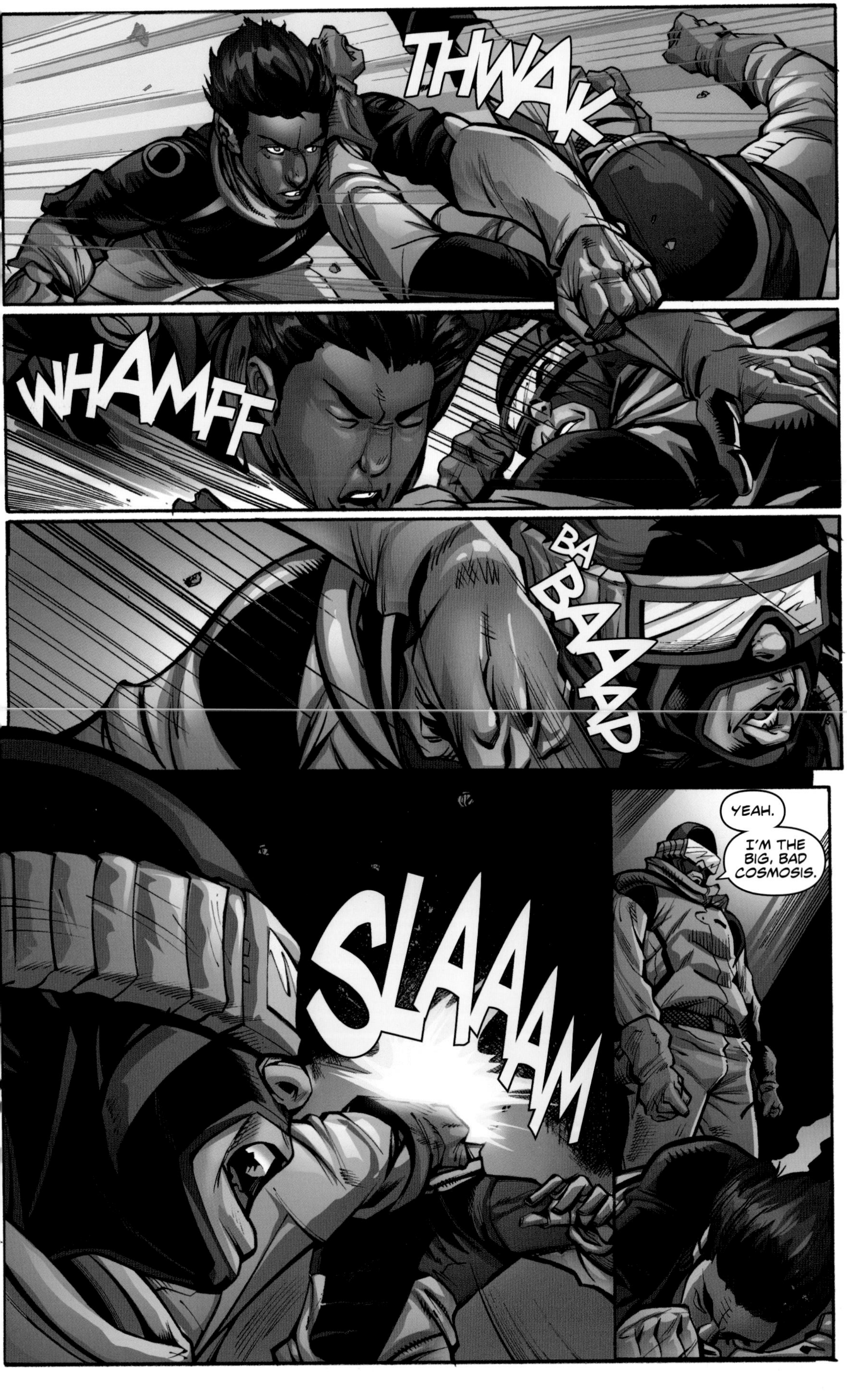

THWAK
WHAMFF
BA BAAAP
SLAAAM
YEAH.
I'M THE BIG, BAD COSMOSIS.

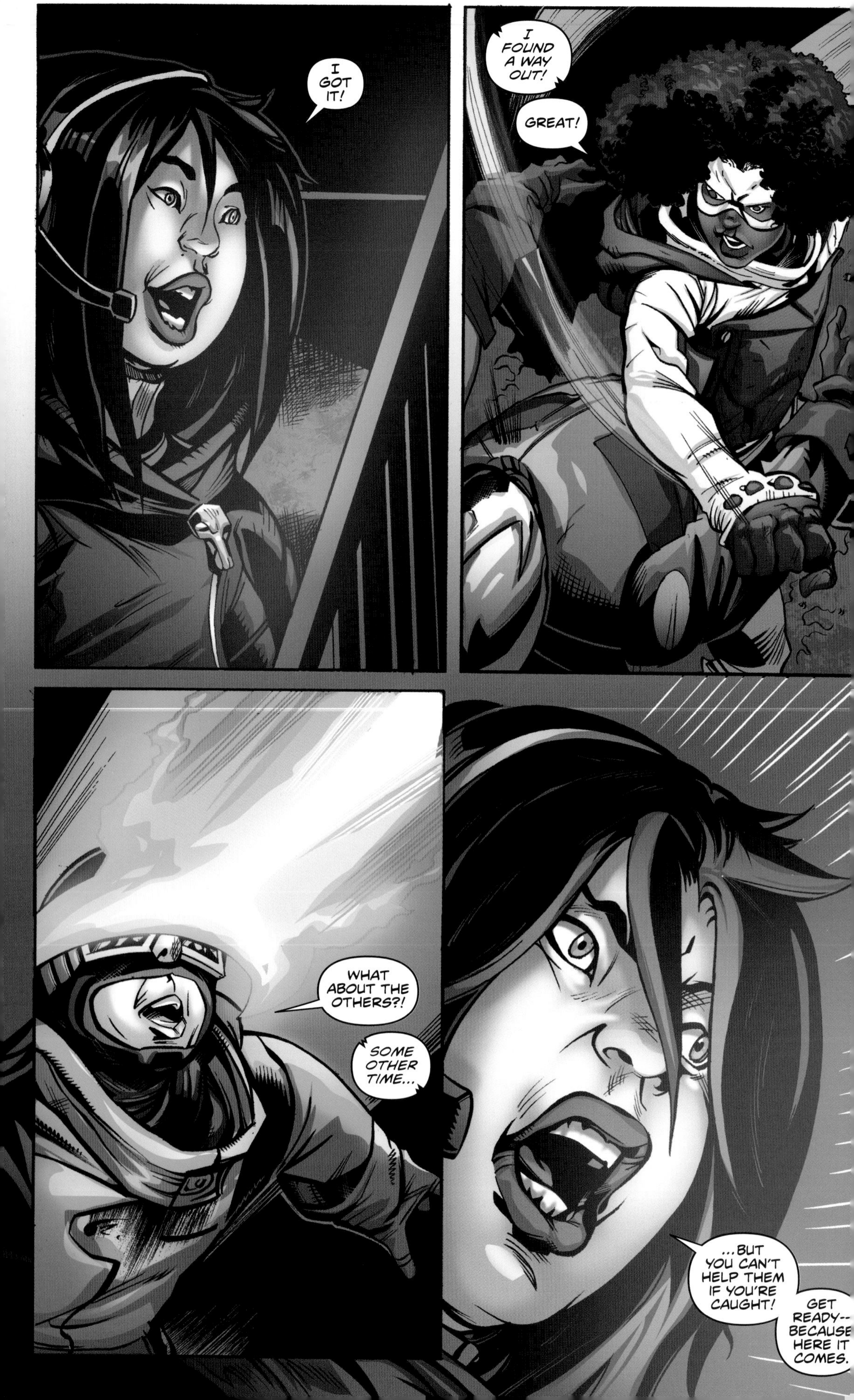

I GOT IT!
I FOUND A WAY OUT!
GREAT!
WHAT ABOUT THE OTHERS?!
SOME OTHER TIME...
...BUT YOU CAN'T HELP THEM IF YOU'RE CAUGHT!
GET READY-- BECAUSE HERE IT COMES.

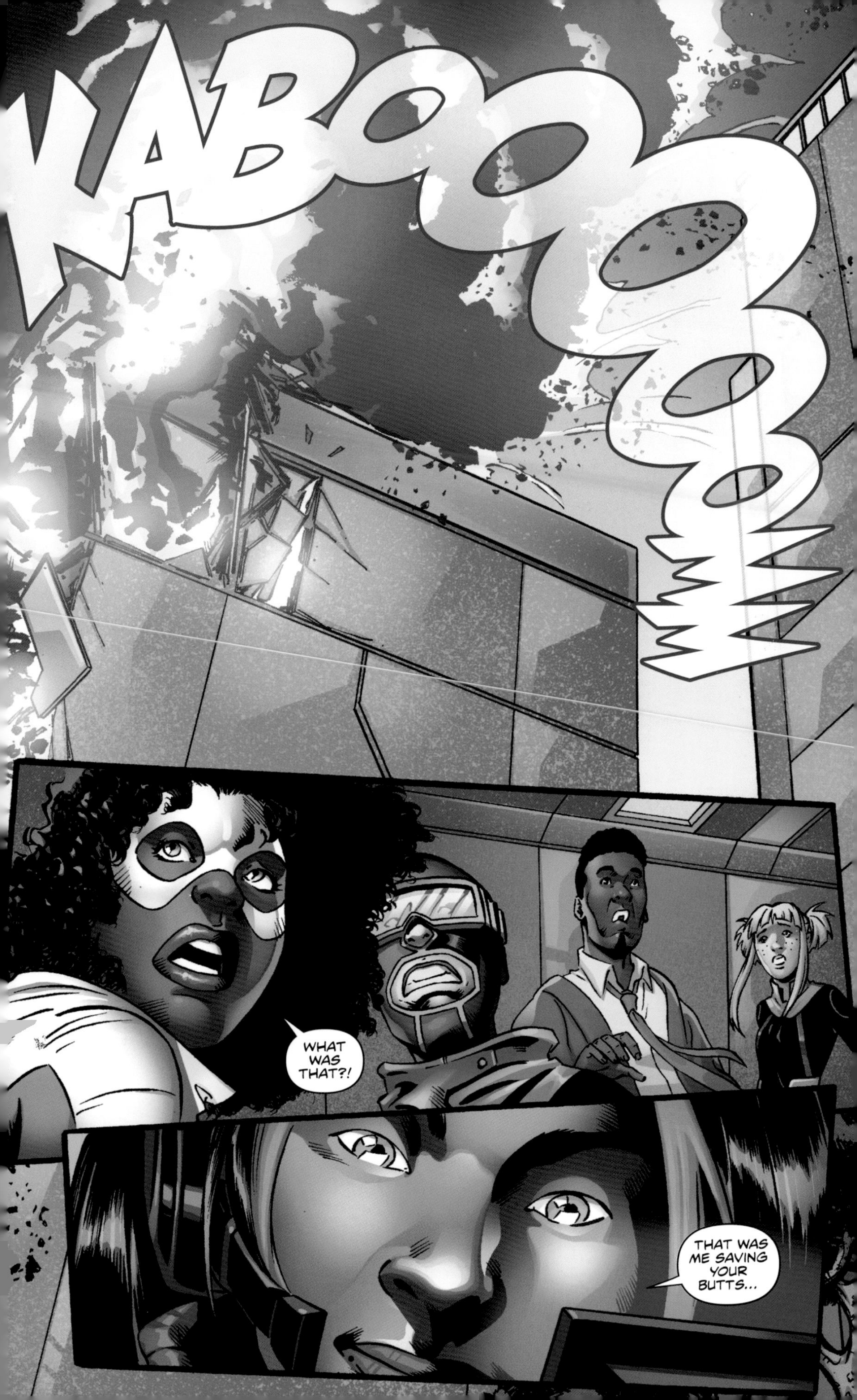
KABOOOOOM
WHAT WAS THAT?!
THAT WAS ME SAVING YOUR BUTTS...

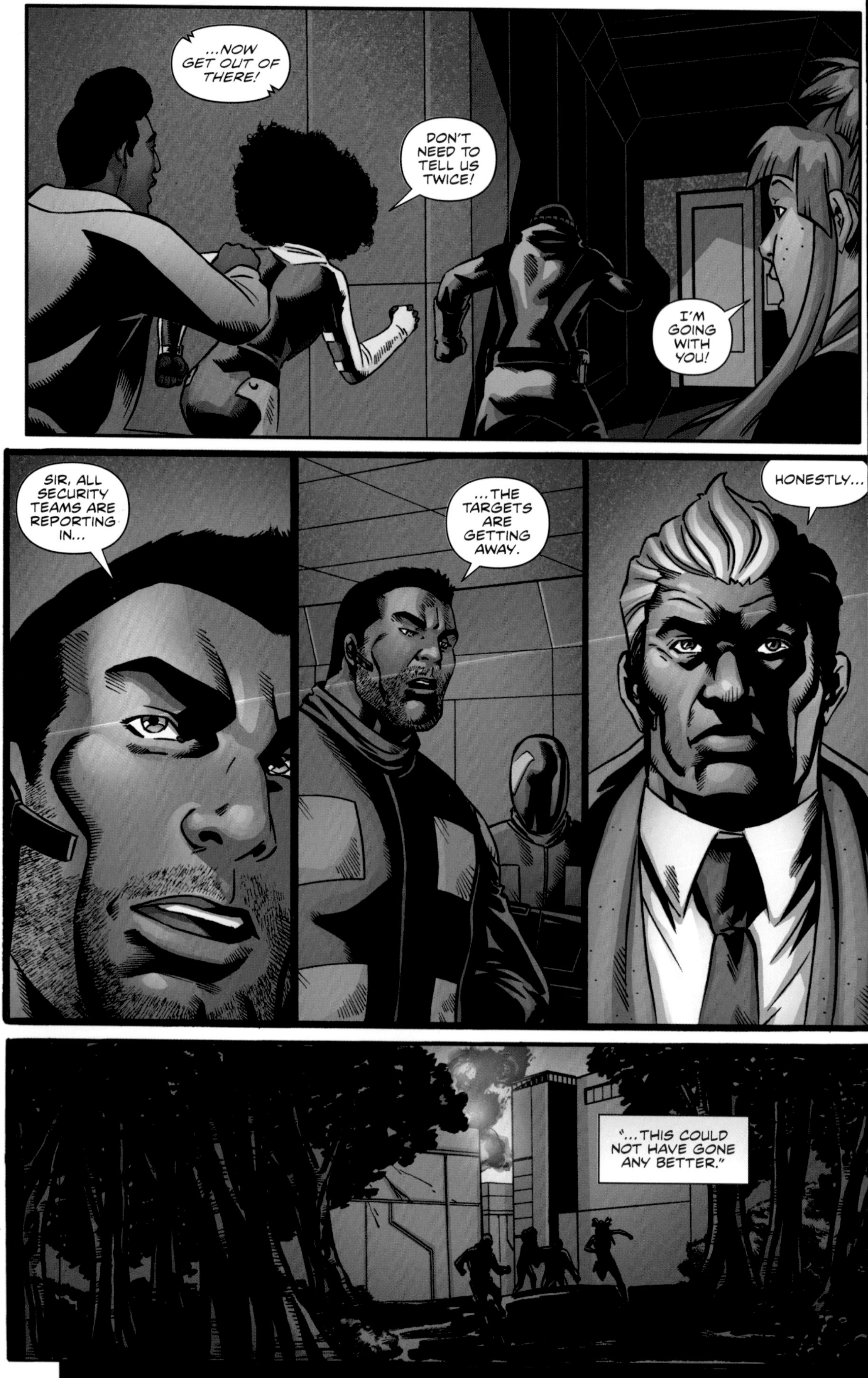
...NOW GET OUT OF THERE!
DON'T NEED TO TELL US TWICE!
I'M GOING WITH YOU!
SIR, ALL SECURITY TEAMS ARE REPORTING IN...
...THE TARGETS ARE GETTING AWAY.
HONESTLY...
"...THIS COULD NOT HAVE GONE ANY BETTER."

CHAPTER THREE

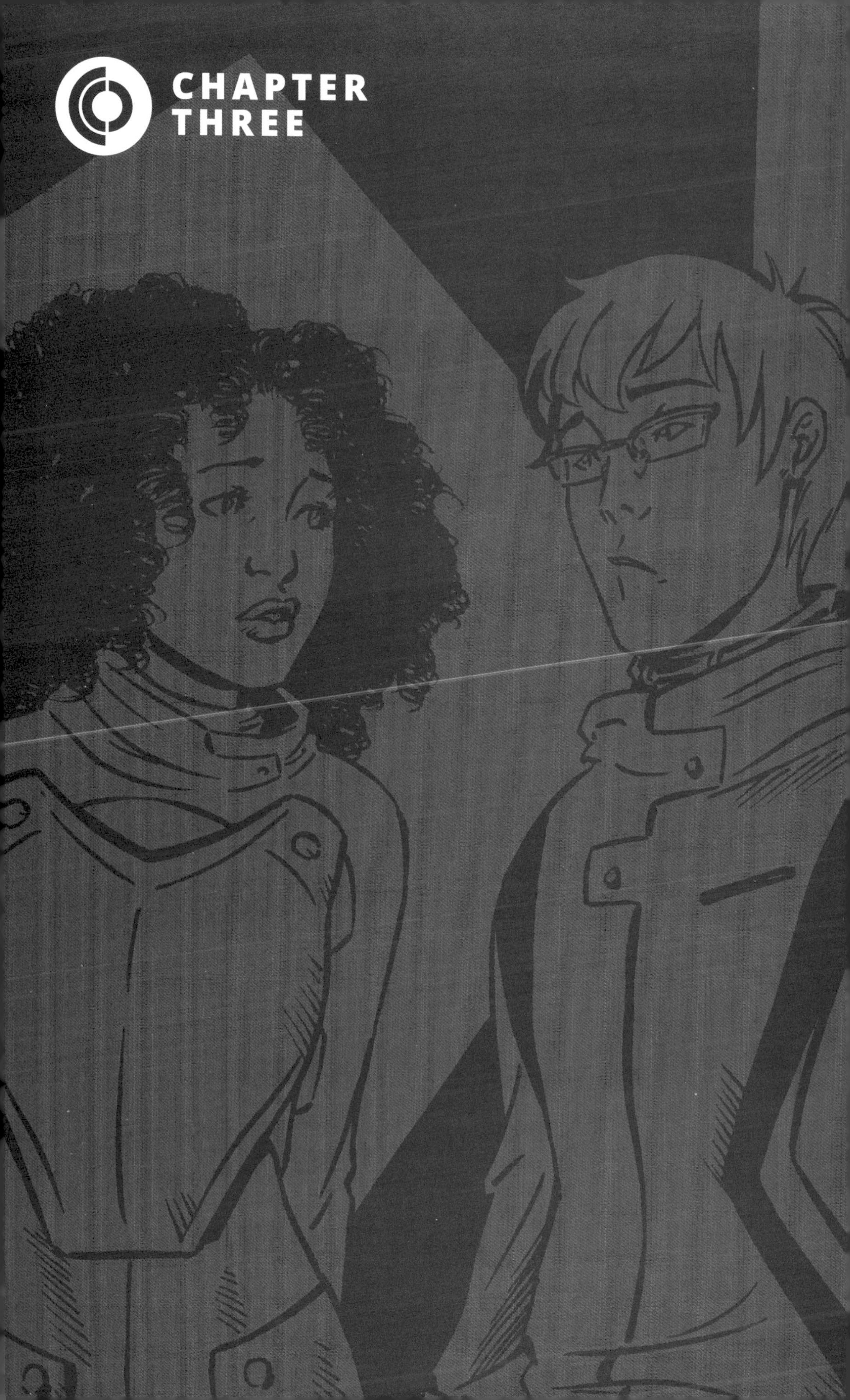

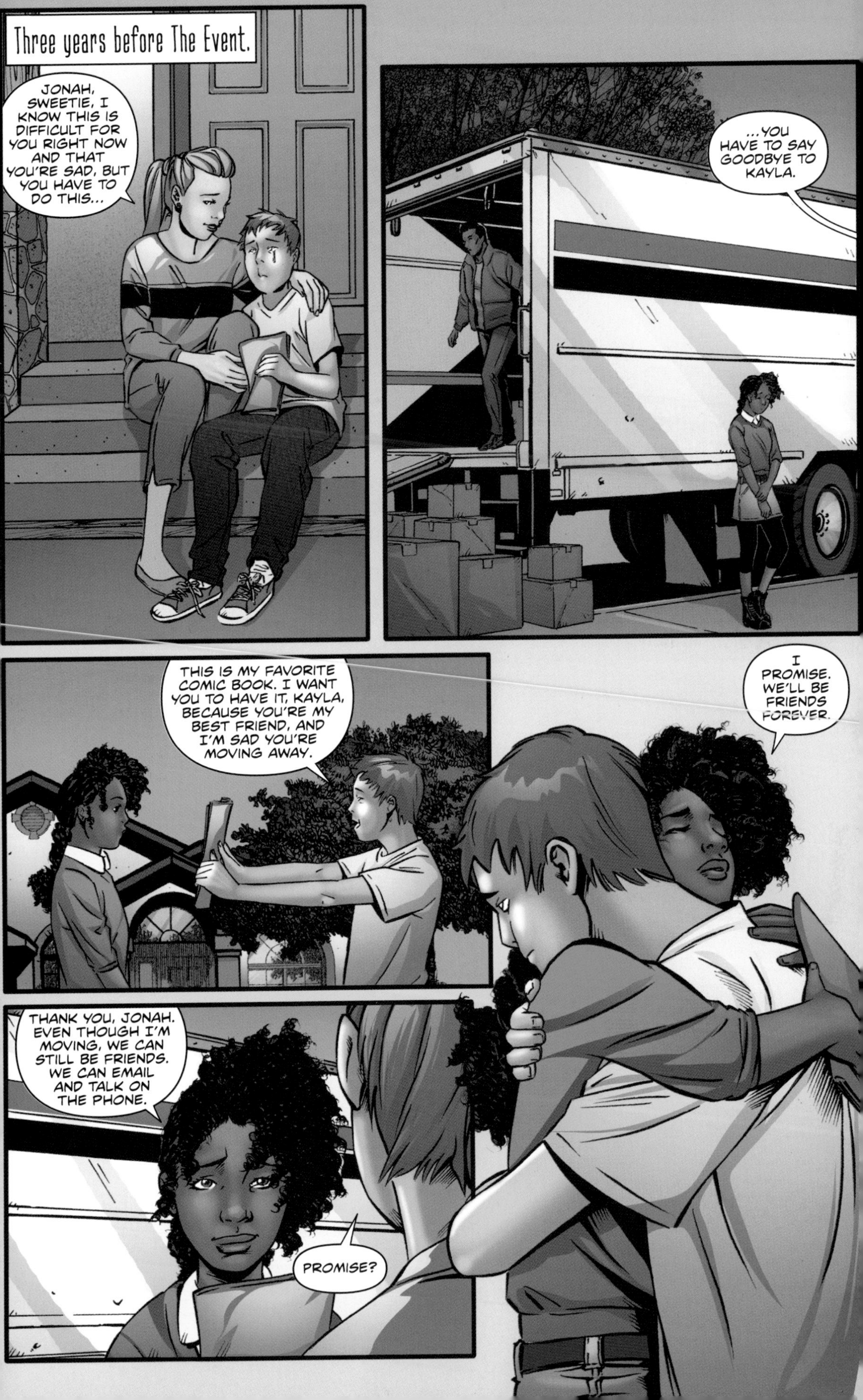
Three years before The Event.
JONAH, SWEETIE, I KNOW THIS IS DIFFICULT FOR YOU RIGHT NOW AND THAT YOU'RE SAD, BUT YOU HAVE TO DO THIS...
...YOU HAVE TO SAY GOODBYE TO KAYLA.
THIS IS MY FAVORITE COMIC BOOK. I WANT YOU TO HAVE IT, KAYLA, BECAUSE YOU'RE MY BEST FRIEND, AND I'M SAD YOU'RE MOVING AWAY.
THANK YOU, JONAH. EVEN THOUGH I'M MOVING, WE CAN STILL BE FRIENDS. WE CAN EMAIL AND TALK ON THE PHONE.
PROMISE?
I PROMISE. WE'LL BE FRIENDS FOREVER.

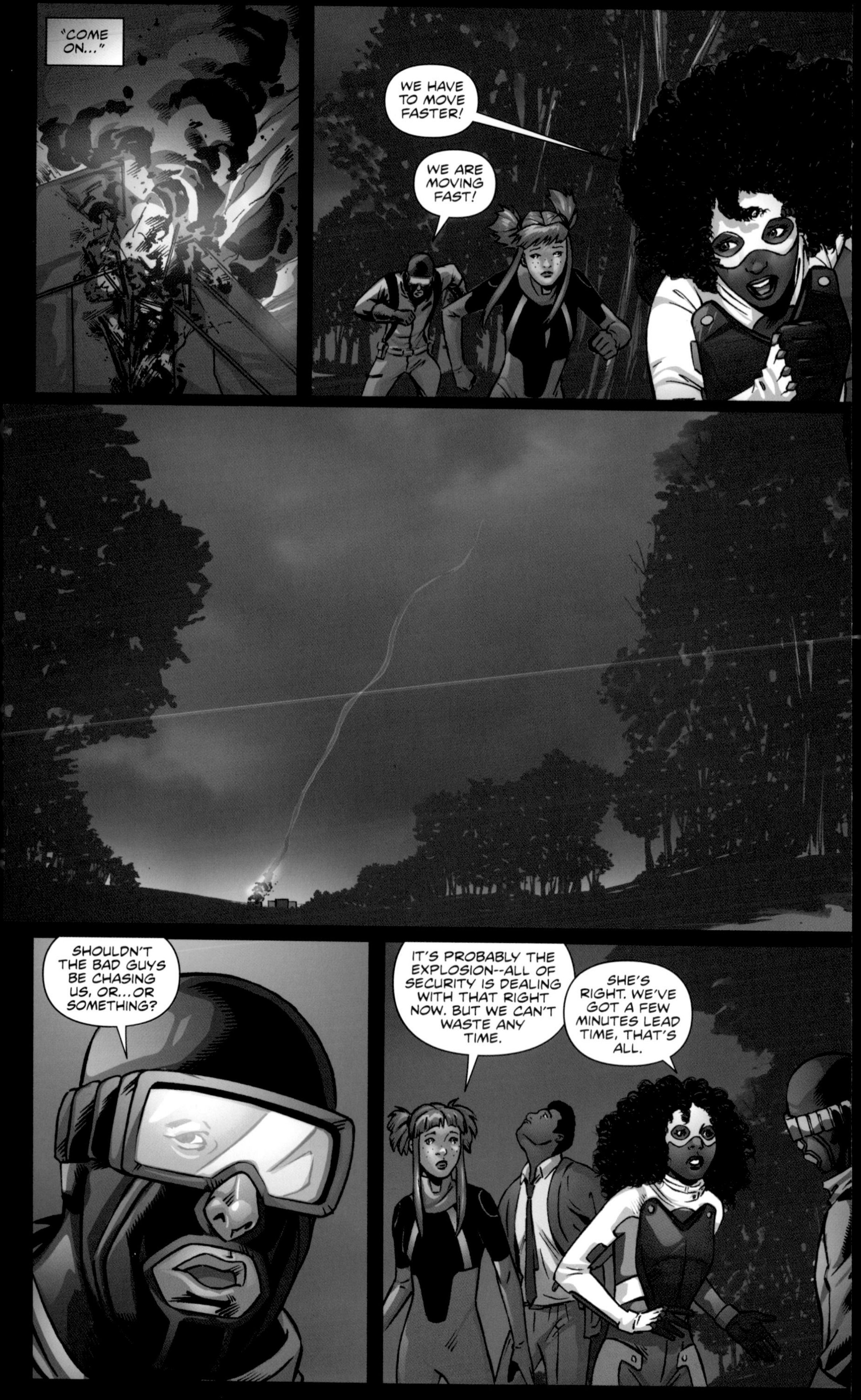
"COME ON..."
WE HAVE TO MOVE FASTER!
WE ARE MOVING FAST!
SHOULDN'T THE BAD GUYS BE CHASING US, OR...OR SOMETHING?
IT'S PROBABLY THE EXPLOSION--ALL OF SECURITY IS DEALING WITH THAT RIGHT NOW. BUT WE CAN'T WASTE ANY TIME.
SHE'S RIGHT. WE'VE GOT A FEW MINUTES LEAD TIME, THAT'S ALL.

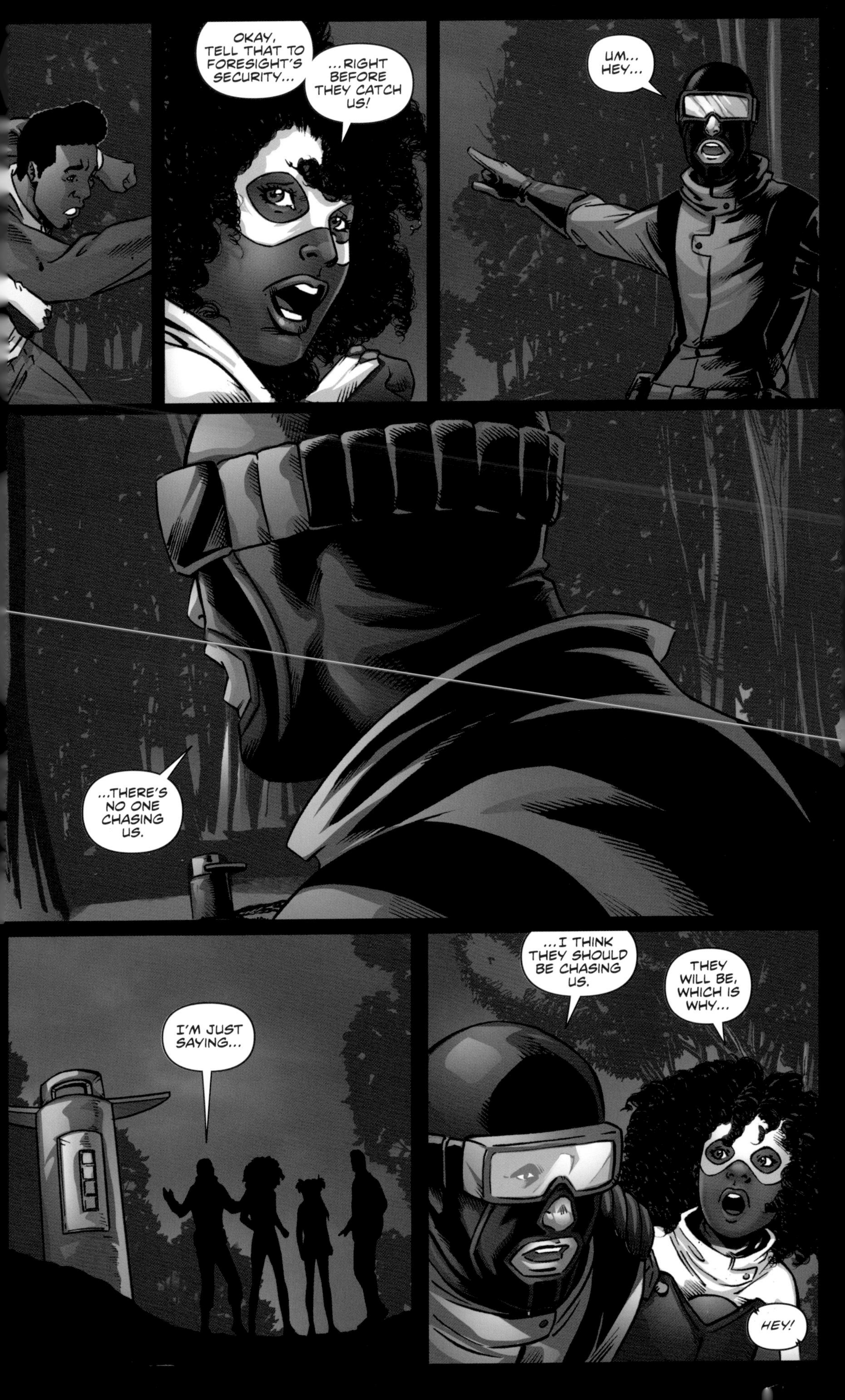

OKAY, TELL THAT TO FORESIGHT'S SECURITY...
...RIGHT BEFORE THEY CATCH US!
UM... HEY...
...THERE'S NO ONE CHASING US.
I'M JUST SAYING...
...I THINK THEY SHOULD BE CHASING US.
THEY WILL BE, WHICH IS WHY...
HEY!

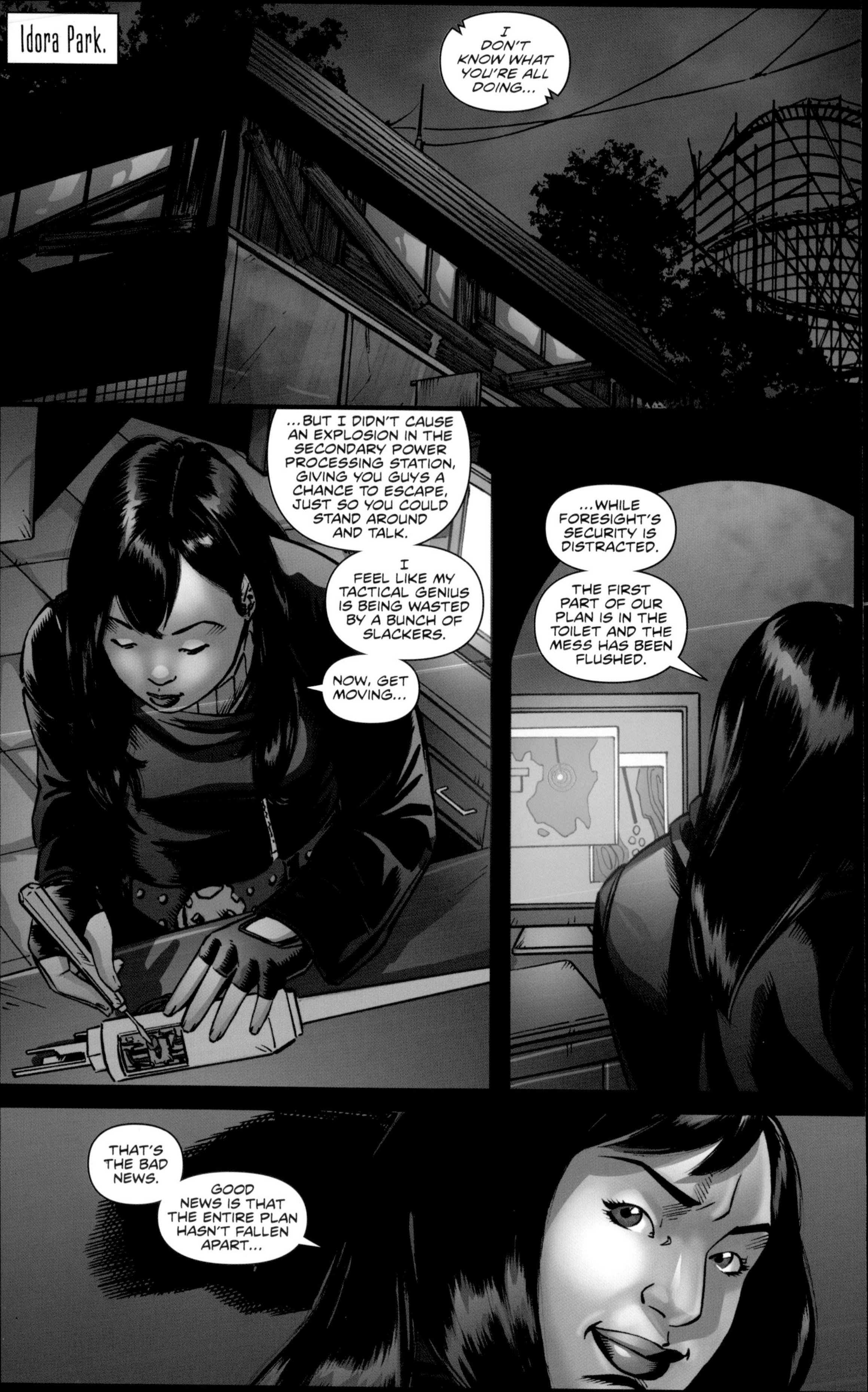

Idora Park.
I DON'T KNOW WHAT YOU'RE ALL DOING...
...BUT I DIDN'T CAUSE AN EXPLOSION IN THE SECONDARY POWER PROCESSING STATION, GIVING YOU GUYS A CHANCE TO ESCAPE, JUST SO YOU COULD STAND AROUND AND TALK.
I FEEL LIKE MY TACTICAL GENIUS IS BEING WASTED BY A BUNCH OF SLACKERS.
NOW, GET MOVING...
...WHILE FORESIGHT'S SECURITY IS DISTRACTED.
THE FIRST PART OF OUR PLAN IS IN THE TOILET AND THE MESS HAS BEEN FLUSHED.
THAT'S THE BAD NEWS.
GOOD NEWS IS THAT THE ENTIRE PLAN HASN'T FALLEN APART...

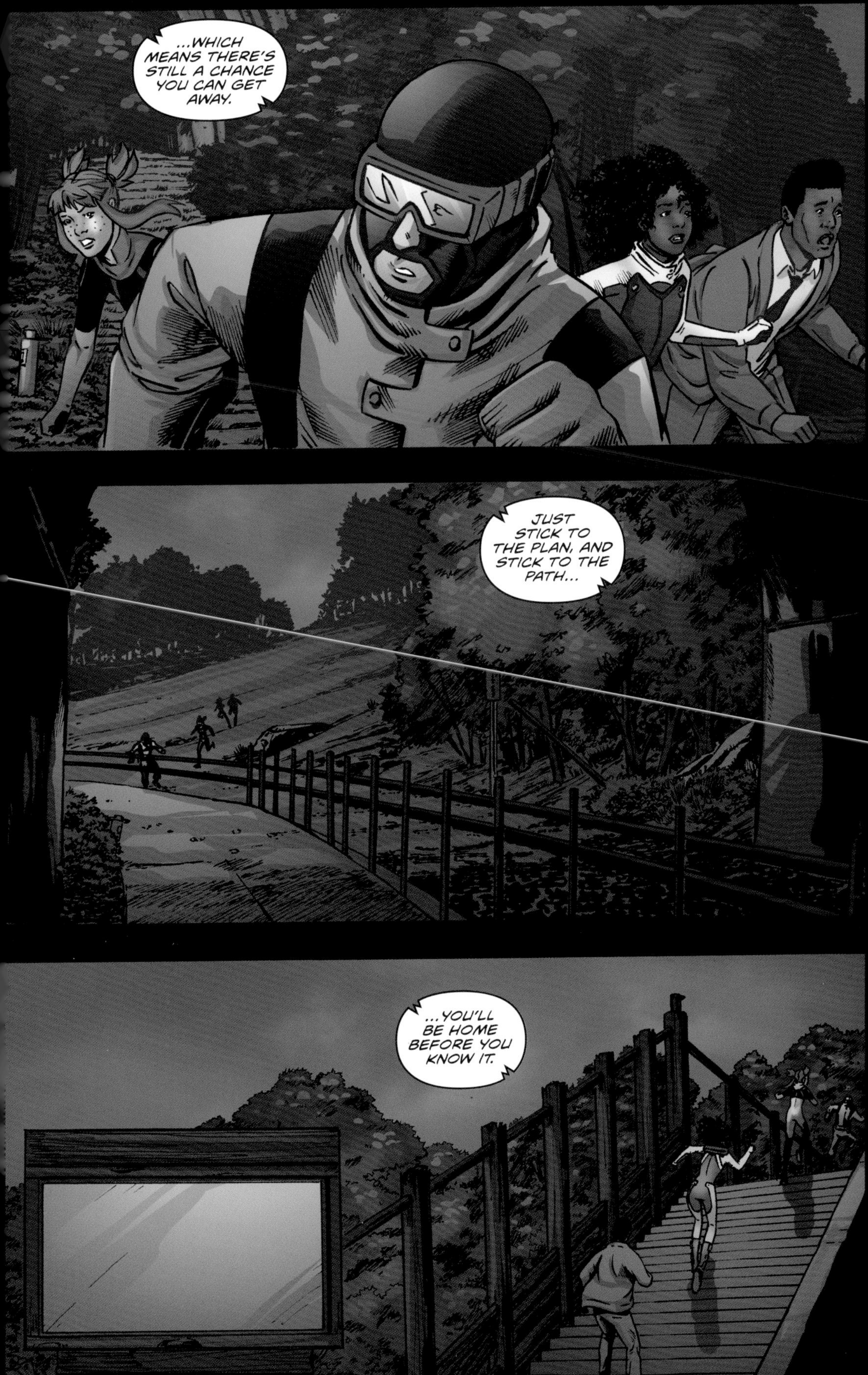
...WHICH MEANS THERE'S STILL A CHANCE YOU CAN GET AWAY.
JUST STICK TO THE PLAN, AND STICK TO THE PATH...
...YOU'LL BE HOME BEFORE YOU KNOW IT.

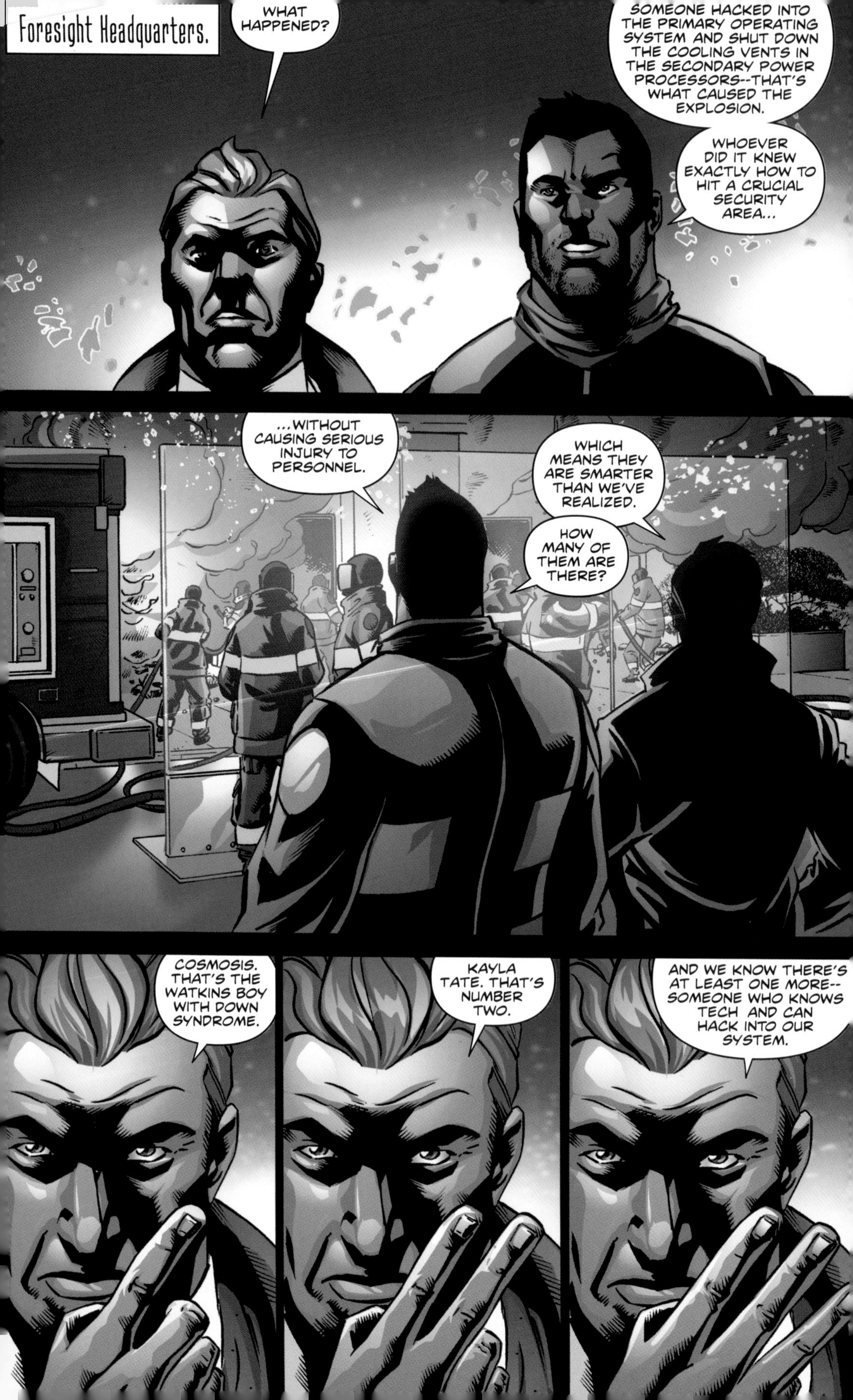
Foresight Headquarters.
WHAT HAPPENED?
SOMEONE HACKED INTO THE PRIMARY OPERATING SYSTEM AND SHUT DOWN THE COOLING VENTS IN THE SECONDARY POWER PROCESSORS--THAT'S WHAT CAUSED THE EXPLOSION.
WHOEVER DID IT KNEW EXACTLY HOW TO HIT A CRUCIAL SECURITY AREA...
...WITHOUT CAUSING SERIOUS INJURY TO PERSONNEL.
WHICH MEANS THEY ARE SMARTER THAN WE'VE REALIZED.
HOW MANY OF THEM ARE THERE?
COSMOSIS. THAT'S THE WATKINS BOY WITH DOWN SYNDROME.
KAYLA TATE. THAT'S NUMBER TWO.
AND WE KNOW THERE'S AT LEAST ONE MORE--SOMEONE WHO KNOWS TECH AND CAN HACK INTO OUR SYSTEM.

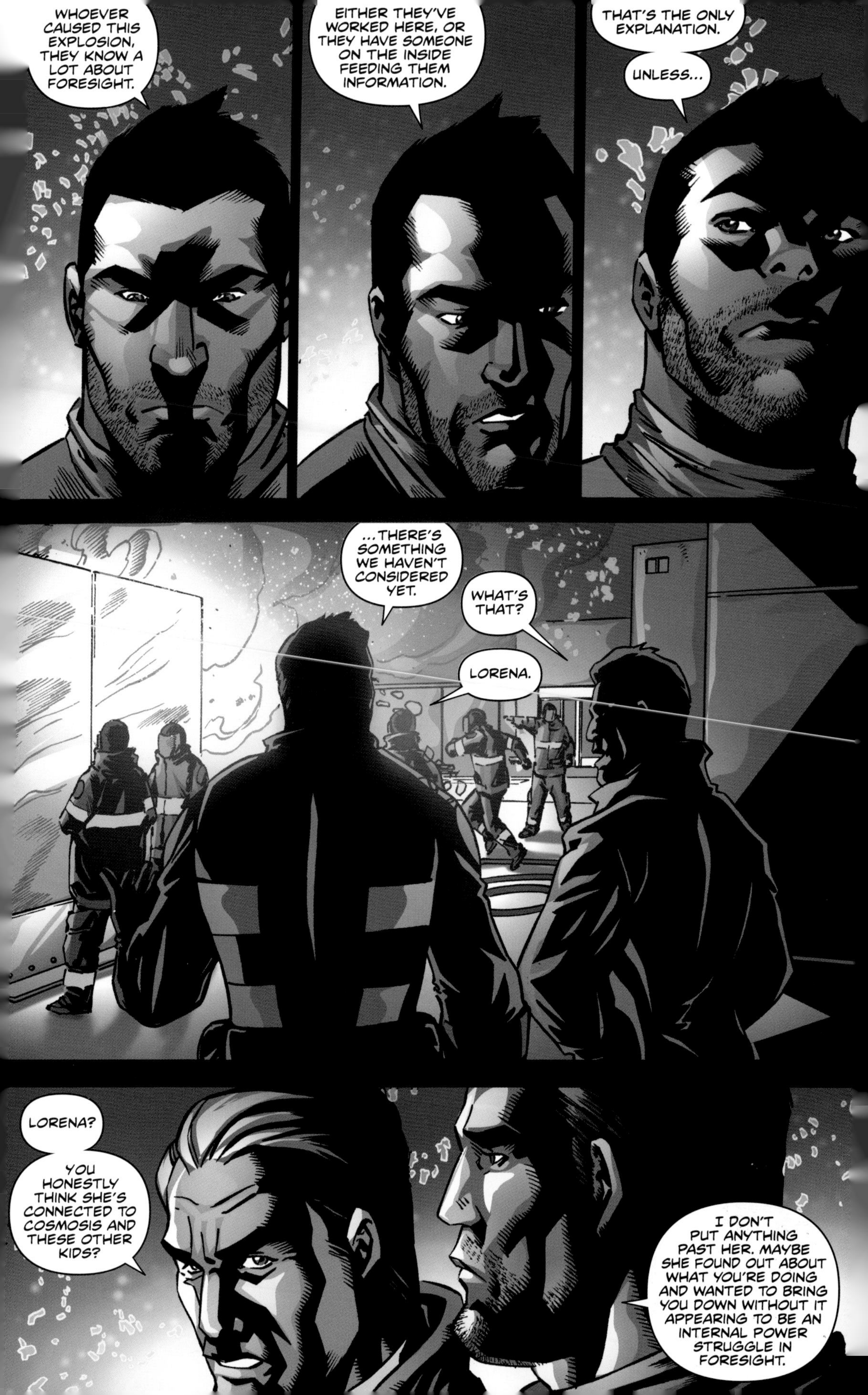
WHOEVER CAUSED THIS EXPLOSION, THEY KNOW A LOT ABOUT FORESIGHT.
EITHER THEY'VE WORKED HERE, OR THEY HAVE SOMEONE ON THE INSIDE FEEDING THEM INFORMATION.
THAT'S THE ONLY EXPLANATION.
UNLESS...
...THERE'S SOMETHING WE HAVEN'T CONSIDERED YET.
WHAT'S THAT?
LORENA.
LORENA?
YOU HONESTLY THINK SHE'S CONNECTED TO COSMOSIS AND THESE OTHER KIDS?
I DON'T PUT ANYTHING PAST HER. MAYBE SHE FOUND OUT ABOUT WHAT YOU'RE DOING AND WANTED TO BRING YOU DOWN WITHOUT IT APPEARING TO BE AN INTERNAL POWER STRUGGLE IN FORESIGHT.

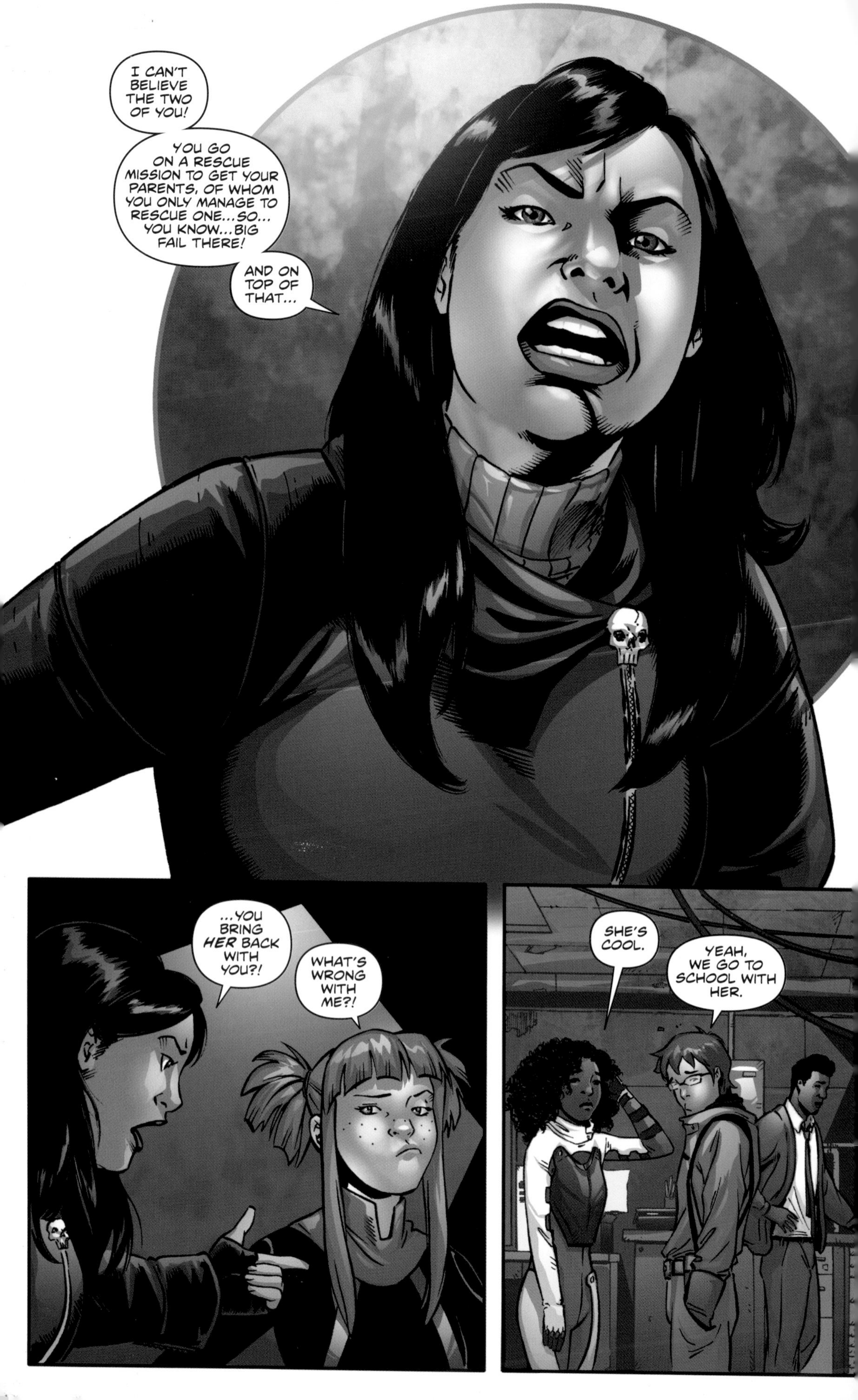
I CAN'T BELIEVE THE TWO OF YOU!
YOU GO ON A RESCUE MISSION TO GET YOUR PARENTS, OF WHOM YOU ONLY MANAGE TO RESCUE ONE...SO... YOU KNOW...BIG FAIL THERE!
AND ON TOP OF THAT...
...YOU BRING HER BACK WITH YOU?!
WHAT'S WRONG WITH ME?!
SHE'S COOL.
YEAH, WE GO TO SCHOOL WITH HER.

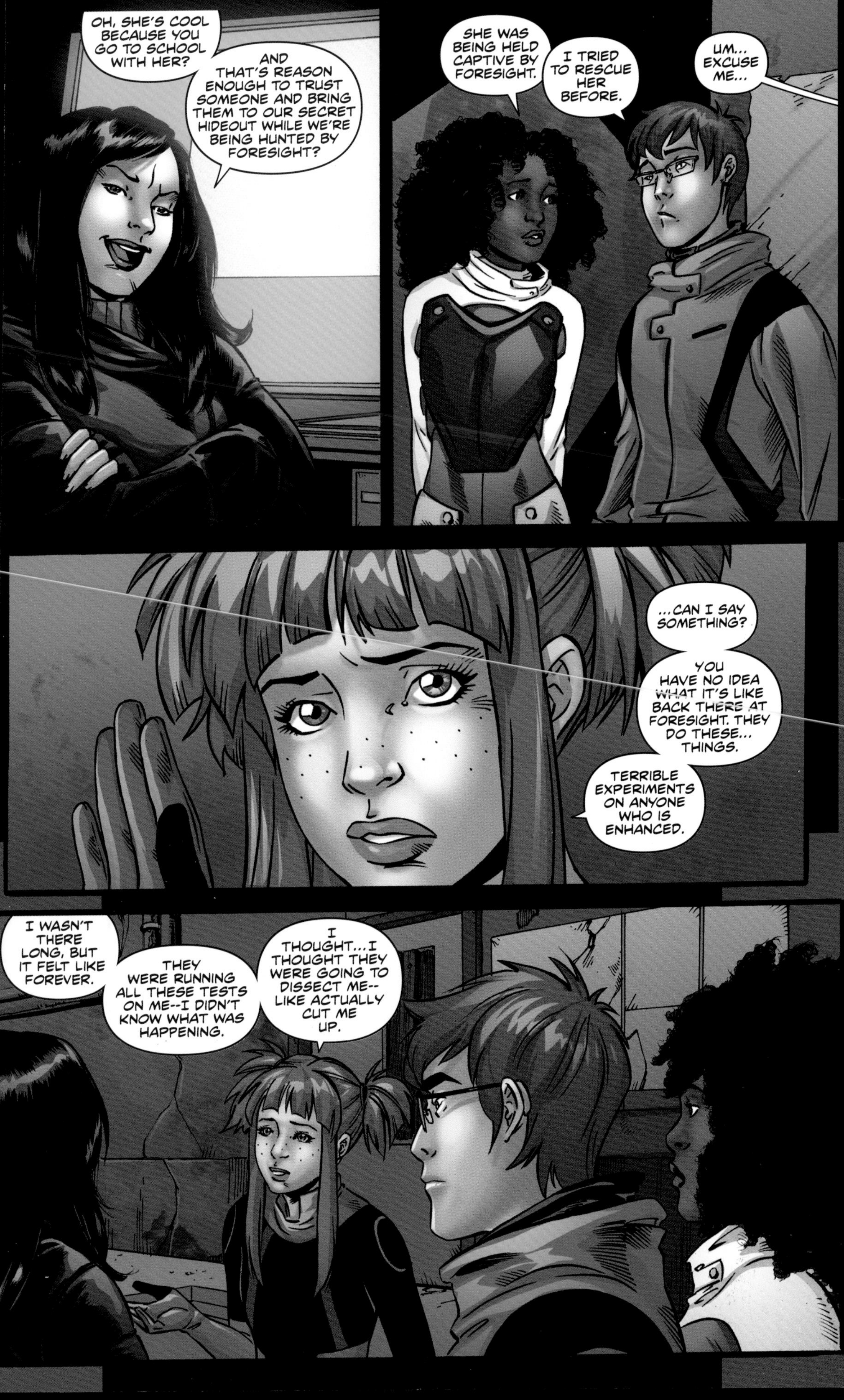

OH, SHE'S COOL BECAUSE YOU GO TO SCHOOL WITH HER?
AND THAT'S REASON ENOUGH TO TRUST SOMEONE AND BRING THEM TO OUR SECRET HIDEOUT WHILE WE'RE BEING HUNTED BY FORESIGHT?
SHE WAS BEING HELD CAPTIVE BY FORESIGHT.
I TRIED TO RESCUE HER BEFORE.
UM... EXCUSE ME...
...CAN I SAY SOMETHING?
YOU HAVE NO IDEA WHAT IT'S LIKE BACK THERE AT FORESIGHT. THEY DO THESE... THINGS.
TERRIBLE EXPERIMENTS ON ANYONE WHO IS ENHANCED.
I WASN'T THERE LONG, BUT IT FELT LIKE FOREVER.
THEY WERE RUNNING ALL THESE TESTS ON ME--I DIDN'T KNOW WHAT WAS HAPPENING.
I THOUGHT...I THOUGHT THEY WERE GOING TO DISSECT ME--LIKE ACTUALLY CUT ME UP.

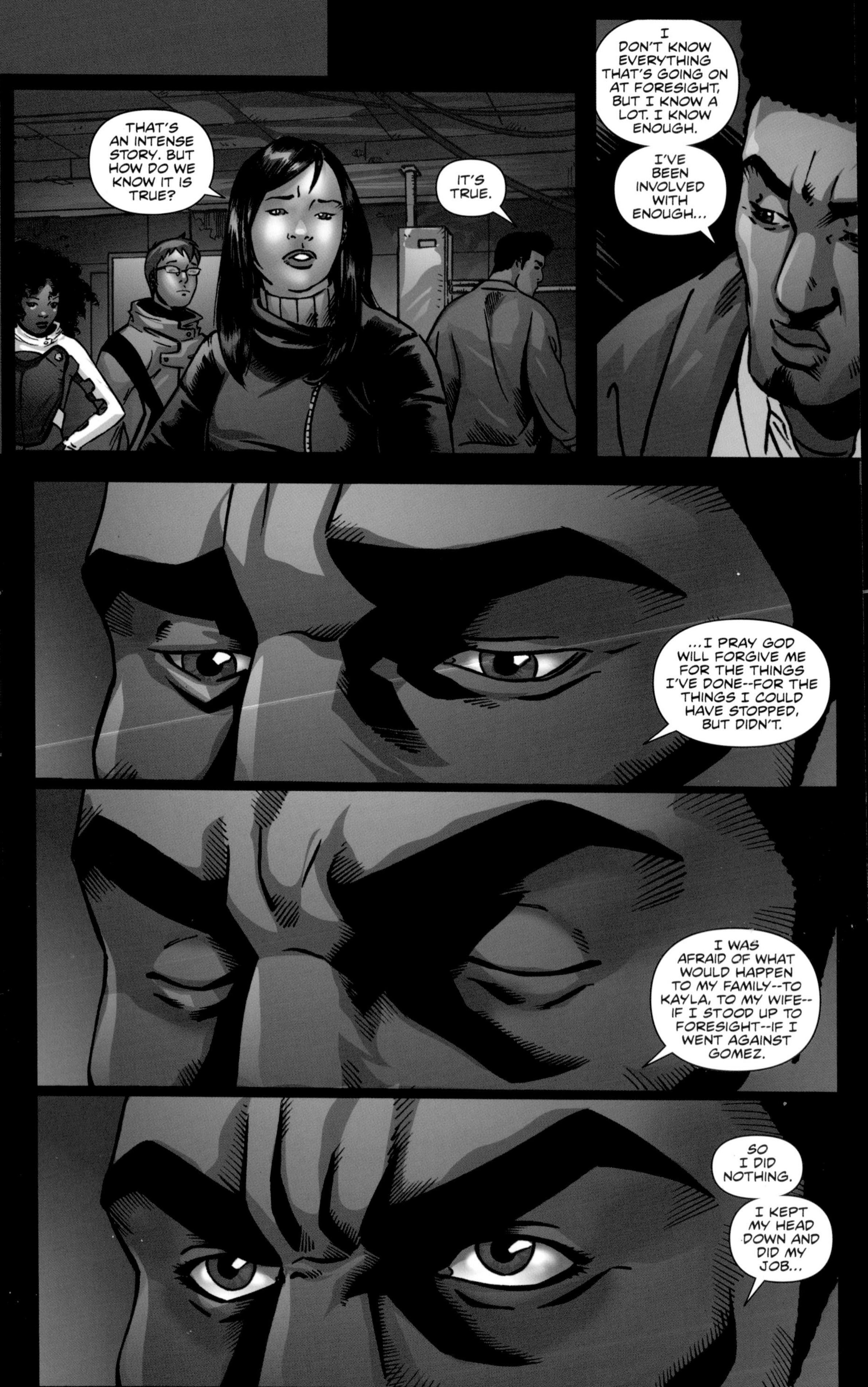
THAT'S AN INTENSE STORY. BUT HOW DO WE KNOW IT IS TRUE?
IT'S TRUE.
I DON'T KNOW EVERYTHING THAT'S GOING ON AT FORESIGHT, BUT I KNOW A LOT. I KNOW ENOUGH.
I'VE BEEN INVOLVED WITH ENOUGH...
...I PRAY GOD WILL FORGIVE ME FOR THE THINGS I'VE DONE--FOR THE THINGS I COULD HAVE STOPPED, BUT DIDN'T.
I WAS AFRAID OF WHAT WOULD HAPPEN TO MY FAMILY--TO KAYLA, TO MY WIFE--IF I STOOD UP TO FORESIGHT--IF I WENT AGAINST GOMEZ.
SO I DID NOTHING.
I KEPT MY HEAD DOWN AND DID MY JOB...

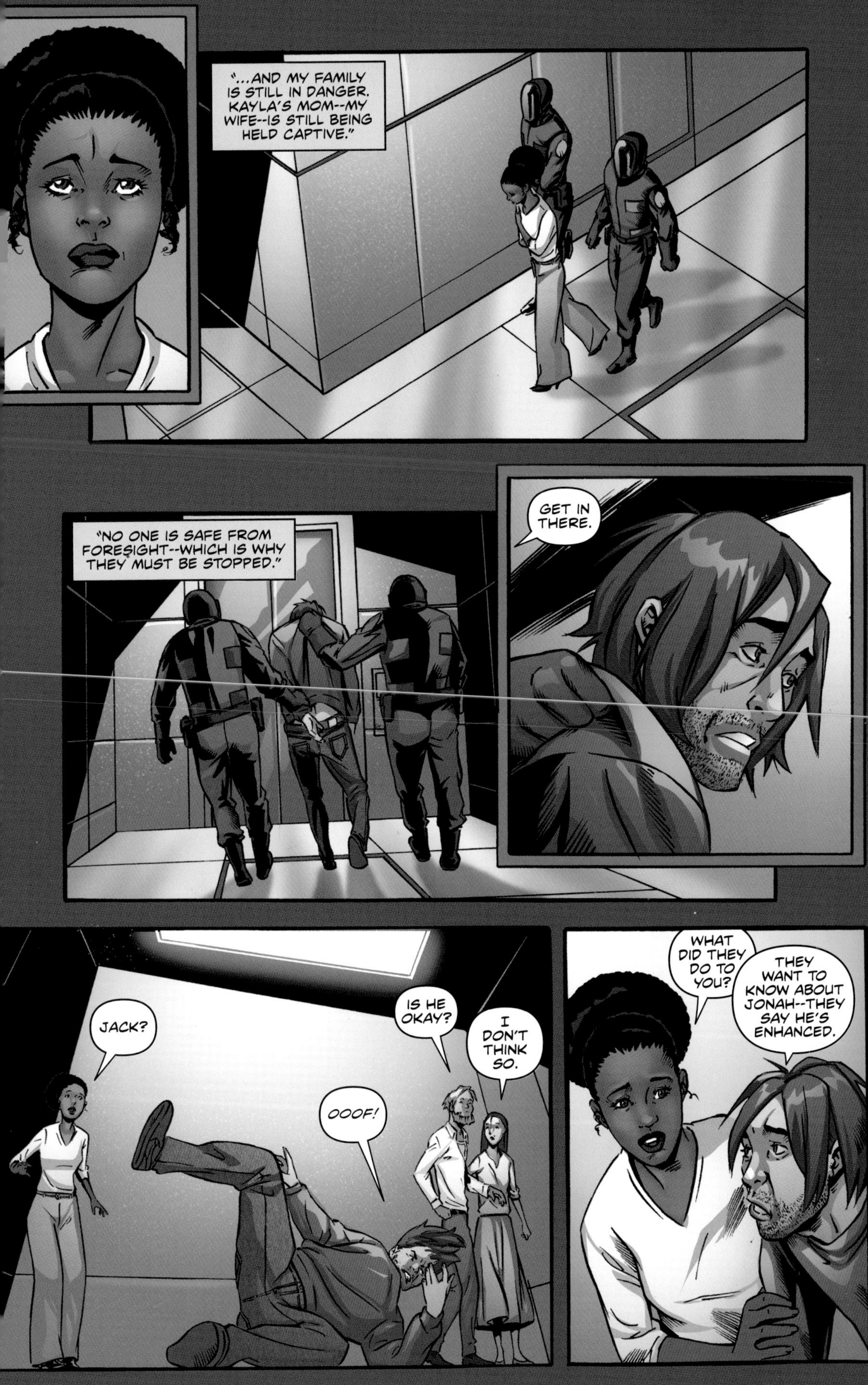
"...AND MY FAMILY IS STILL IN DANGER. KAYLA'S MOM--MY WIFE--IS STILL BEING HELD CAPTIVE."
"NO ONE IS SAFE FROM FORESIGHT--WHICH IS WHY THEY MUST BE STOPPED."
GET IN THERE.
JACK?
IS HE OKAY?
I DON'T THINK SO.
OOOF!
WHAT DID THEY DO TO YOU?
THEY WANT TO KNOW ABOUT JONAH--THEY SAY HE'S ENHANCED.

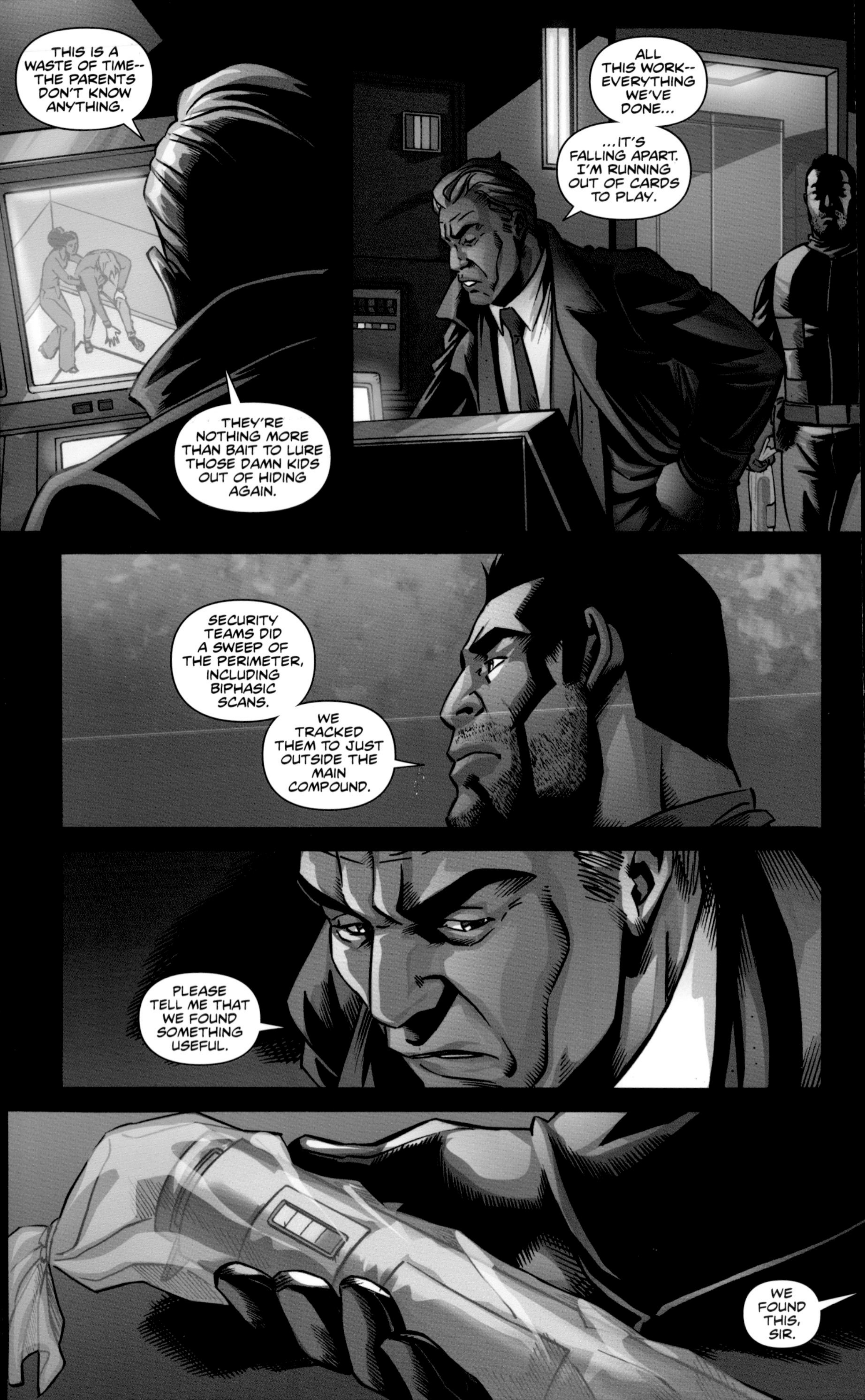
THIS IS A WASTE OF TIME-- THE PARENTS DON'T KNOW ANYTHING.
THEY'RE NOTHING MORE THAN BAIT TO LURE THOSE DAMN KIDS OUT OF HIDING AGAIN.
ALL THIS WORK-- EVERYTHING WE'VE DONE...
...IT'S FALLING APART. I'M RUNNING OUT OF CARDS TO PLAY.
SECURITY TEAMS DID A SWEEP OF THE PERIMETER, INCLUDING BIPHASIC SCANS.
WE TRACKED THEM TO JUST OUTSIDE THE MAIN COMPOUND.
PLEASE TELL ME THAT WE FOUND SOMETHING USEFUL.
WE FOUND THIS, SIR.

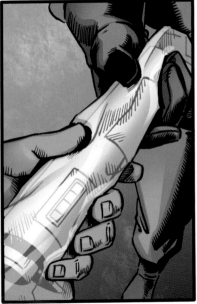

THERE'S NO WAY TEENAGERS PLAYING SUPERHERO CAN GET THEIR HANDS ON THESE.

I KNOW.

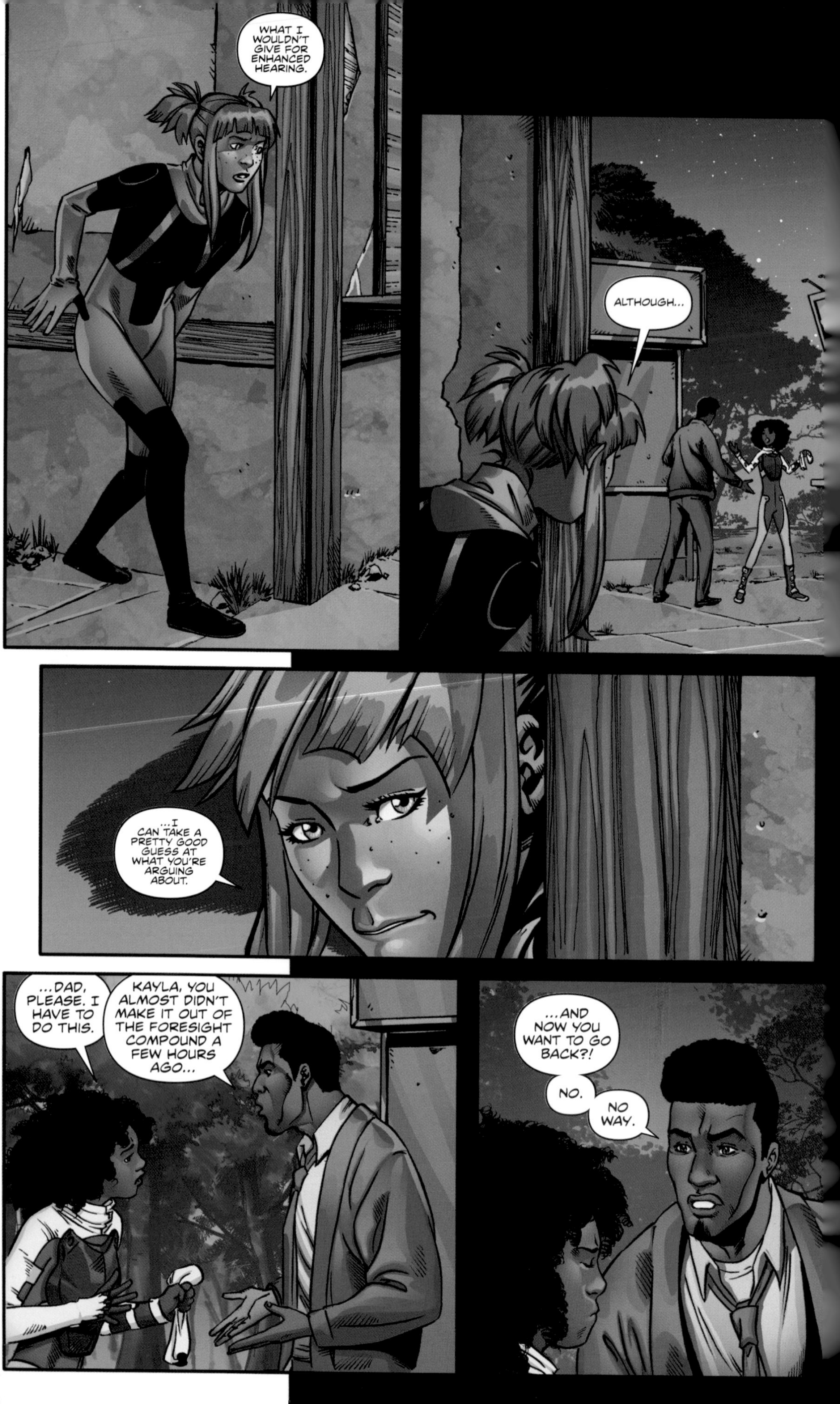
WHAT I WOULDN'T GIVE FOR ENHANCED HEARING.
ALTHOUGH...
...I CAN TAKE A PRETTY GOOD GUESS AT WHAT YOU'RE ARGUING ABOUT.
...DAD, PLEASE. I HAVE TO DO THIS.
KAYLA, YOU ALMOST DIDN'T MAKE IT OUT OF THE FORESIGHT COMPOUND A FEW HOURS AGO...
...AND NOW YOU WANT TO GO BACK?!
NO.
NO WAY.

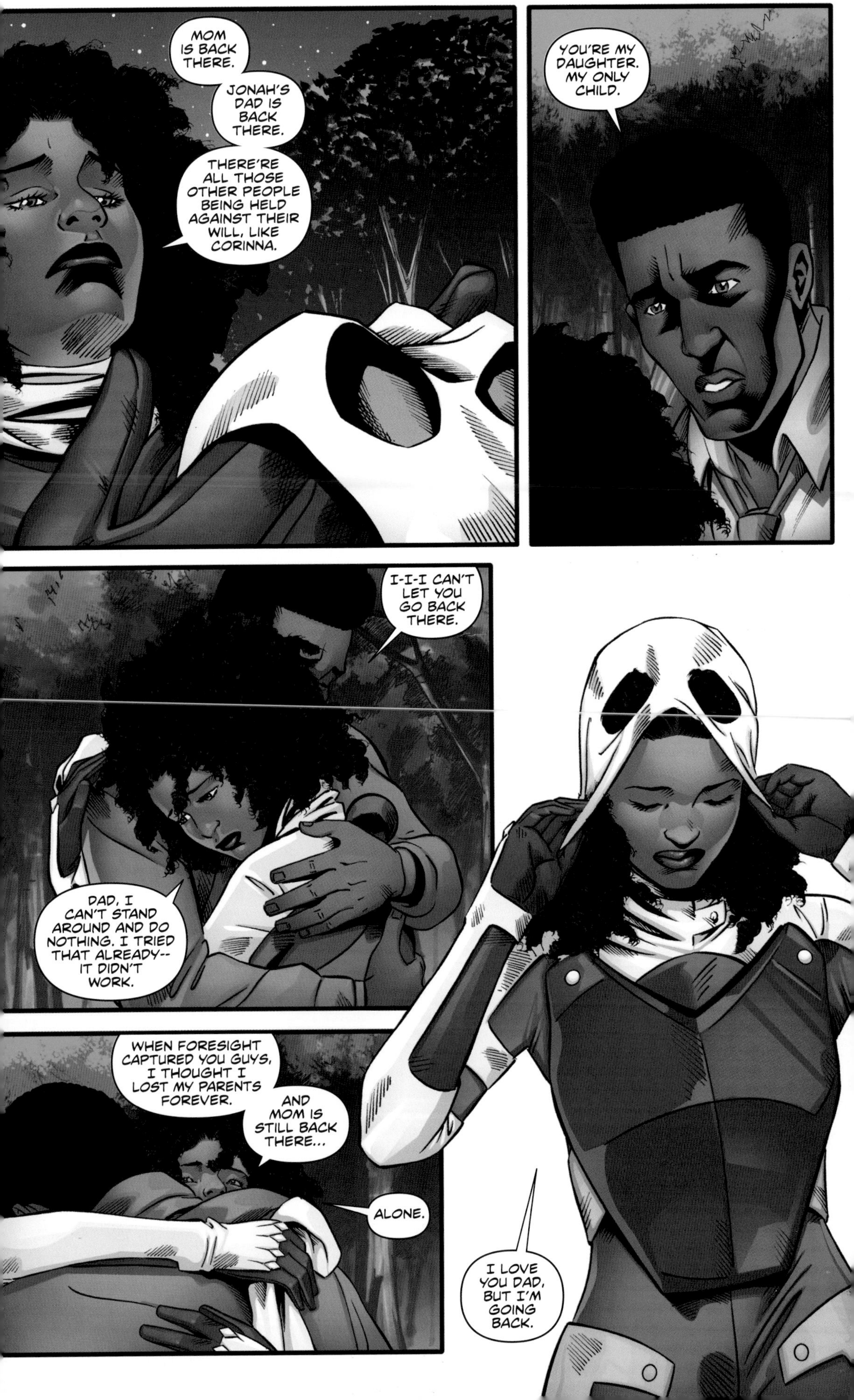
MOM IS BACK THERE.
JONAH'S DAD IS BACK THERE.
THERE'RE ALL THOSE OTHER PEOPLE BEING HELD AGAINST THEIR WILL, LIKE CORINNA.
YOU'RE MY DAUGHTER. MY ONLY CHILD.
I-I-I CAN'T LET YOU GO BACK THERE.
DAD, I CAN'T STAND AROUND AND DO NOTHING. I TRIED THAT ALREADY-- IT DIDN'T WORK.
WHEN FORESIGHT CAPTURED YOU GUYS, I THOUGHT I LOST MY PARENTS FOREVER.
AND MOM IS STILL BACK THERE...
ALONE.
I LOVE YOU DAD, BUT I'M GOING BACK.

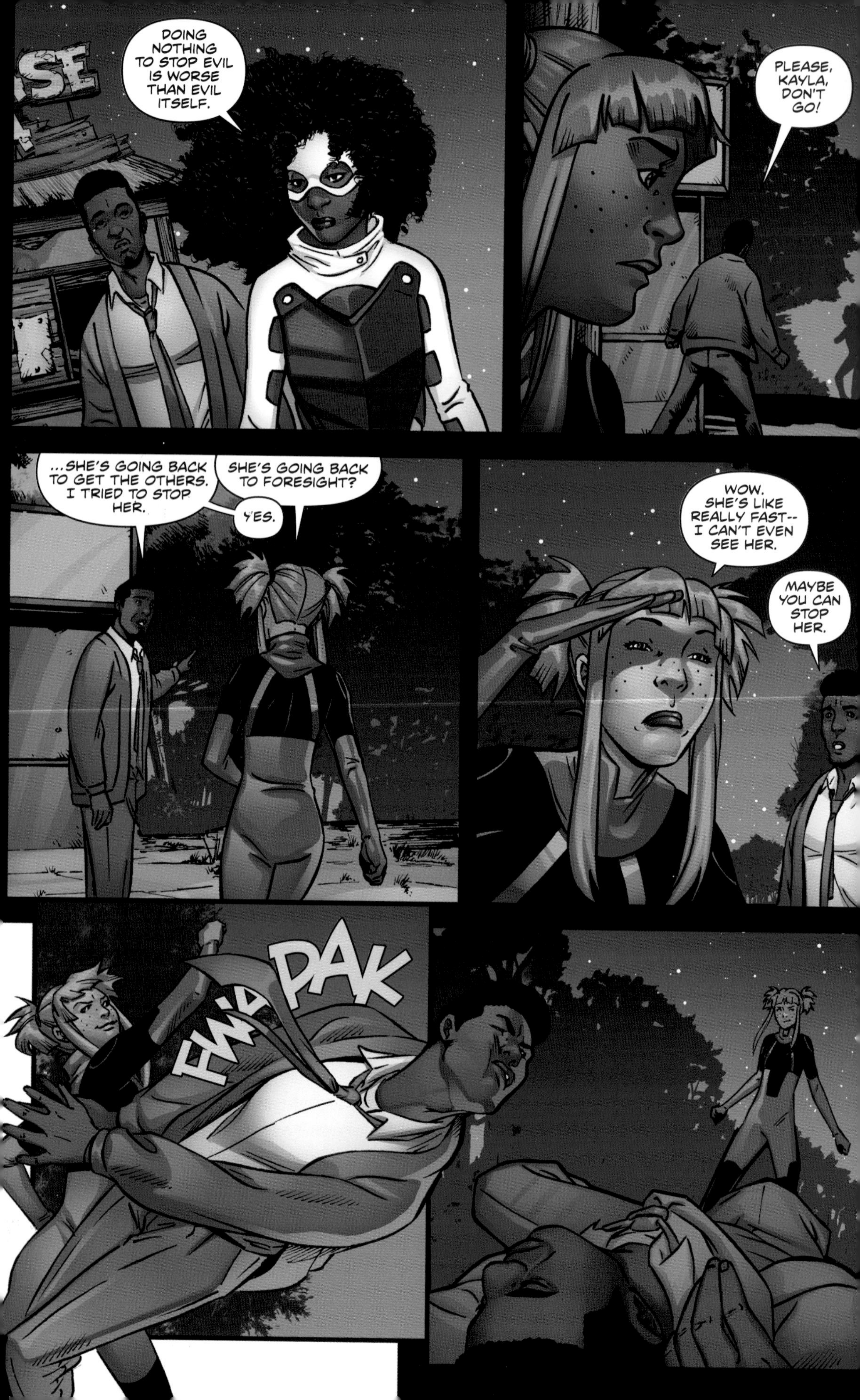
DOING NOTHING TO STOP EVIL IS WORSE THAN EVIL ITSELF.
PLEASE, KAYLA, DON'T GO!
...SHE'S GOING BACK TO GET THE OTHERS. I TRIED TO STOP HER.
SHE'S GOING BACK TO FORESIGHT?
YES.
WOW. SHE'S LIKE REALLY FAST-- I CAN'T EVEN SEE HER.
MAYBE YOU CAN STOP HER.
PAK
FWiP

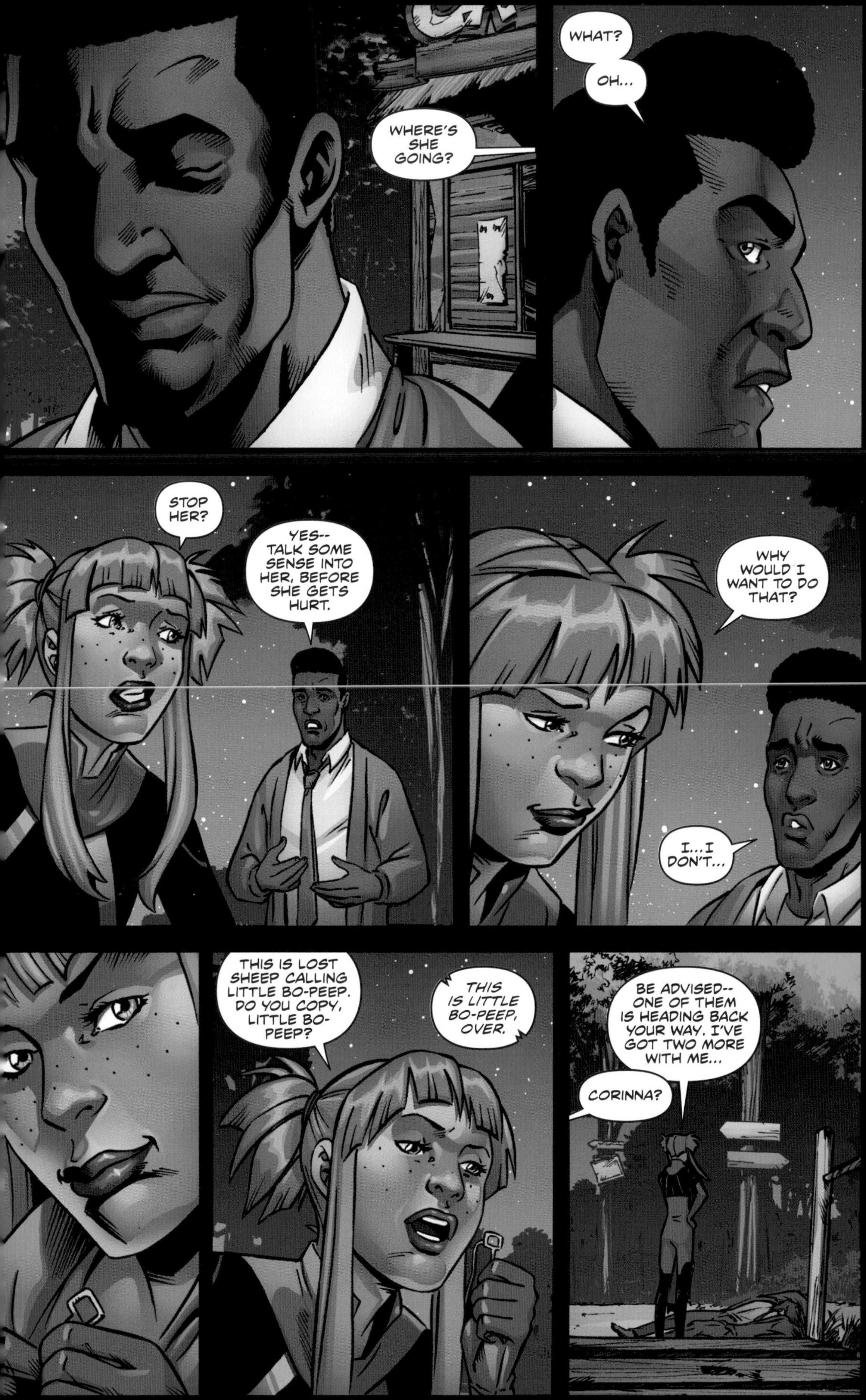
WHERE'S SHE GOING?
WHAT?
OH...
STOP HER?
YES-- TALK SOME SENSE INTO HER, BEFORE SHE GETS HURT.
WHY WOULD I WANT TO DO THAT?
I...I DON'T...
THIS IS LOST SHEEP CALLING LITTLE BO-PEEP. DO YOU COPY, LITTLE BO-PEEP?
THIS IS LITTLE BO-PEEP, OVER.
BE ADVISED-- ONE OF THEM IS HEADING BACK YOUR WAY. I'VE GOT TWO MORE WITH ME...
CORINNA?

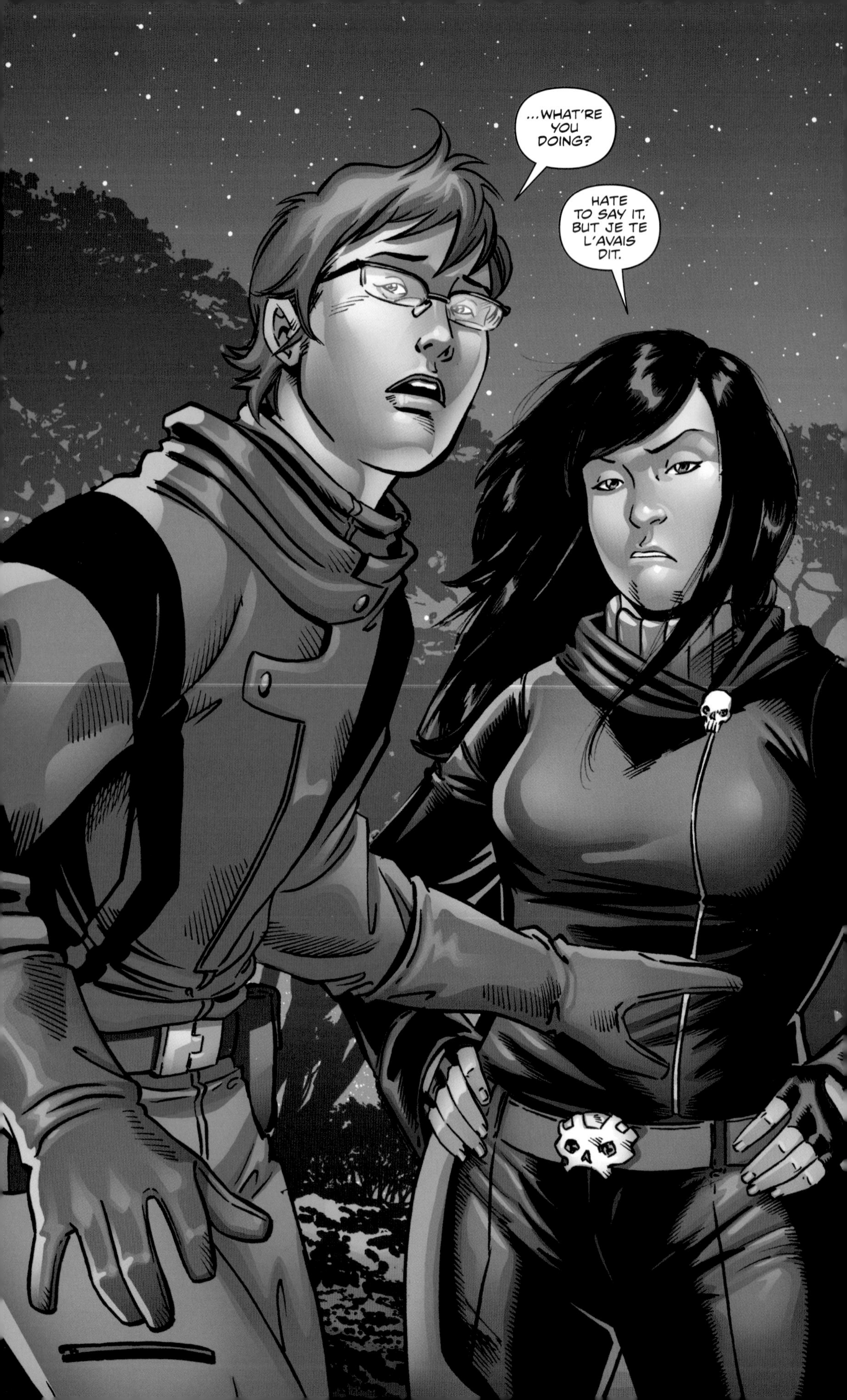
...WHAT'RE YOU DOING?
HATE TO SAY IT, BUT JE TE L'AVAIS DIT.

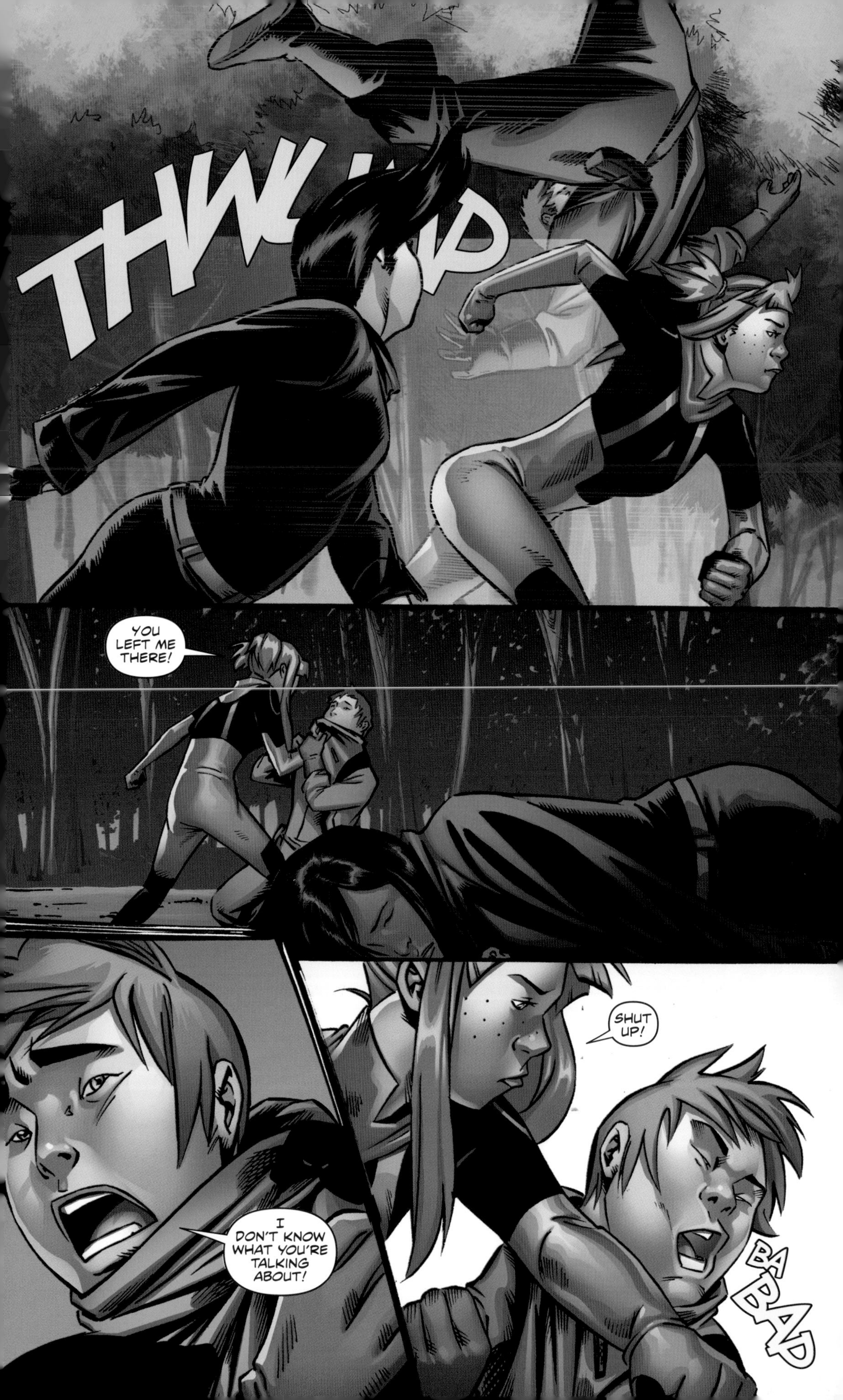
THWUMP
YOU LEFT ME THERE!
I DON'T KNOW WHAT YOU'RE TALKING ABOUT!
SHUT UP!
BABAD

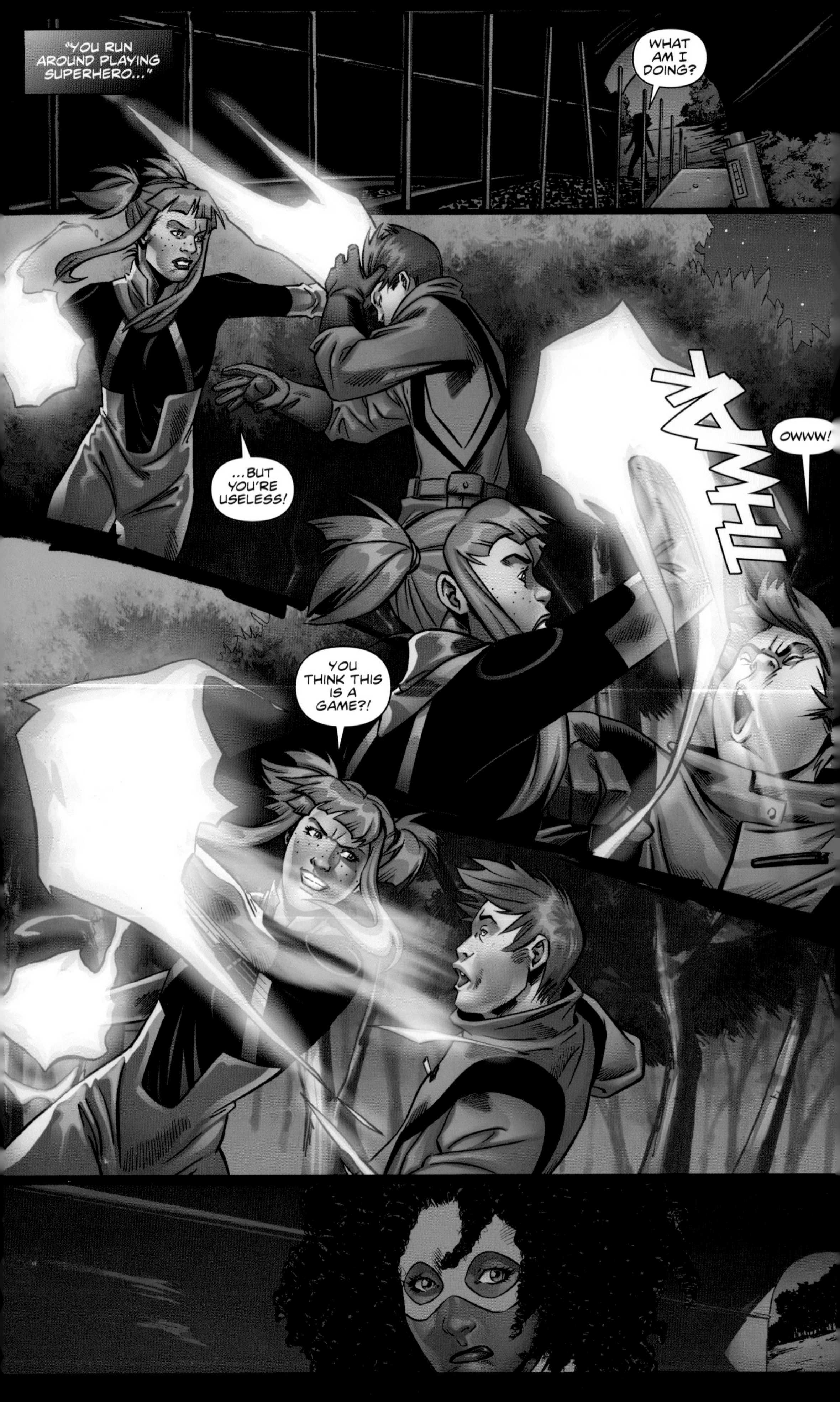
"YOU RUN AROUND PLAYING SUPERHERO..."
WHAT AM I DOING?
...BUT YOU'RE USELESS!
THWAK
OWWW!
YOU THINK THIS IS A GAME?!

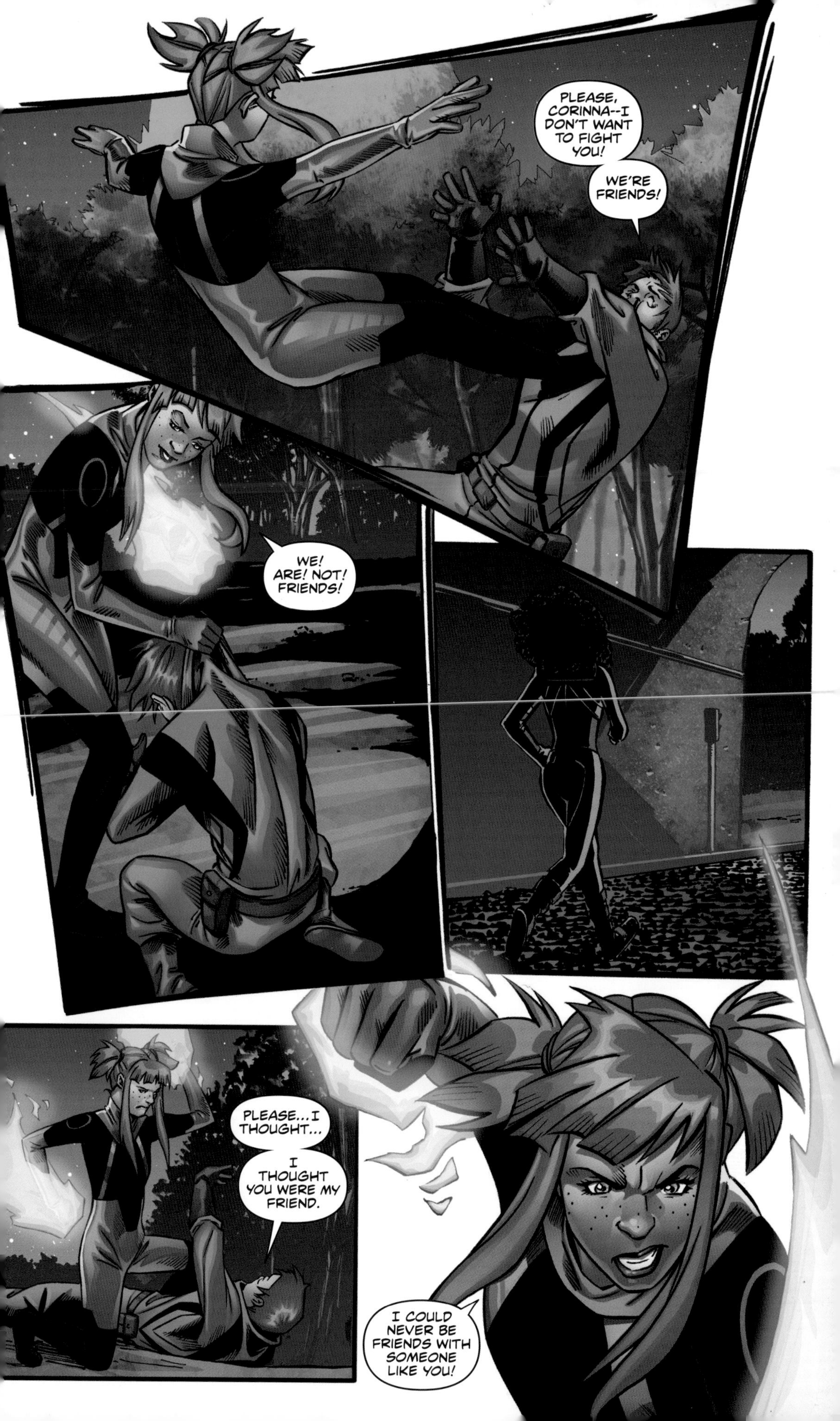
PLEASE, CORINNA--I DON'T WANT TO FIGHT YOU!
WE'RE FRIENDS!
WE! ARE! NOT! FRIENDS!
PLEASE...I THOUGHT...
I THOUGHT YOU WERE MY FRIEND.
I COULD NEVER BE FRIENDS WITH SOMEONE LIKE YOU!

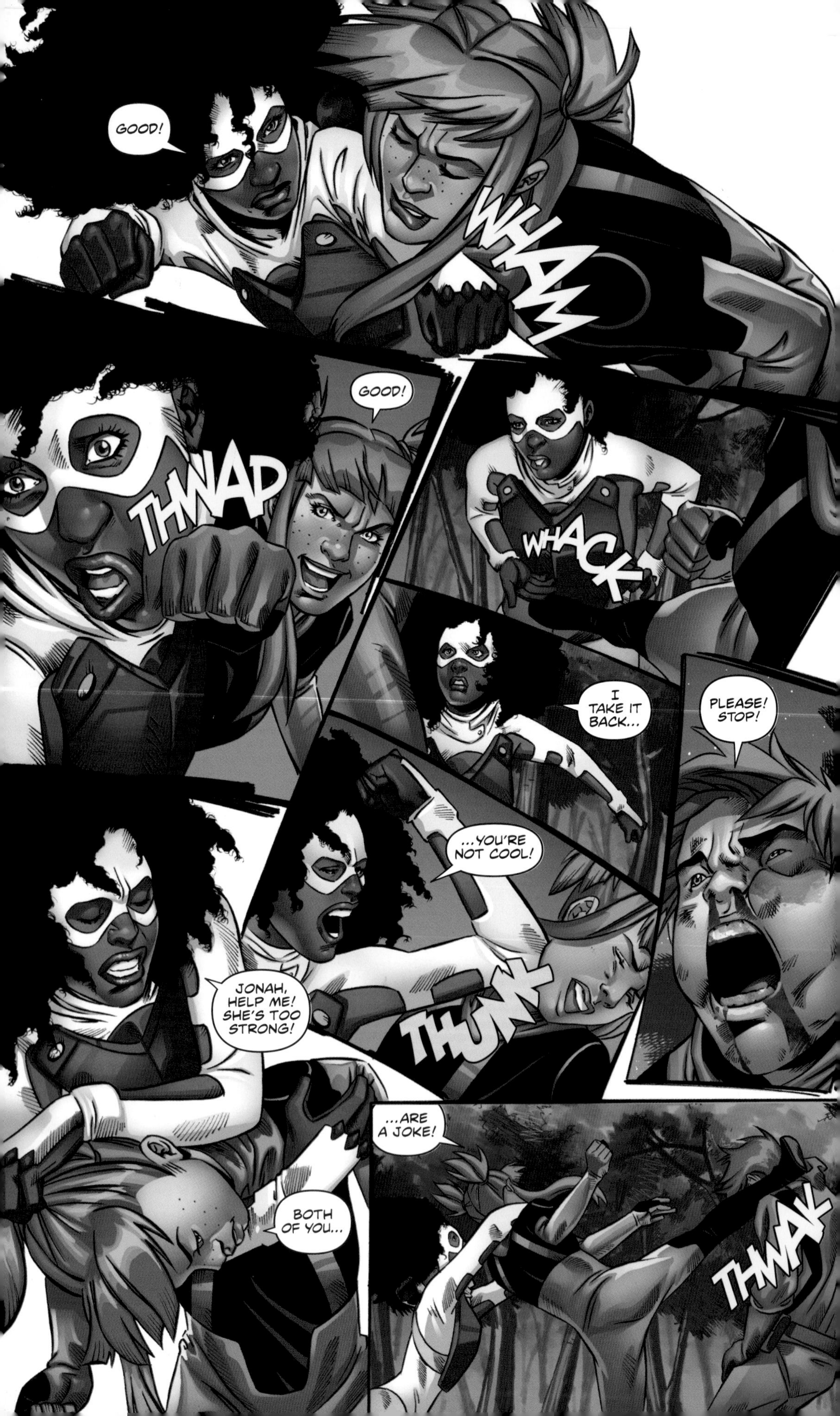
GOOD!
WHAM
GOOD!
THWAP
WHACK
I TAKE IT BACK...
PLEASE! STOP!
...YOU'RE NOT COOL!
JONAH, HELP ME! SHE'S TOO STRONG!
THUNK
BOTH OF YOU...
...ARE A JOKE!
THWAK

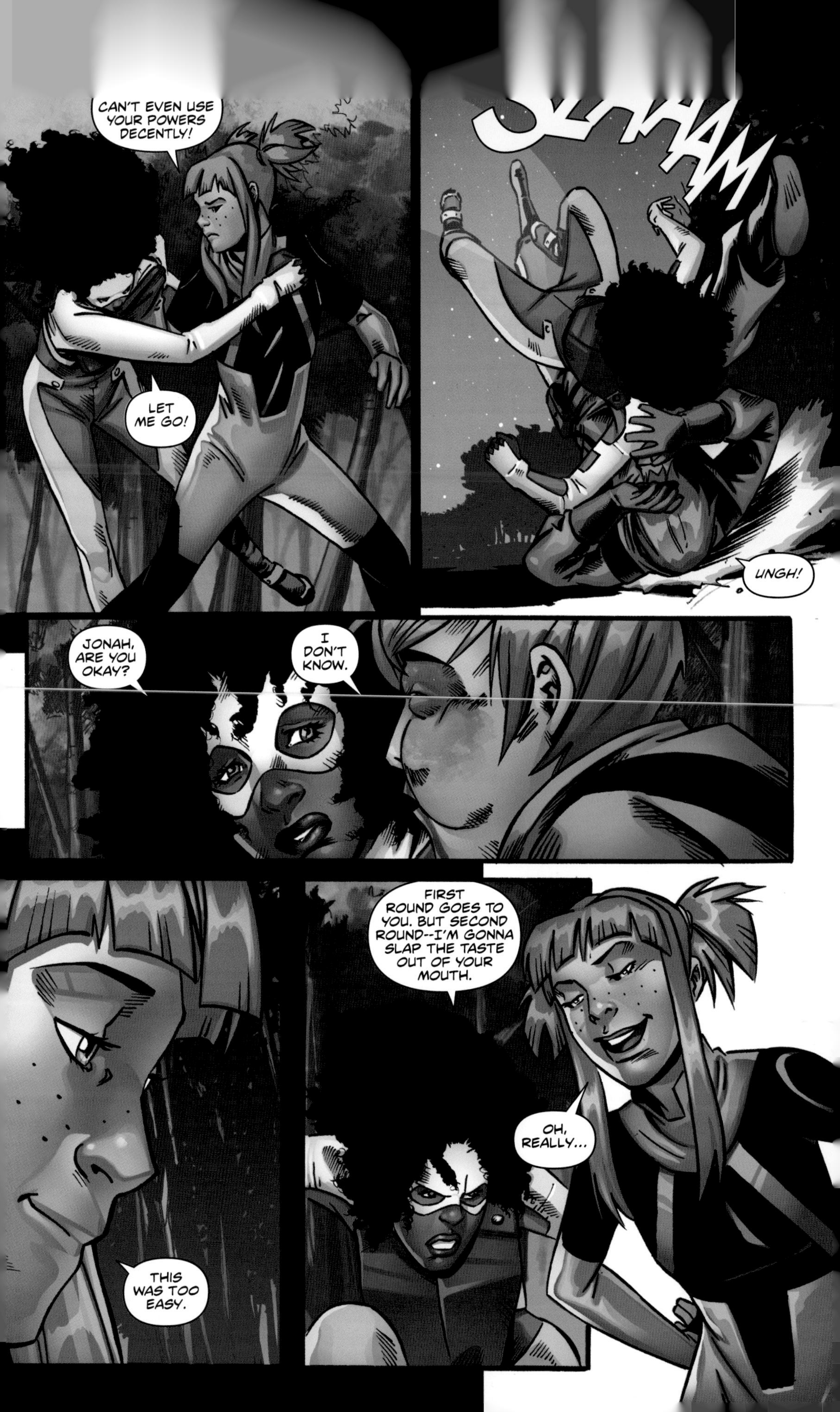
CAN'T EVEN USE YOUR POWERS DECENTLY!
LET ME GO!
UNGH!
JONAH, ARE YOU OKAY?
I DON'T KNOW.
THIS WAS TOO EASY.
FIRST ROUND GOES TO YOU. BUT SECOND ROUND--I'M GONNA SLAP THE TASTE OUT OF YOUR MOUTH.
OH, REALLY...

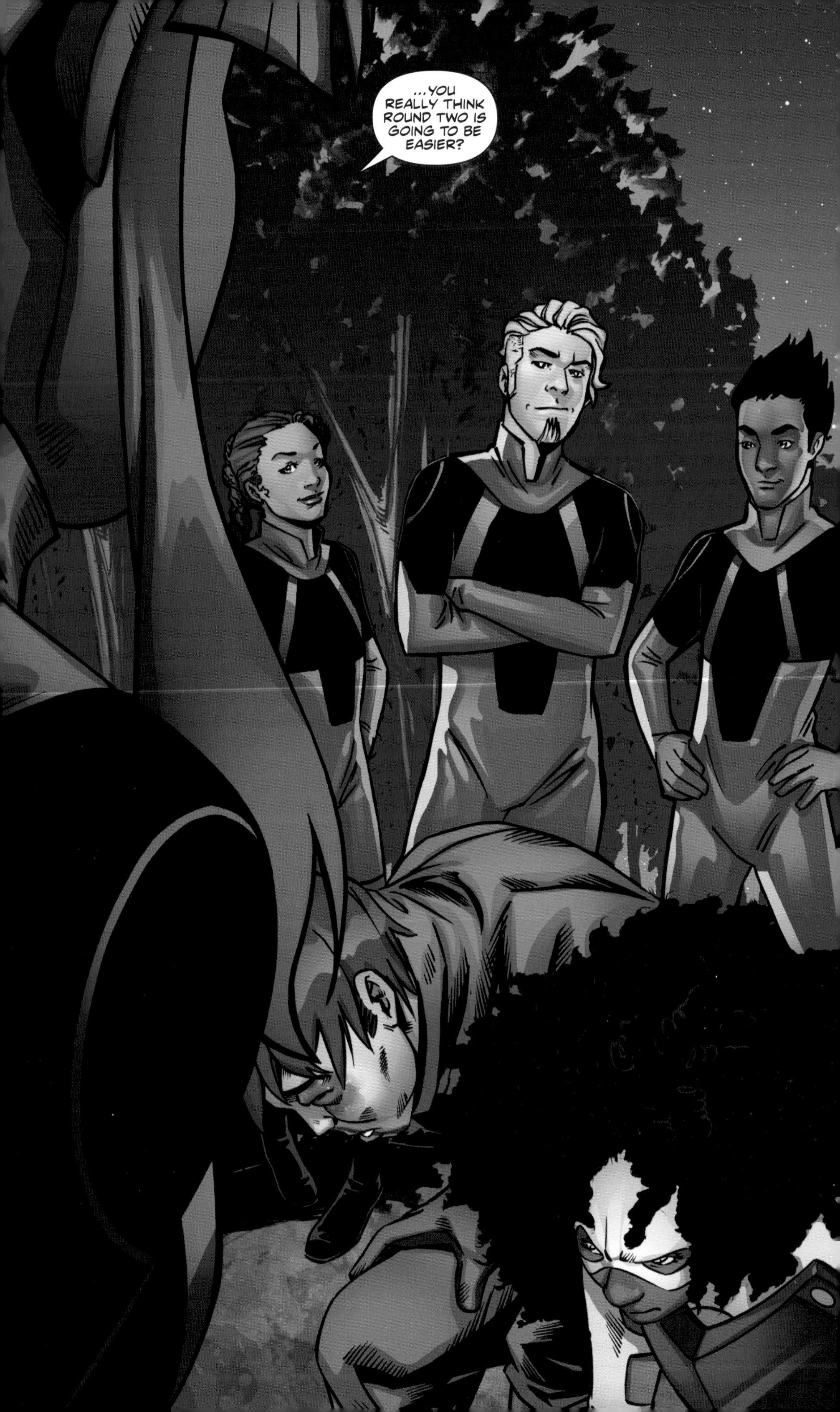
...YOU REALLY THINK ROUND TWO IS GOING TO BE EASIER?

CHAPTER FOUR

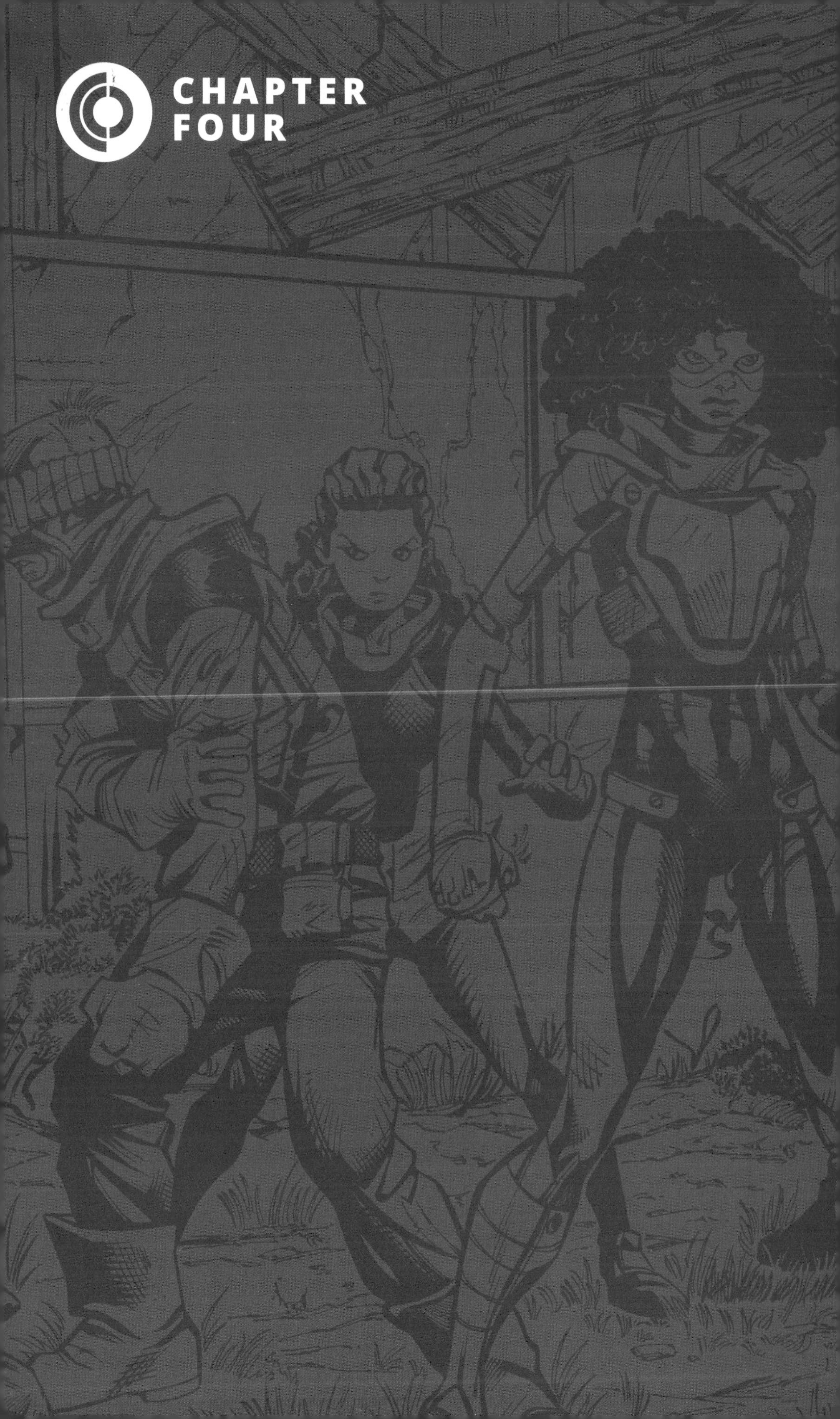

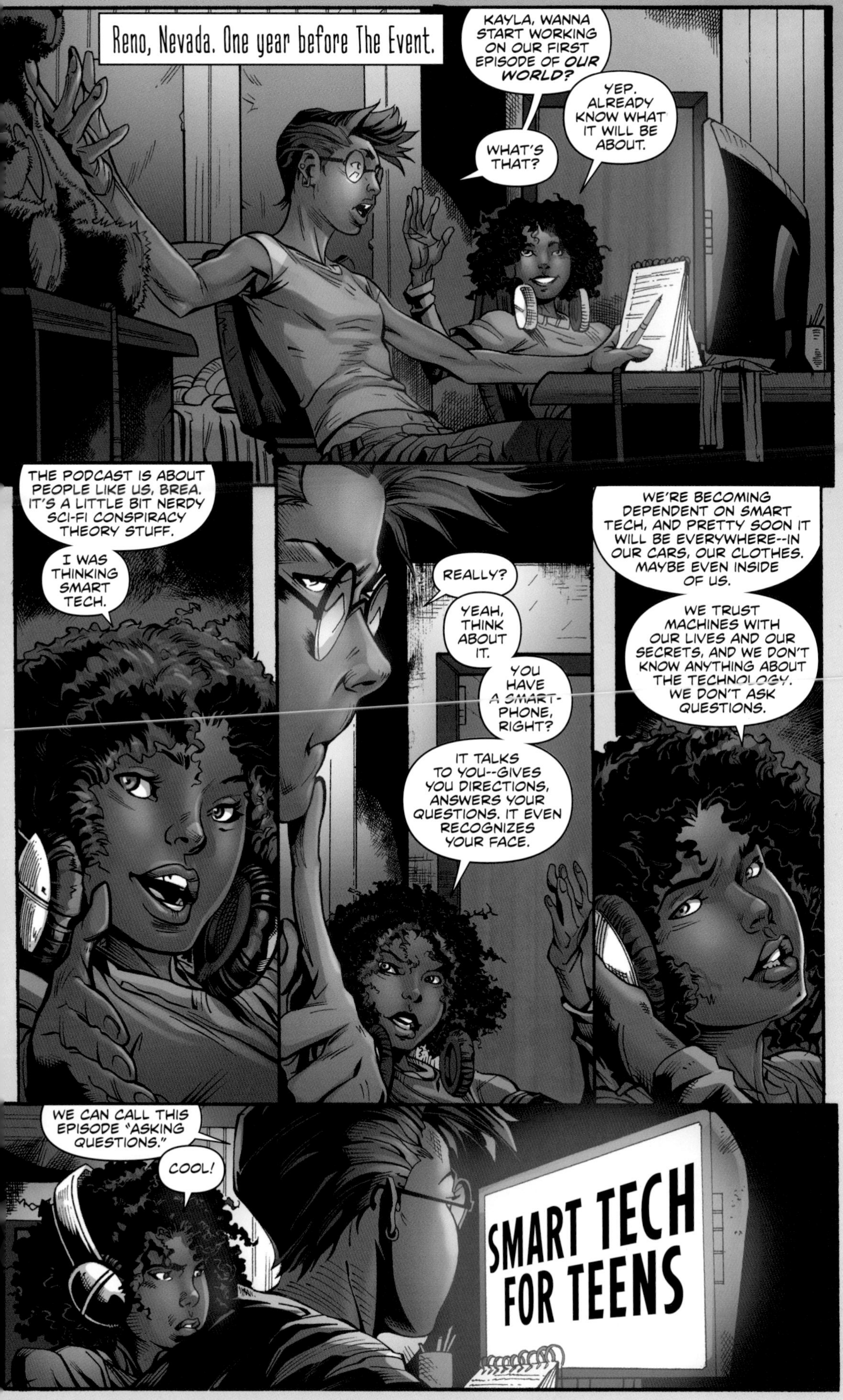
Reno, Nevada. One year before The Event.
KAYLA, WANNA START WORKING ON OUR FIRST EPISODE OF OUR WORLD?
WHAT'S THAT?
YEP. ALREADY KNOW WHAT IT WILL BE ABOUT.
THE PODCAST IS ABOUT PEOPLE LIKE US, BREA. IT'S A LITTLE BIT NERDY SCI-FI CONSPIRACY THEORY STUFF.
I WAS THINKING SMART TECH.
REALLY?
YEAH, THINK ABOUT IT.
YOU HAVE A SMART-PHONE, RIGHT?
IT TALKS TO YOU--GIVES YOU DIRECTIONS, ANSWERS YOUR QUESTIONS. IT EVEN RECOGNIZES YOUR FACE.
WE'RE BECOMING DEPENDENT ON SMART TECH, AND PRETTY SOON IT WILL BE EVERYWHERE--IN OUR CARS, OUR CLOTHES. MAYBE EVEN INSIDE OF US.
WE TRUST MACHINES WITH OUR LIVES AND OUR SECRETS, AND WE DON'T KNOW ANYTHING ABOUT THE TECHNOLOGY. WE DON'T ASK QUESTIONS.
WE CAN CALL THIS EPISODE "ASKING QUESTIONS."
COOL!
SMART TECH FOR TEENS

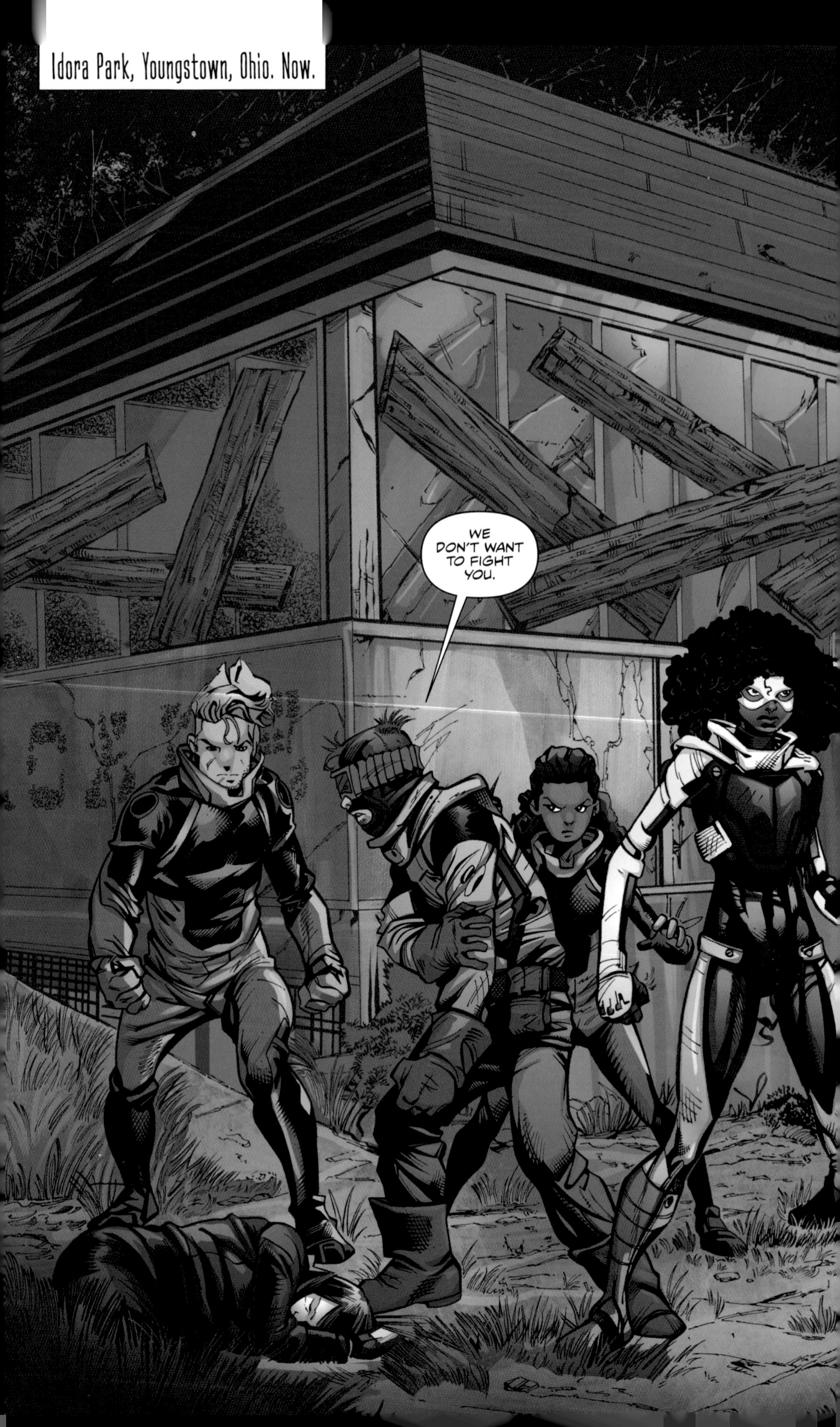
Idora Park, Youngstown, Ohio. Now.
WE DON'T WANT TO FIGHT YOU.

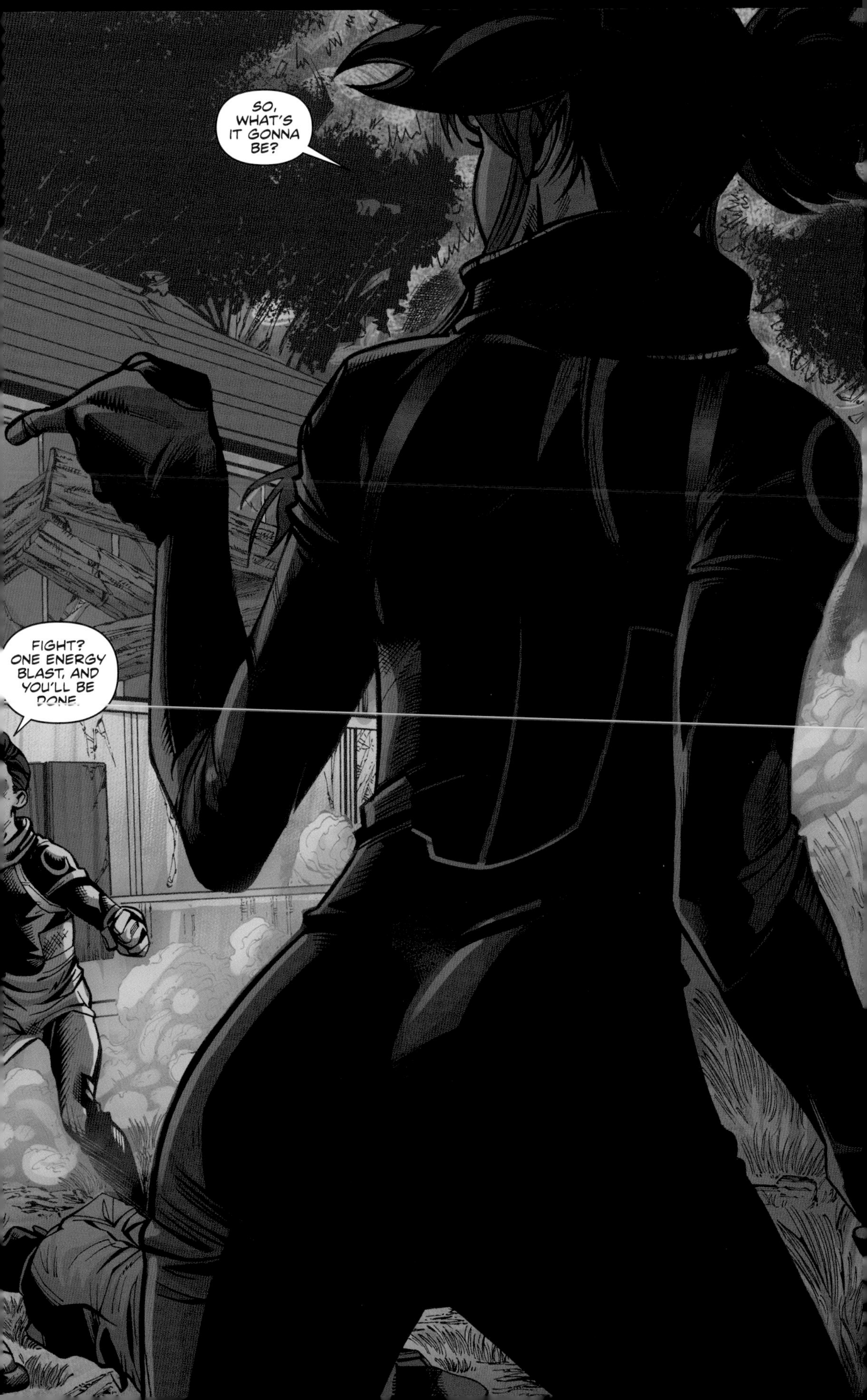
SO, WHAT'S IT GONNA BE?
FIGHT? ONE ENERGY BLAST, AND YOU'LL BE DONE.

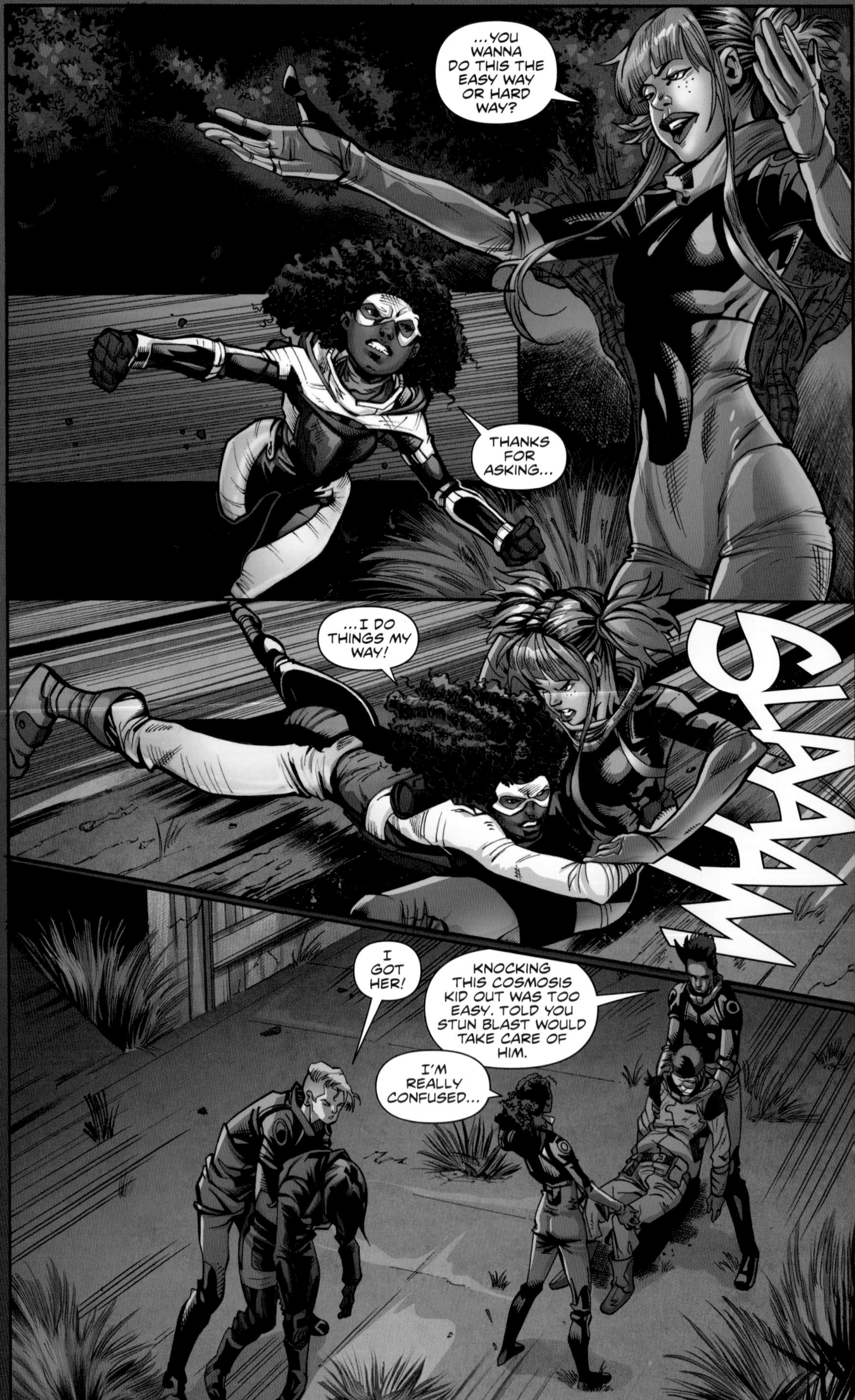
...YOU WANNA DO THIS THE EASY WAY OR HARD WAY?
THANKS FOR ASKING...
...I DO THINGS MY WAY!
SLAAAM
I GOT HER!
KNOCKING THIS COSMOSIS KID OUT WAS TOO EASY. TOLD YOU STUN BLAST WOULD TAKE CARE OF HIM.
I'M REALLY CONFUSED...

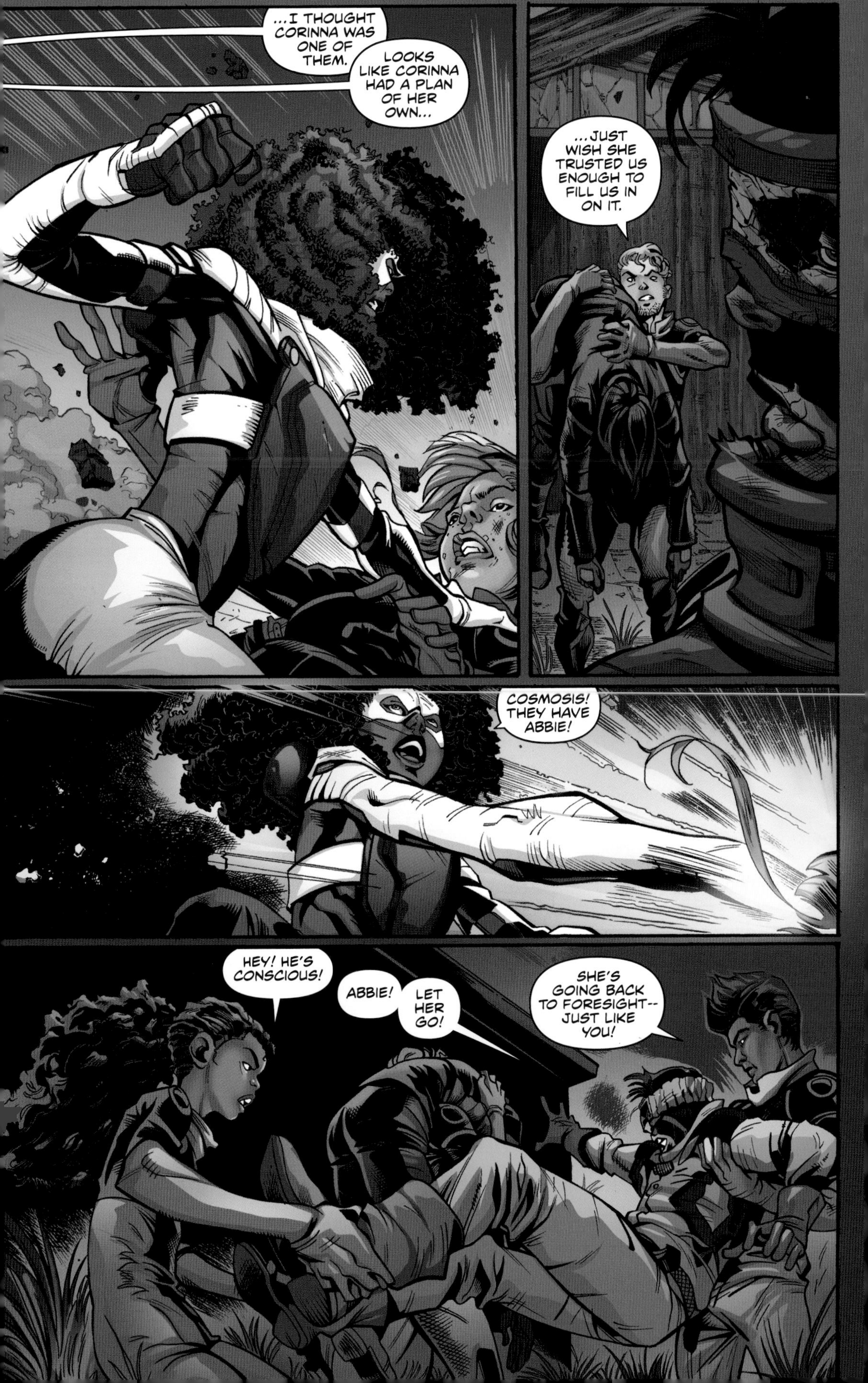
...I THOUGHT CORINNA WAS ONE OF THEM.
LOOKS LIKE CORINNA HAD A PLAN OF HER OWN...
...JUST WISH SHE TRUSTED US ENOUGH TO FILL US IN ON IT.
COSMOSIS! THEY HAVE ABBIE!
HEY! HE'S CONSCIOUS!
ABBIE!
LET HER GO!
SHE'S GOING BACK TO FORESIGHT-- JUST LIKE YOU!

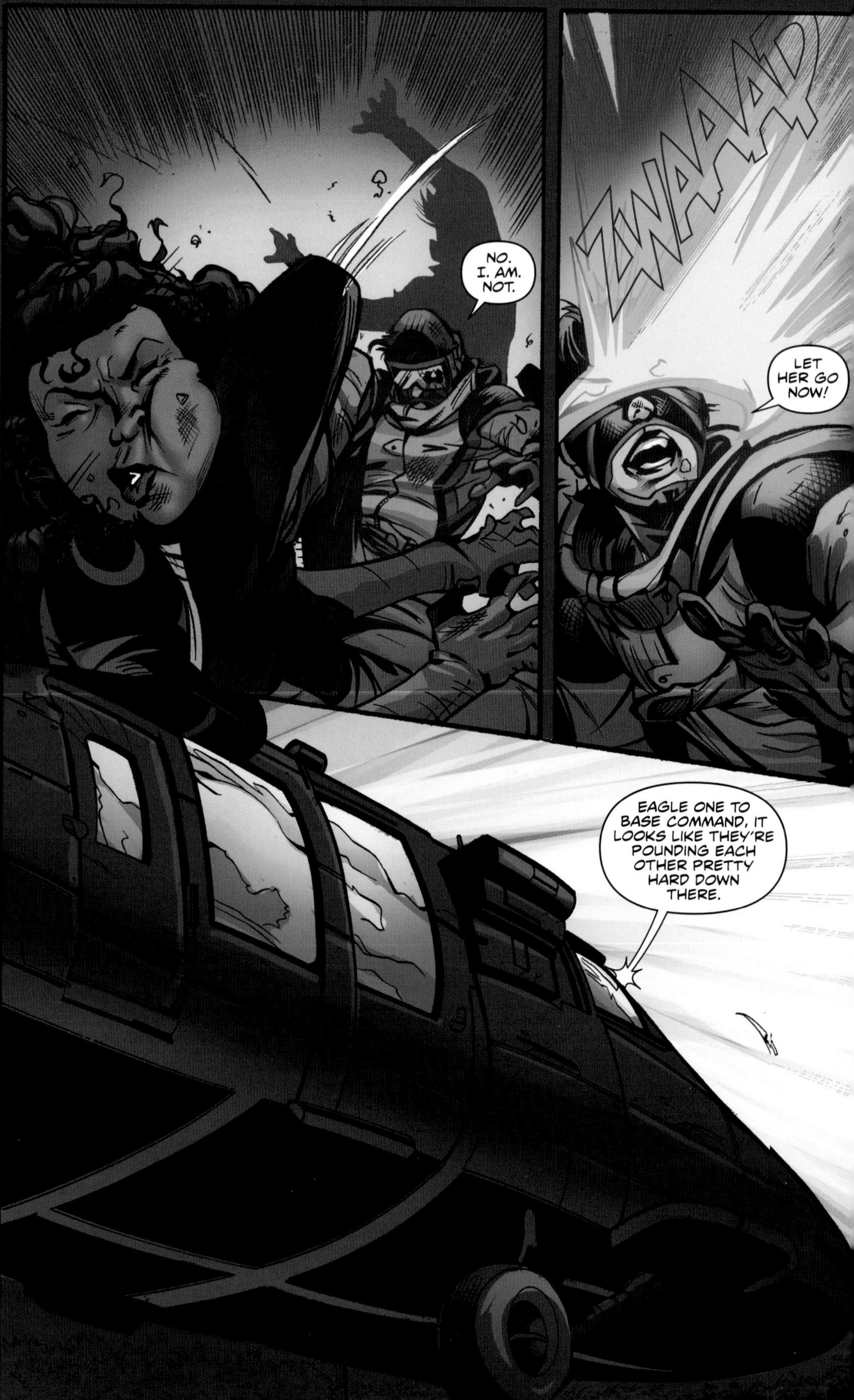
NO. I. AM. NOT.
ZWAAAP
LET HER GO NOW!
EAGLE ONE TO BASE COMMAND, IT LOOKS LIKE THEY'RE POUNDING EACH OTHER PRETTY HARD DOWN THERE.

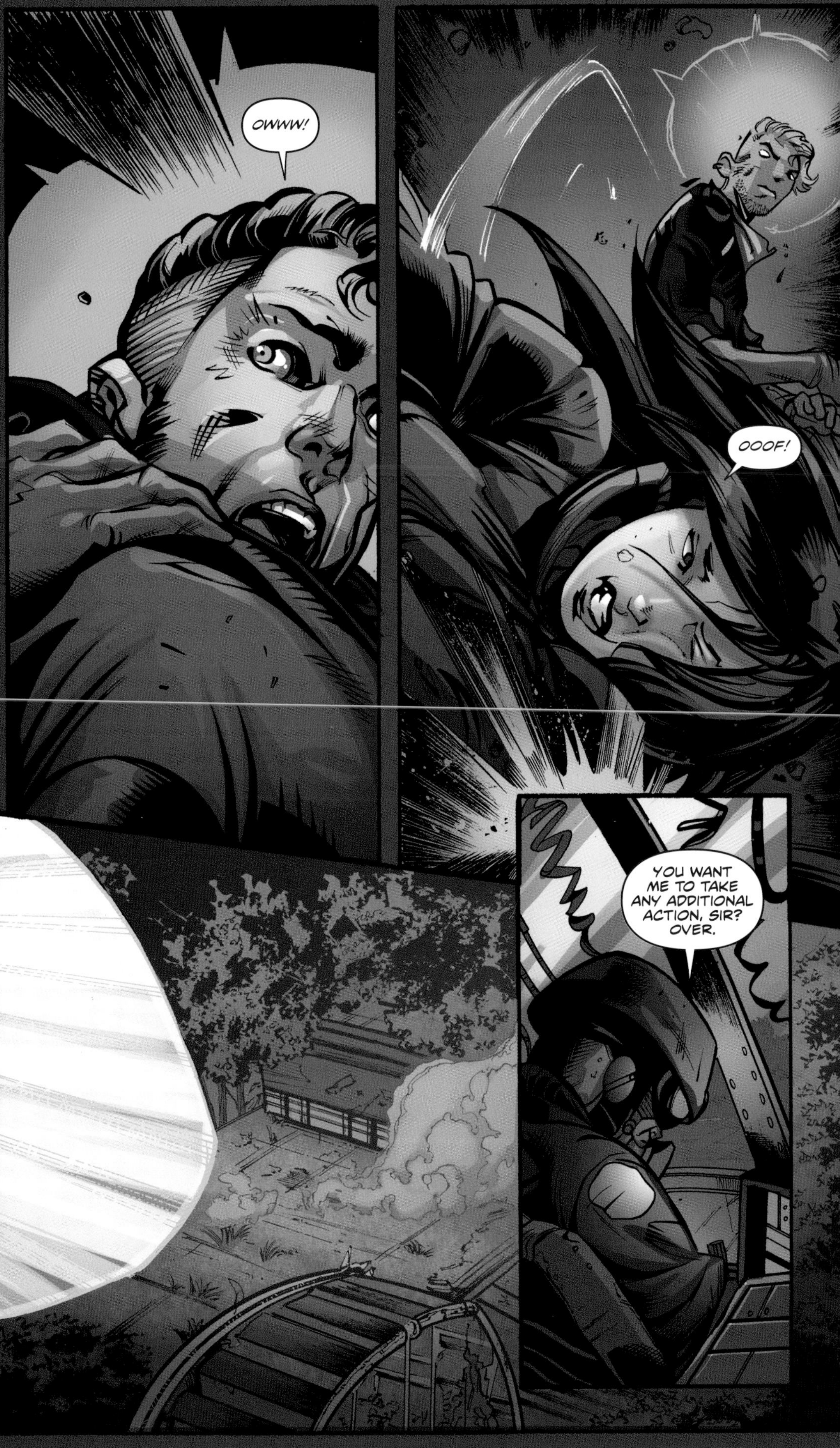
OWWW!
OOOF!
YOU WANT ME TO TAKE ANY ADDITIONAL ACTION, SIR? OVER.

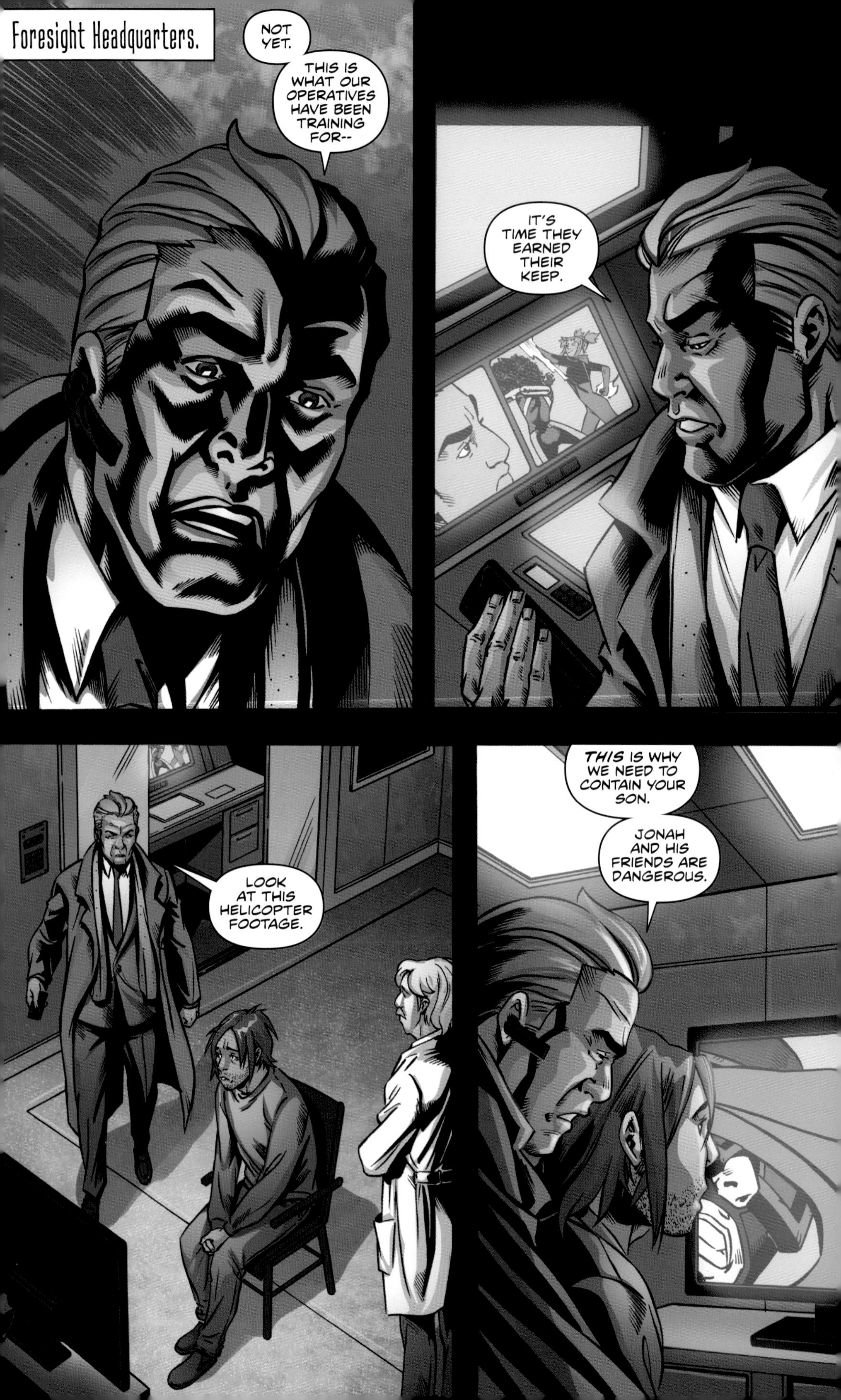
Foresight Headquarters.
NOT YET.
THIS IS WHAT OUR OPERATIVES HAVE BEEN TRAINING FOR--
IT'S TIME THEY EARNED THEIR KEEP.
LOOK AT THIS HELICOPTER FOOTAGE.
THIS IS WHY WE NEED TO CONTAIN YOUR SON.
JONAH AND HIS FRIENDS ARE DANGEROUS.

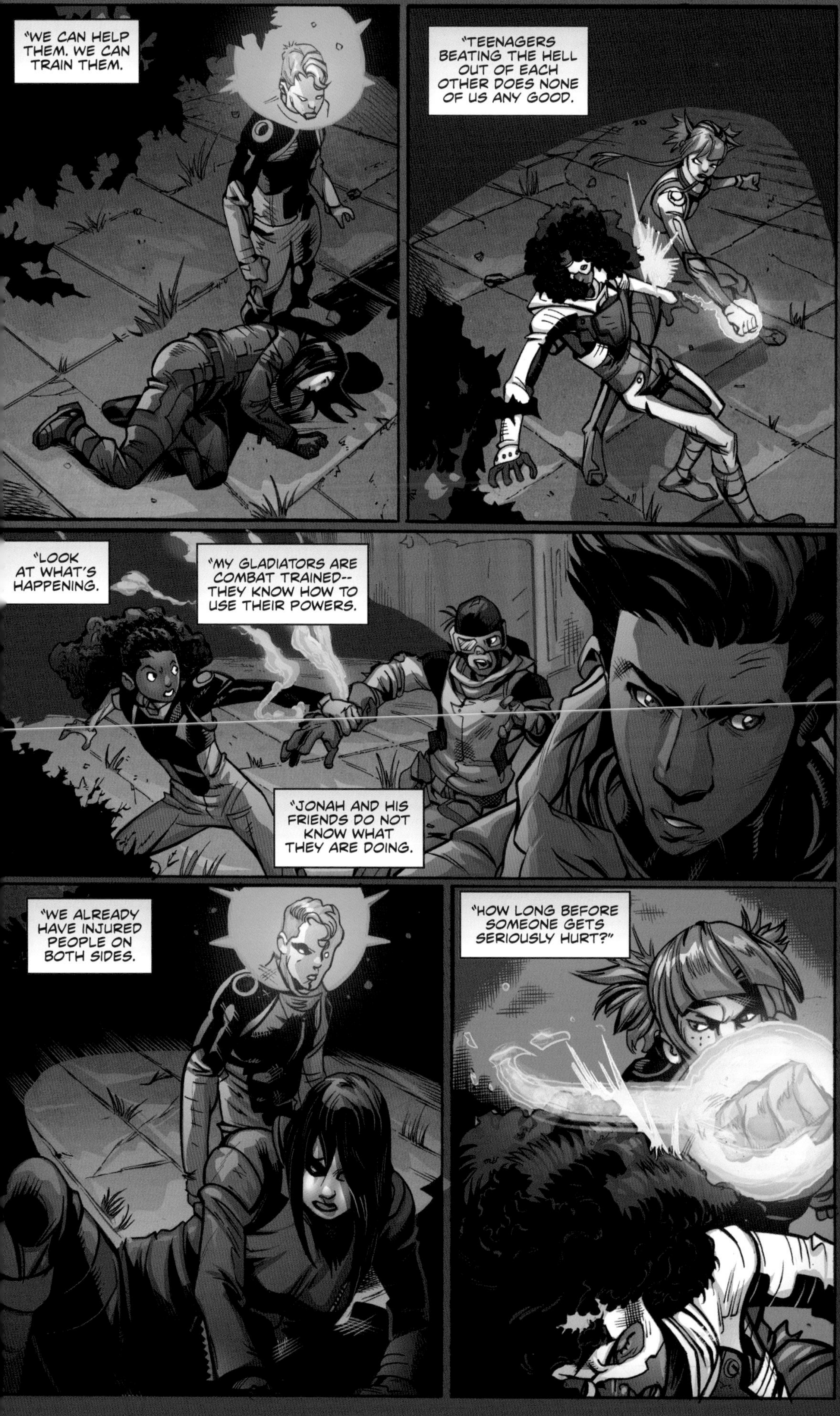
"WE CAN HELP THEM. WE CAN TRAIN THEM.
"TEENAGERS BEATING THE HELL OUT OF EACH OTHER DOES NONE OF US ANY GOOD.
"LOOK AT WHAT'S HAPPENING.
"MY GLADIATORS ARE COMBAT TRAINED-- THEY KNOW HOW TO USE THEIR POWERS.
"JONAH AND HIS FRIENDS DO NOT KNOW WHAT THEY ARE DOING.
"WE ALREADY HAVE INJURED PEOPLE ON BOTH SIDES.
"HOW LONG BEFORE SOMEONE GETS SERIOUSLY HURT?"

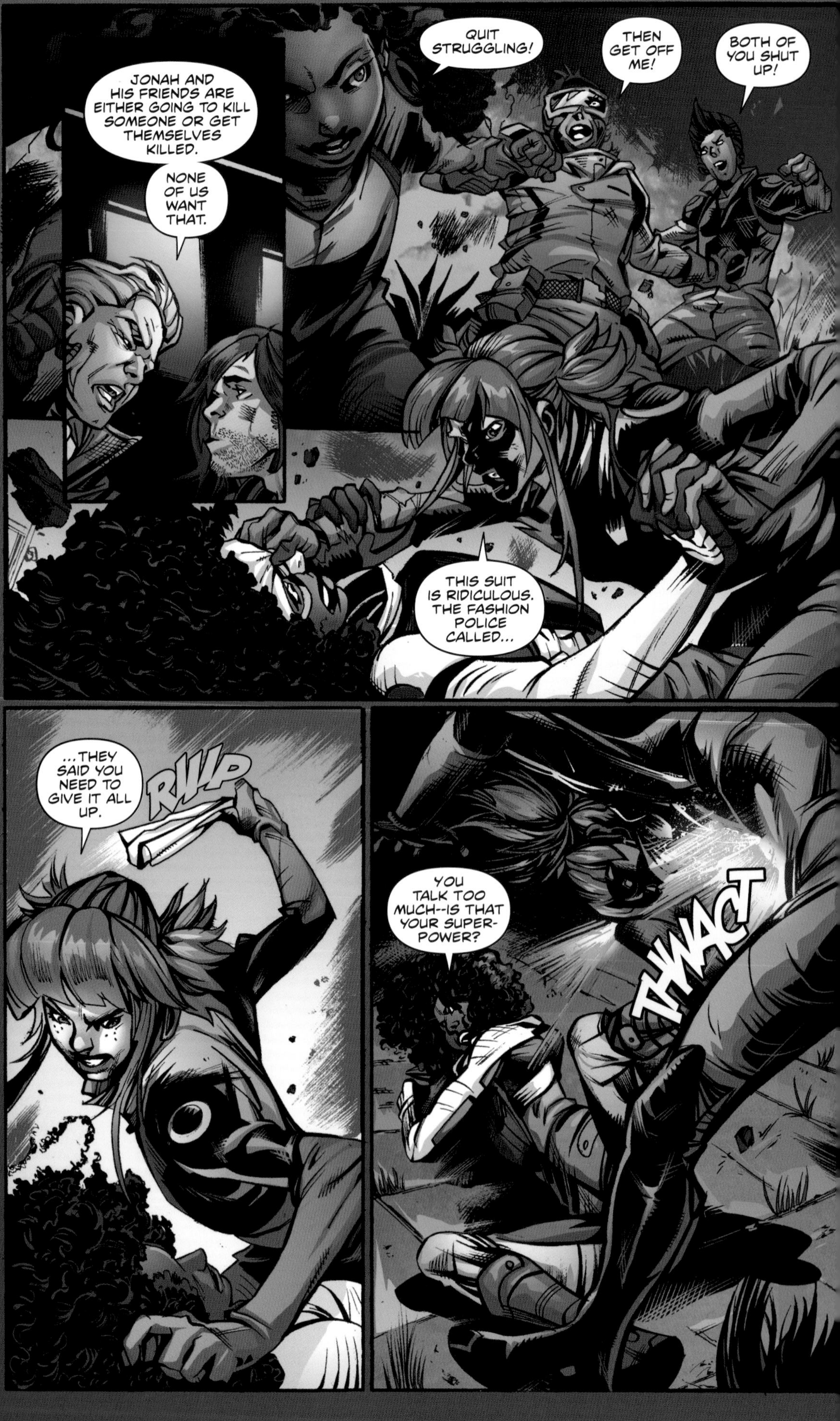

JONAH AND HIS FRIENDS ARE EITHER GOING TO KILL SOMEONE OR GET THEMSELVES KILLED.
NONE OF US WANT THAT.
QUIT STRUGGLING!
THEN GET OFF ME!
BOTH OF YOU SHUT UP!
THIS SUIT IS RIDICULOUS. THE FASHION POLICE CALLED...
...THEY SAID YOU NEED TO GIVE IT ALL UP.
RIIIP
YOU TALK TOO MUCH--IS THAT YOUR SUPER-POWER?
THWACT

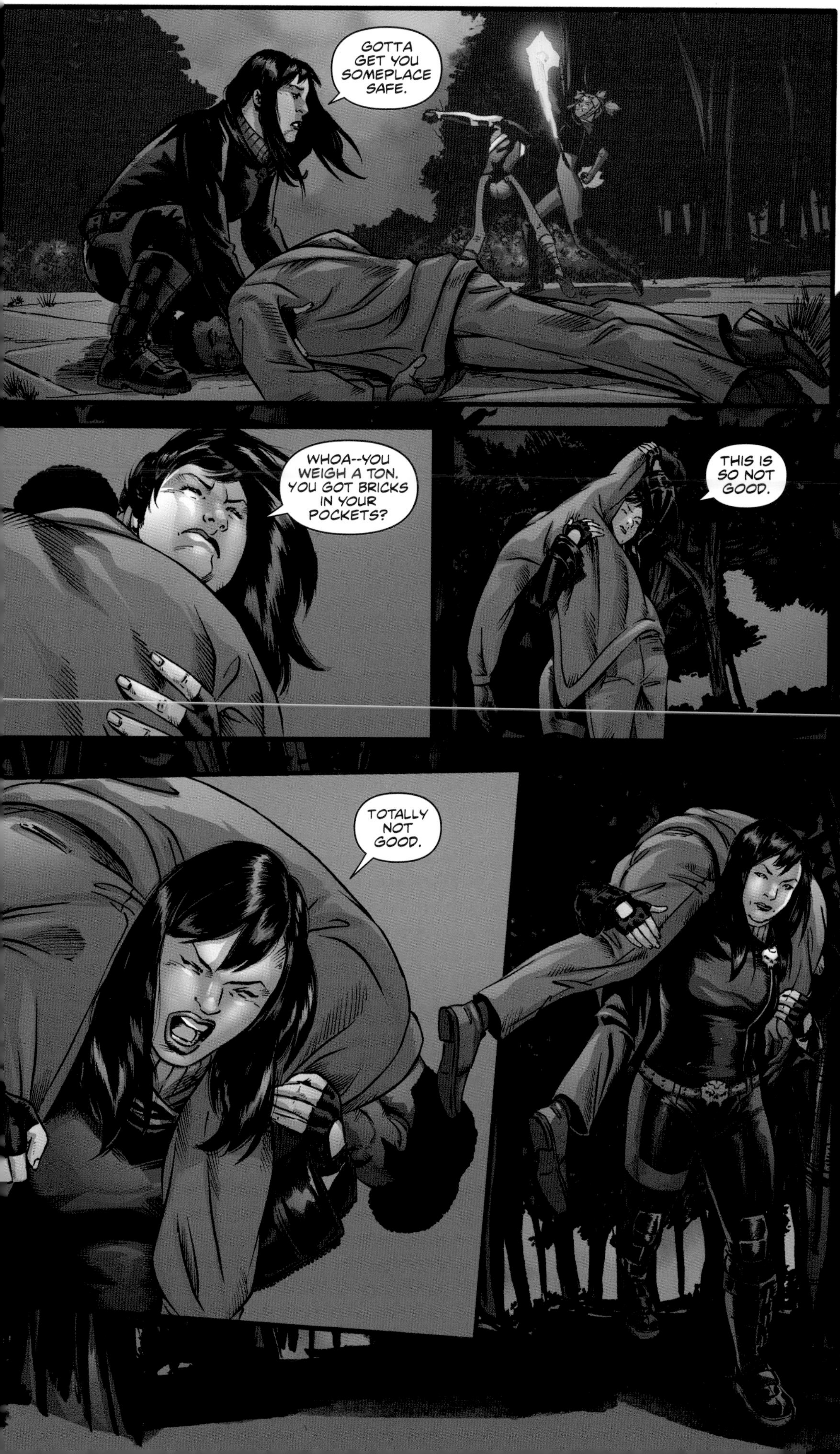
GOTTA GET YOU SOMEPLACE SAFE.
WHOA--YOU WEIGH A TON. YOU GOT BRICKS IN YOUR POCKETS?
THIS IS SO NOT GOOD.
TOTALLY NOT GOOD.

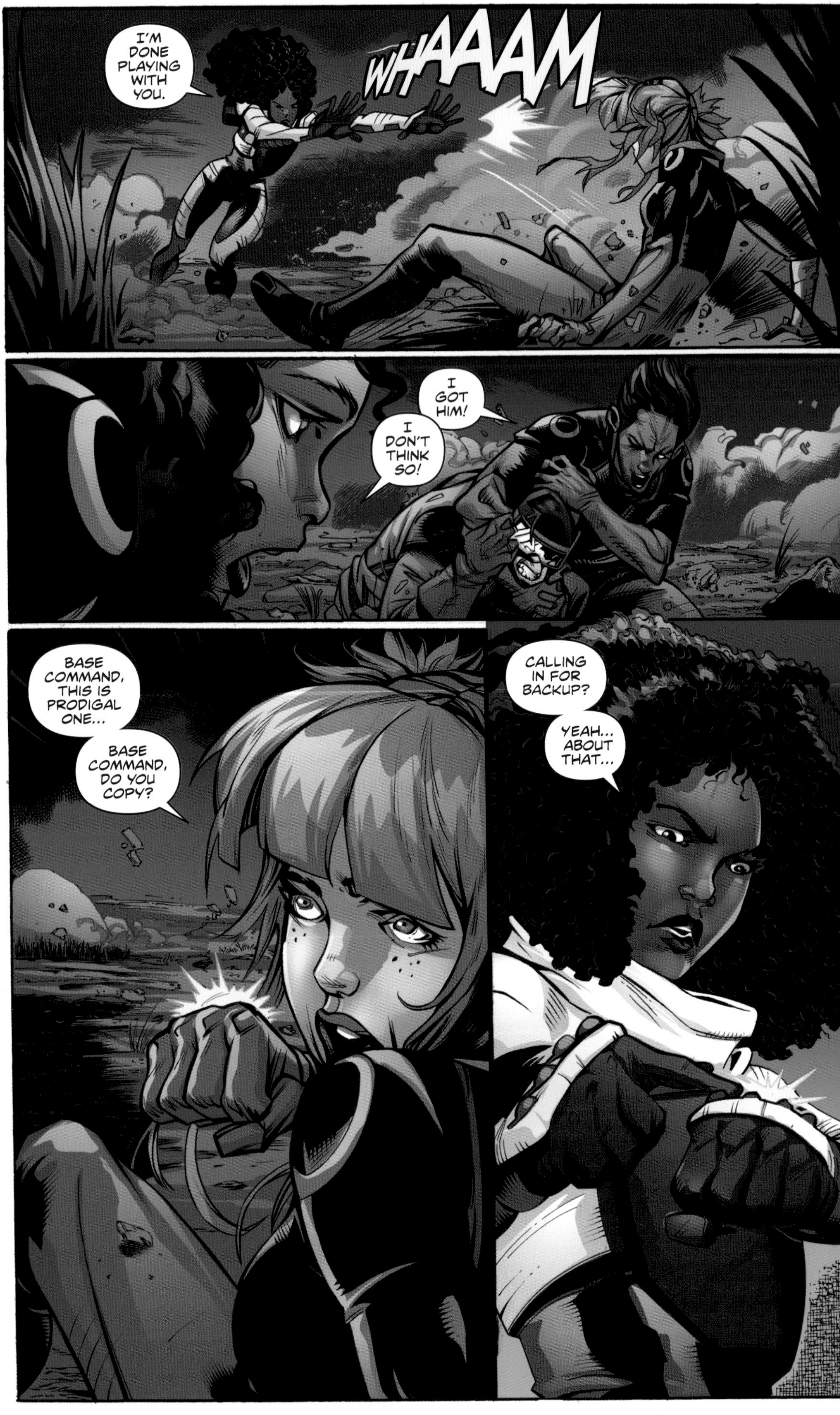
I'M DONE PLAYING WITH YOU.
WHAAAM
I GOT HIM!
I DON'T THINK SO!
BASE COMMAND, THIS IS PRODIGAL ONE...
BASE COMMAND, DO YOU COPY?
CALLING IN FOR BACKUP?
YEAH... ABOUT THAT...

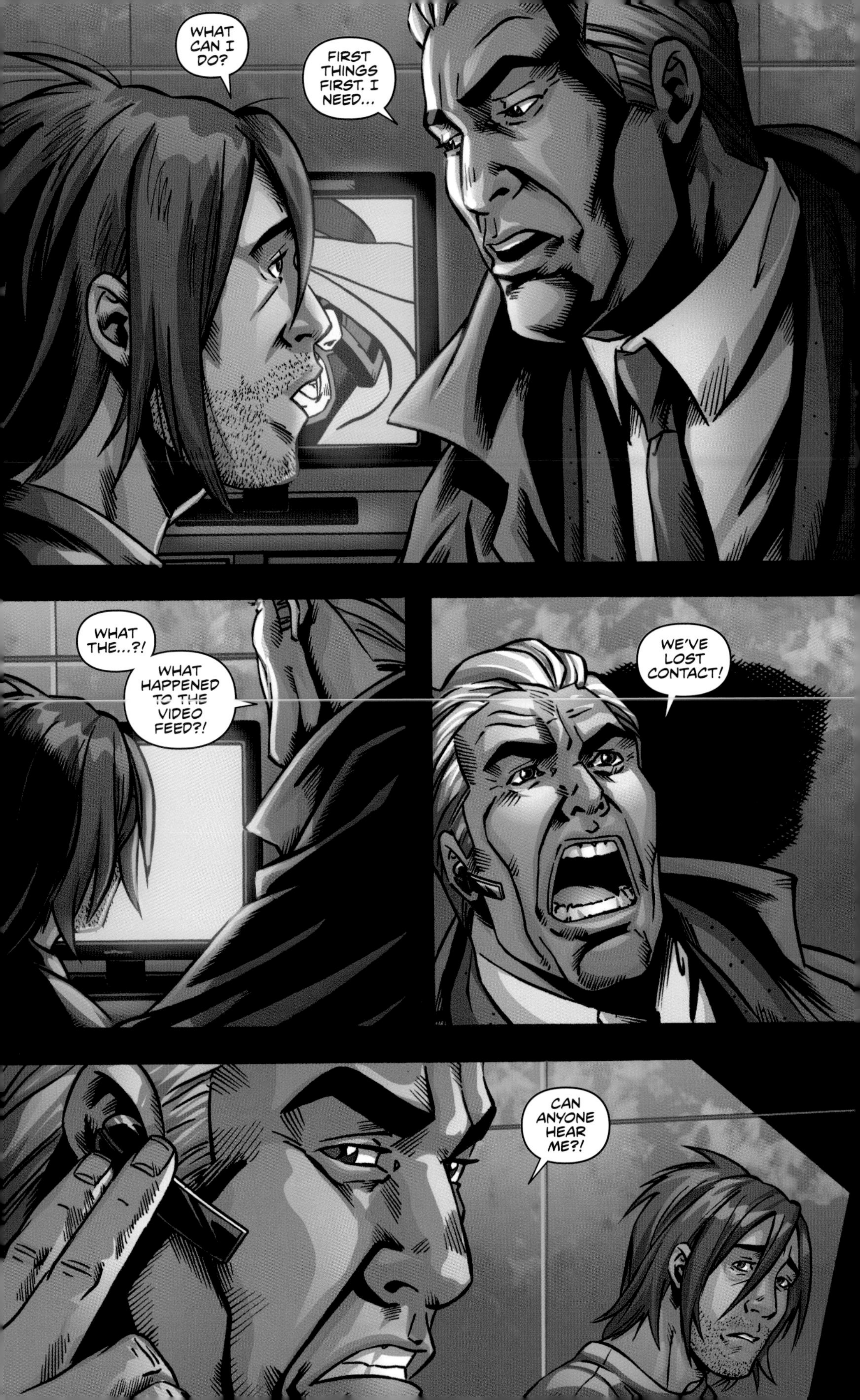
WHAT CAN I DO?
FIRST THINGS FIRST. I NEED...
WHAT THE...?!
WHAT HAPPENED TO THE VIDEO FEED?!
WE'VE LOST CONTACT!
CAN ANYONE HEAR ME?!

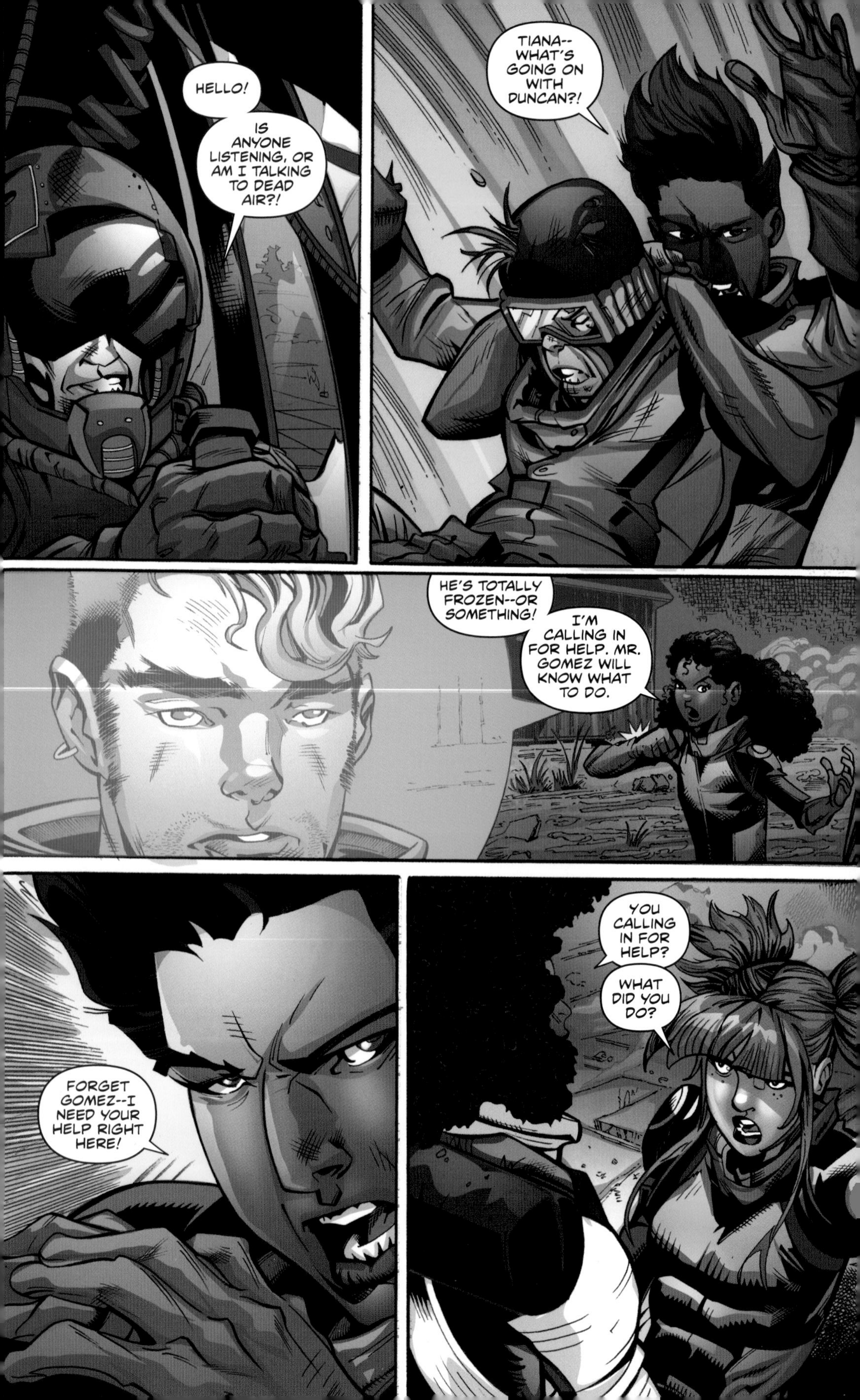
HELLO!
IS ANYONE LISTENING, OR AM I TALKING TO DEAD AIR?!
TIANA-- WHAT'S GOING ON WITH DUNCAN?!
HE'S TOTALLY FROZEN--OR SOMETHING!
I'M CALLING IN FOR HELP. MR. GOMEZ WILL KNOW WHAT TO DO.
FORGET GOMEZ--I NEED YOUR HELP RIGHT HERE!
YOU CALLING IN FOR HELP?
WHAT DID YOU DO?

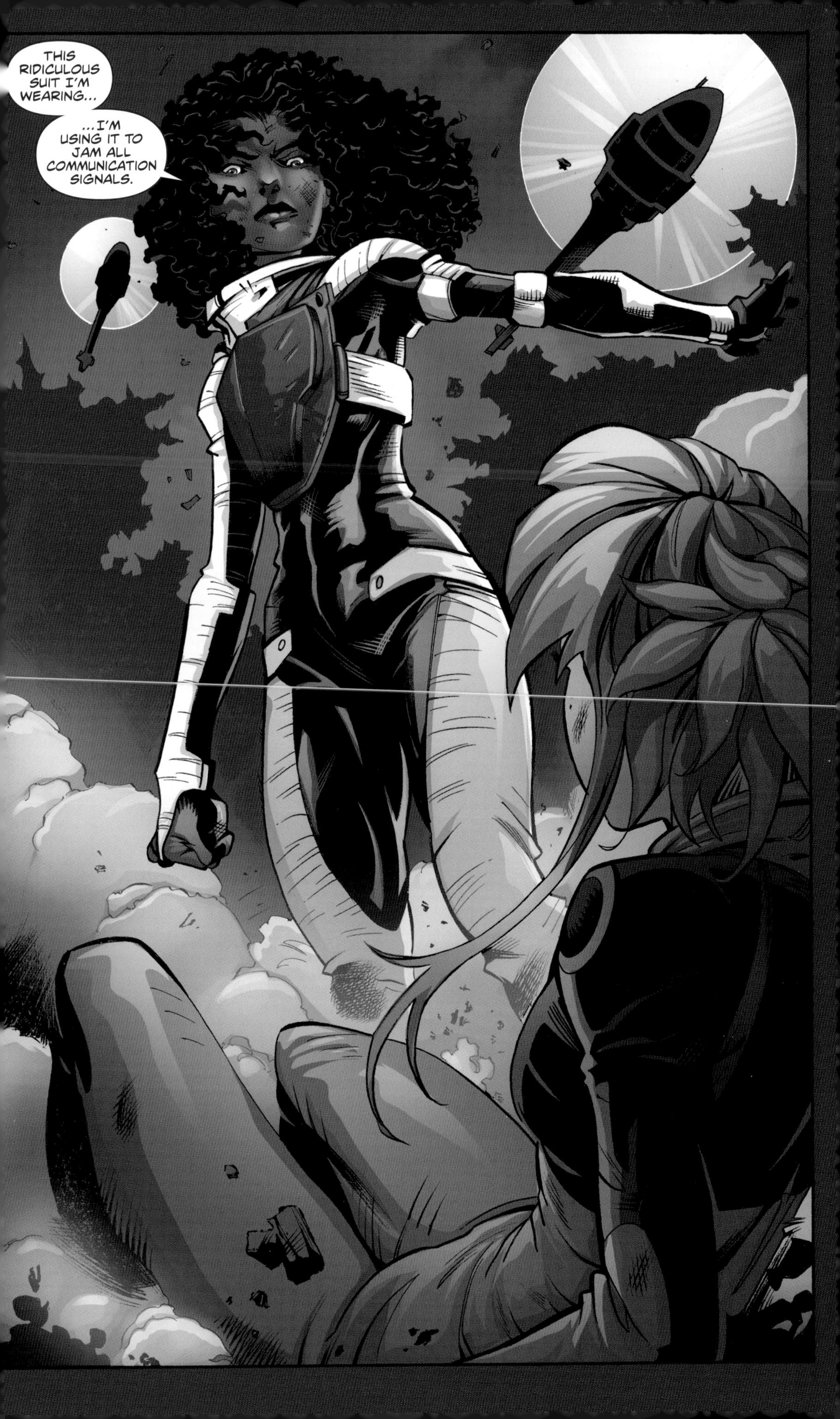
THIS RIDICULOUS SUIT I'M WEARING...
...I'M USING IT TO JAM ALL COMMUNICATION SIGNALS.

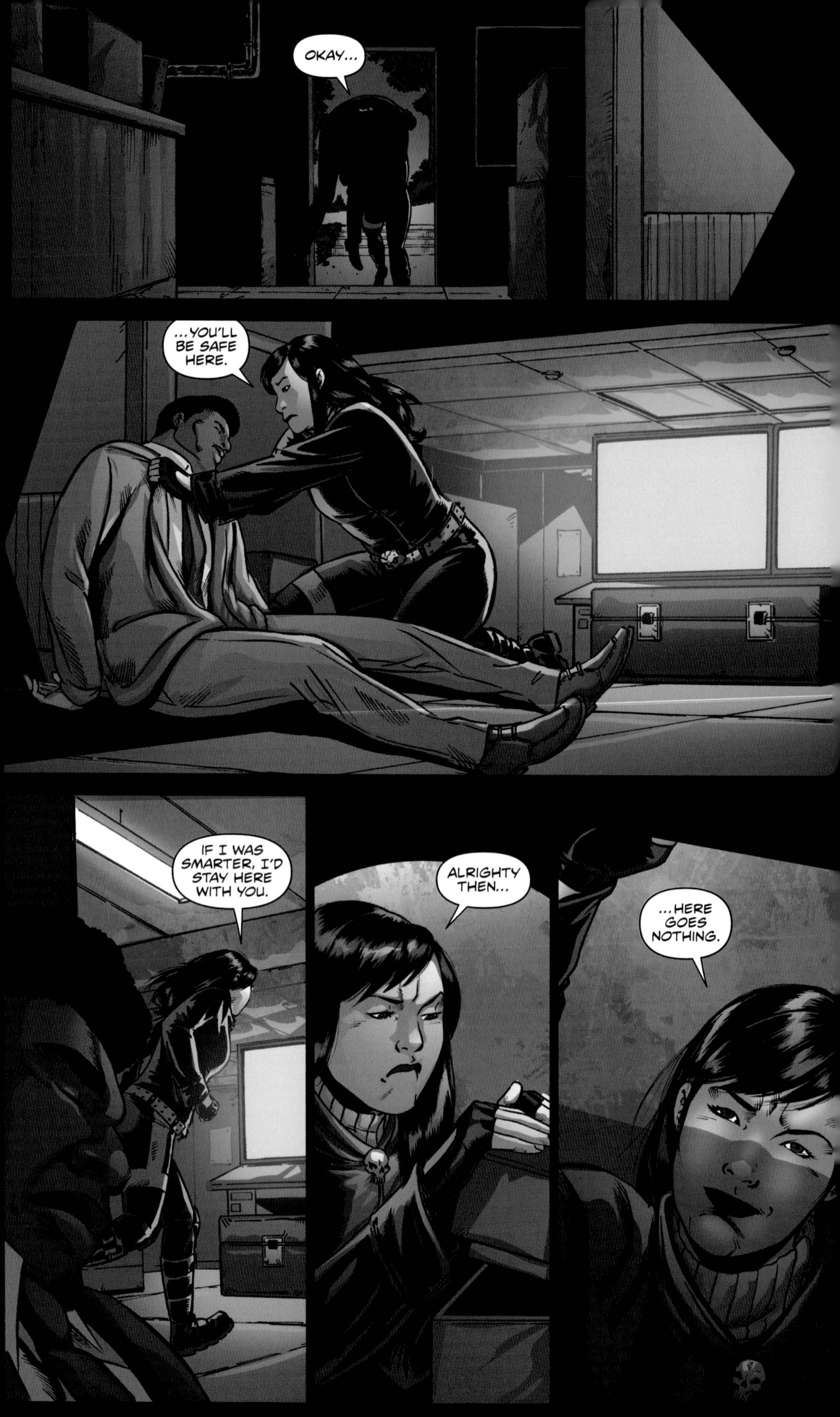
OKAY...
...YOU'LL BE SAFE HERE.
IF I WAS SMARTER, I'D STAY HERE WITH YOU.
ALRIGHTY THEN...
...HERE GOES NOTHING.

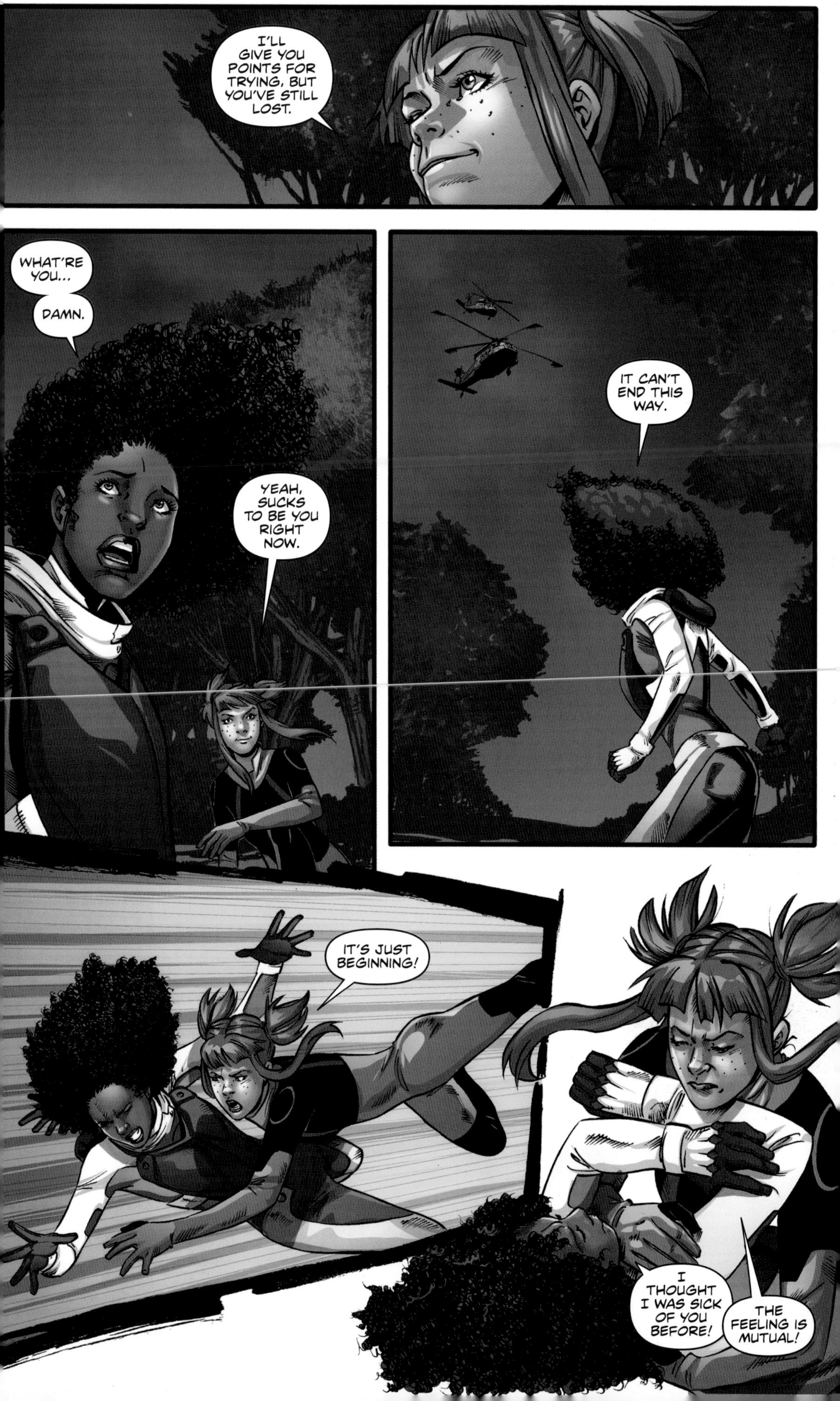
I'LL GIVE YOU POINTS FOR TRYING, BUT YOU'VE STILL LOST.
WHAT'RE YOU...
DAMN.
YEAH, SUCKS TO BE YOU RIGHT NOW.
IT CAN'T END THIS WAY.
IT'S JUST BEGINNING!
I THOUGHT I WAS SICK OF YOU BEFORE!
THE FEELING IS MUTUAL!

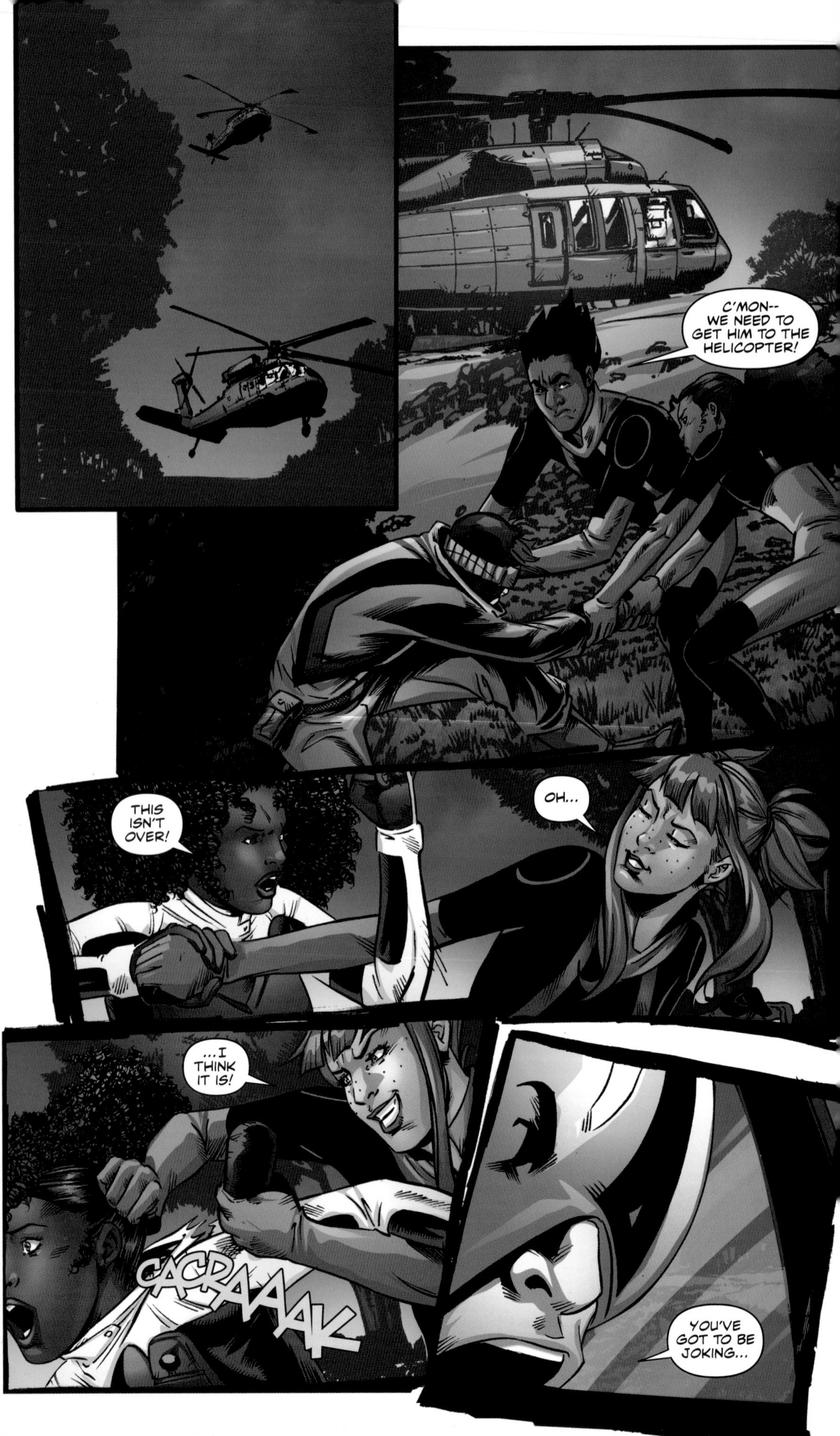
C'MON--
WE NEED TO
GET HIM TO THE
HELICOPTER!
THIS
ISN'T
OVER!
OH...
...I
THINK
IT IS!
CACRAAAK
YOU'VE
GOT TO BE
JOKING...

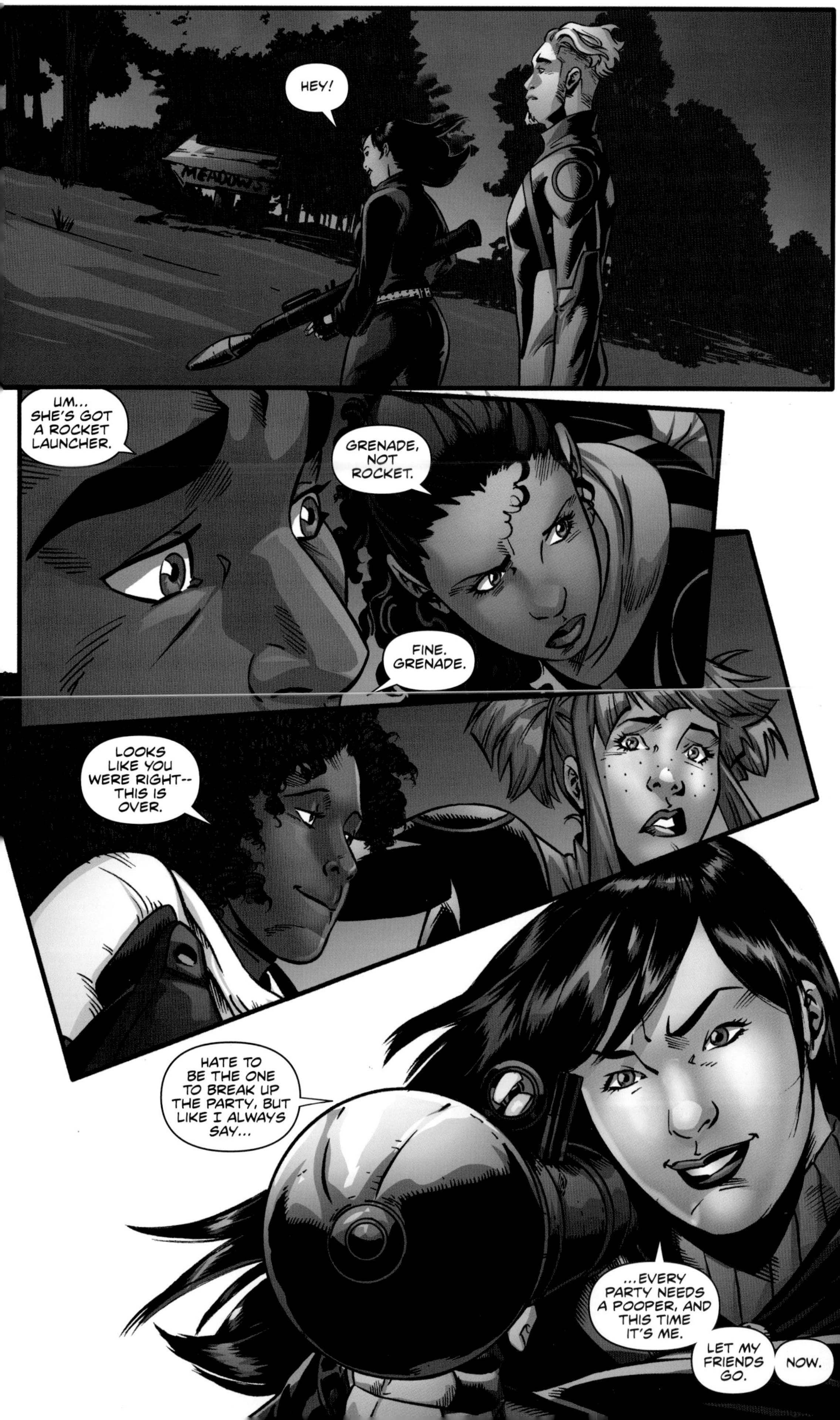
HEY!
MEADOW
UM... SHE'S GOT A ROCKET LAUNCHER.
GRENADE, NOT ROCKET.
FINE. GRENADE.
LOOKS LIKE YOU WERE RIGHT-- THIS IS OVER.
HATE TO BE THE ONE TO BREAK UP THE PARTY, BUT LIKE I ALWAYS SAY...
...EVERY PARTY NEEDS A POOPER, AND THIS TIME IT'S ME.
LET MY FRIENDS GO.
NOW.

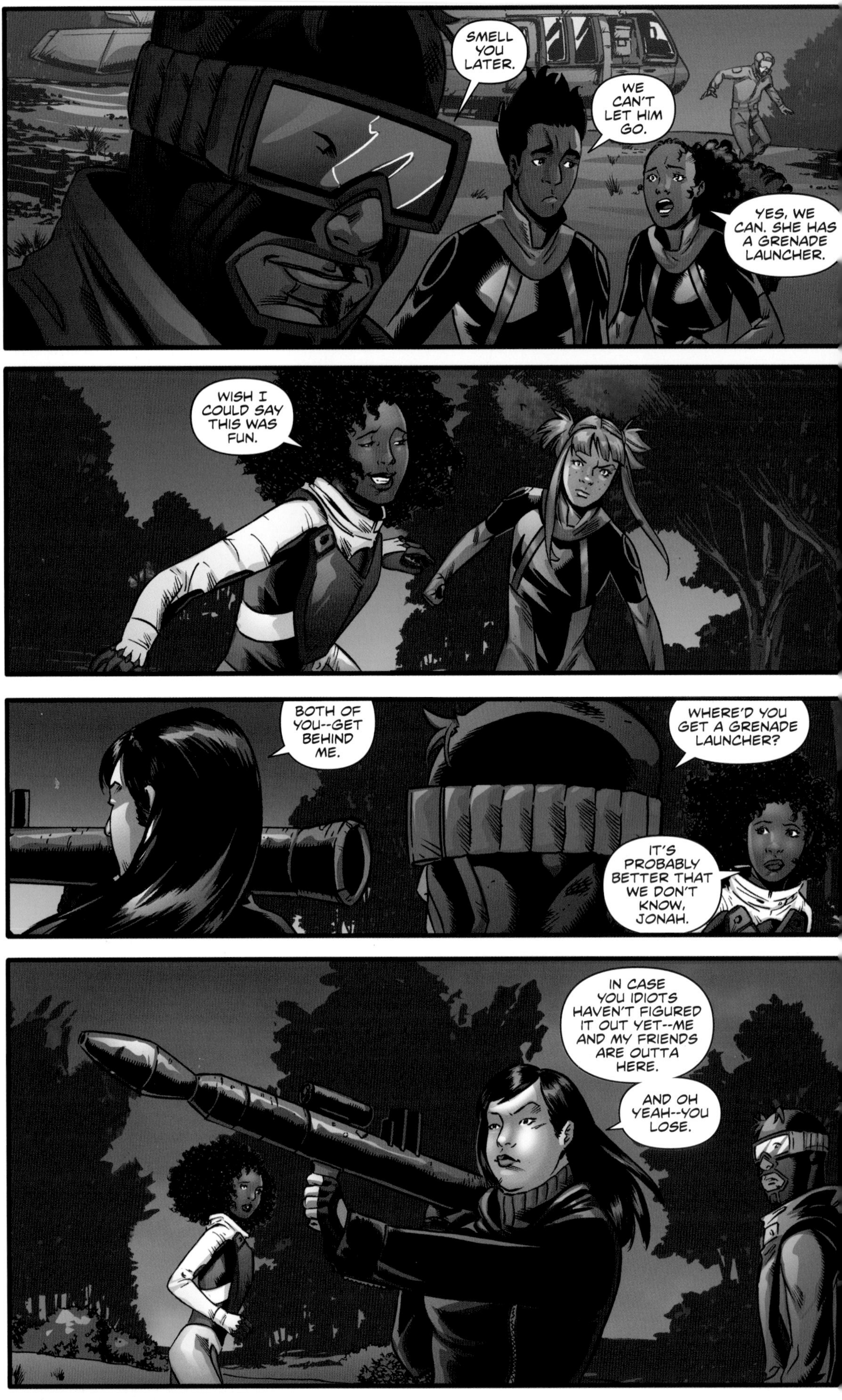
SMELL YOU LATER.
WE CAN'T LET HIM GO.
YES, WE CAN. SHE HAS A GRENADE LAUNCHER.
WISH I COULD SAY THIS WAS FUN.
BOTH OF YOU--GET BEHIND ME.
WHERE'D YOU GET A GRENADE LAUNCHER?
IT'S PROBABLY BETTER THAT WE DON'T KNOW, JONAH.
IN CASE YOU IDIOTS HAVEN'T FIGURED IT OUT YET--ME AND MY FRIENDS ARE OUTTA HERE.
AND OH YEAH--YOU LOSE.

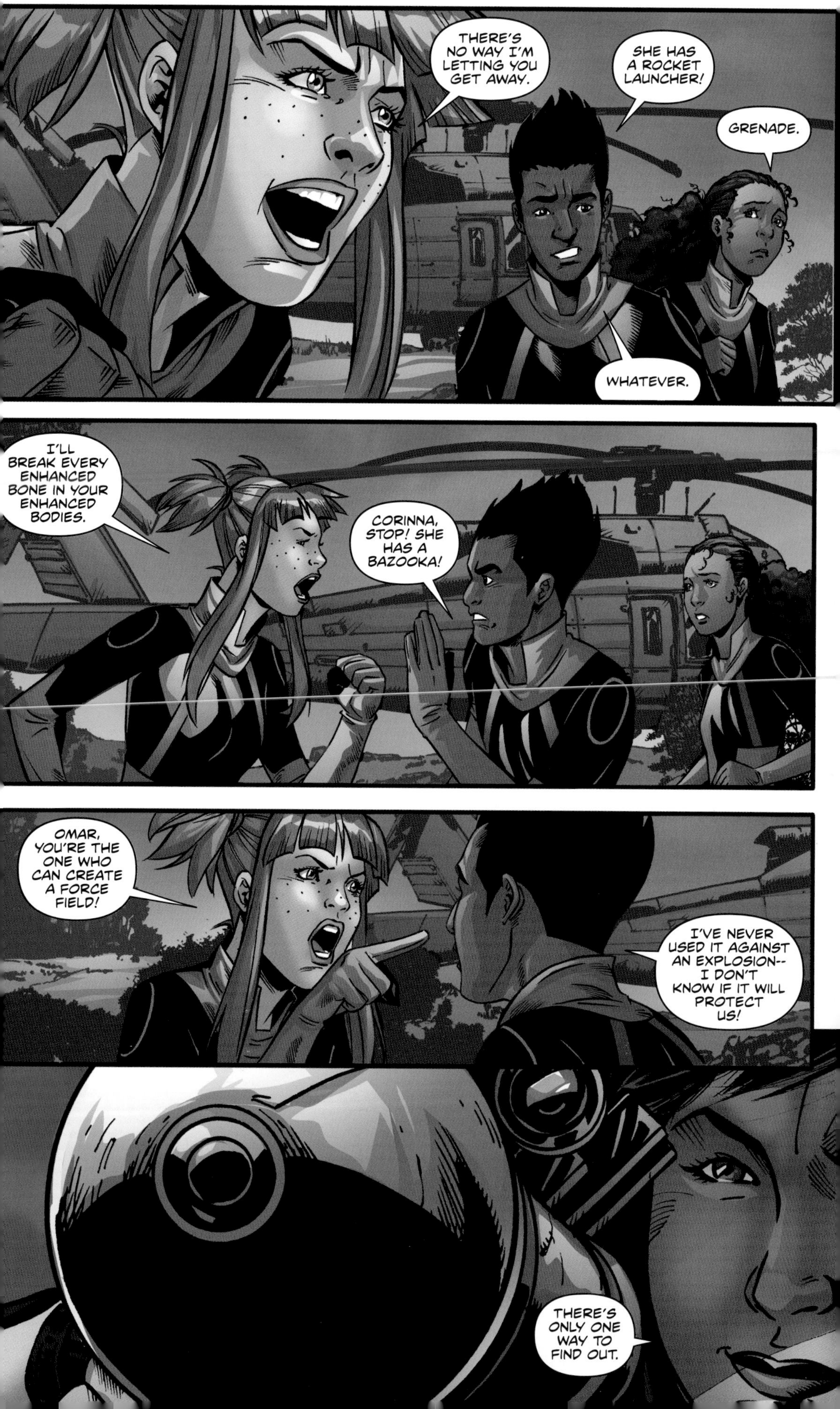
THERE'S NO WAY I'M LETTING YOU GET AWAY.
SHE HAS A ROCKET LAUNCHER!
GRENADE.
WHATEVER.
I'LL BREAK EVERY ENHANCED BONE IN YOUR ENHANCED BODIES.
CORINNA, STOP! SHE HAS A BAZOOKA!
OMAR, YOU'RE THE ONE WHO CAN CREATE A FORCE FIELD!
I'VE NEVER USED IT AGAINST AN EXPLOSION-- I DON'T KNOW IF IT WILL PROTECT US!
THERE'S ONLY ONE WAY TO FIND OUT.

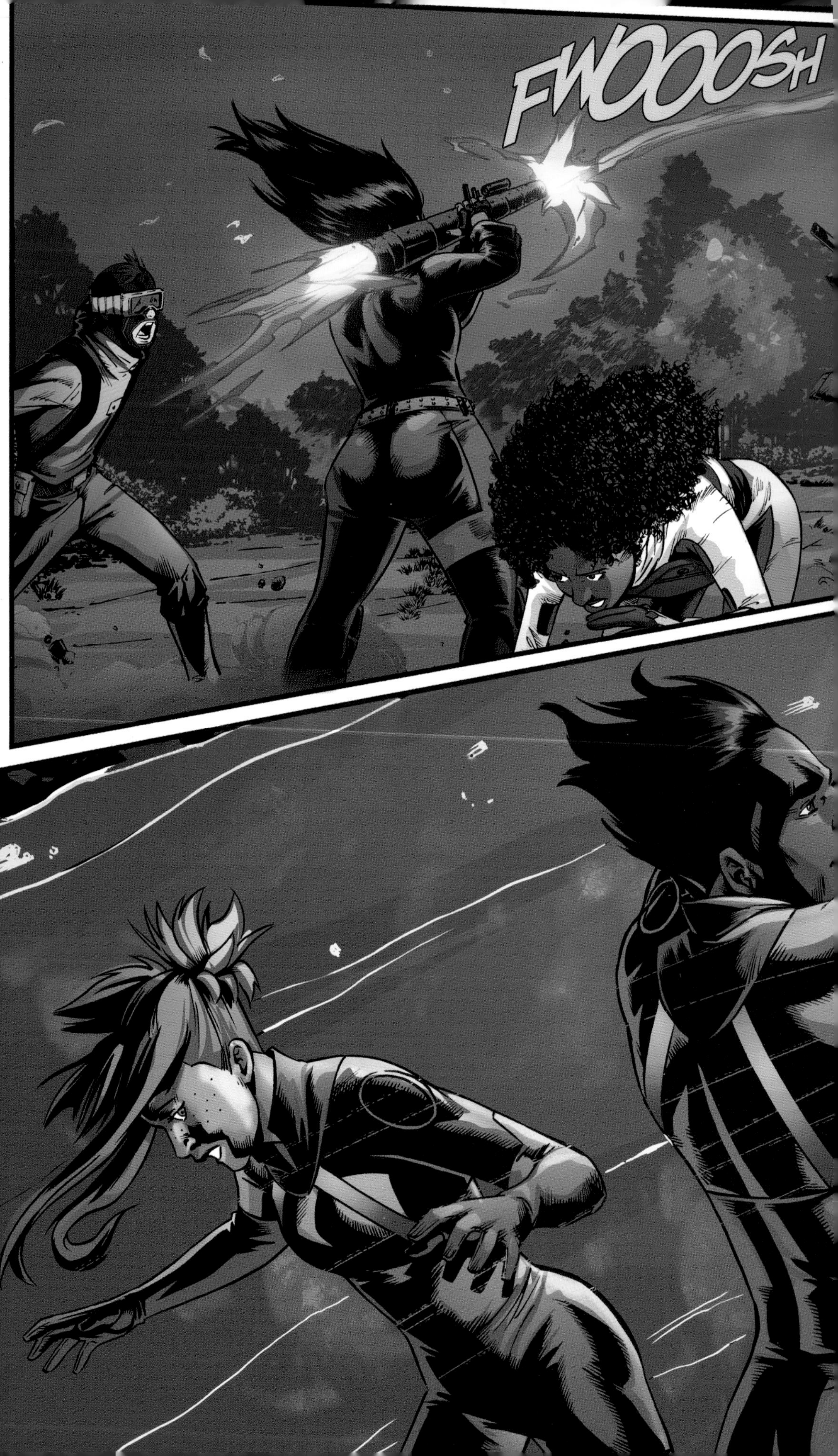
FWOOOSH

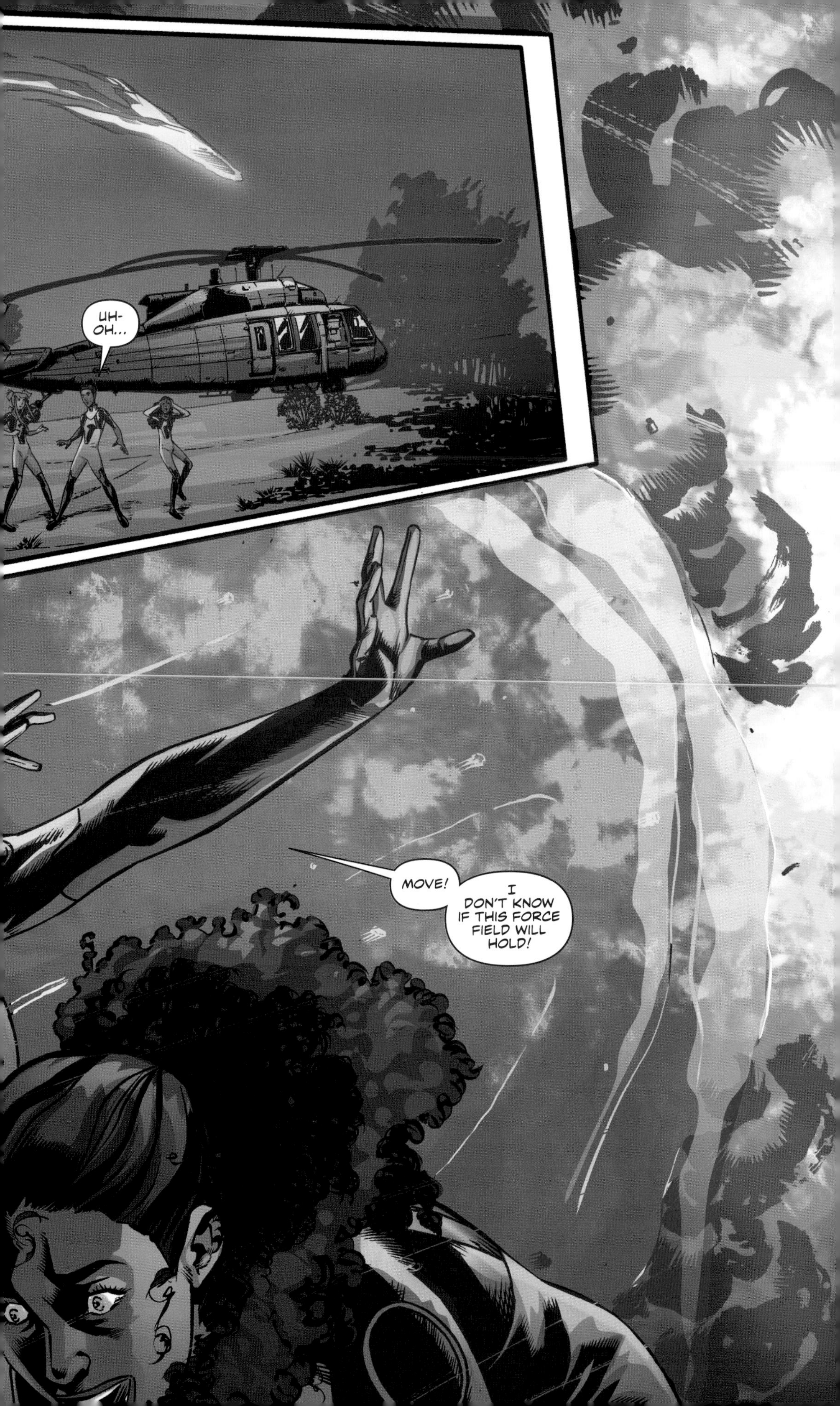
UH-
OH...
MOVE!
I DON'T KNOW IF THIS FORCE FIELD WILL HOLD!

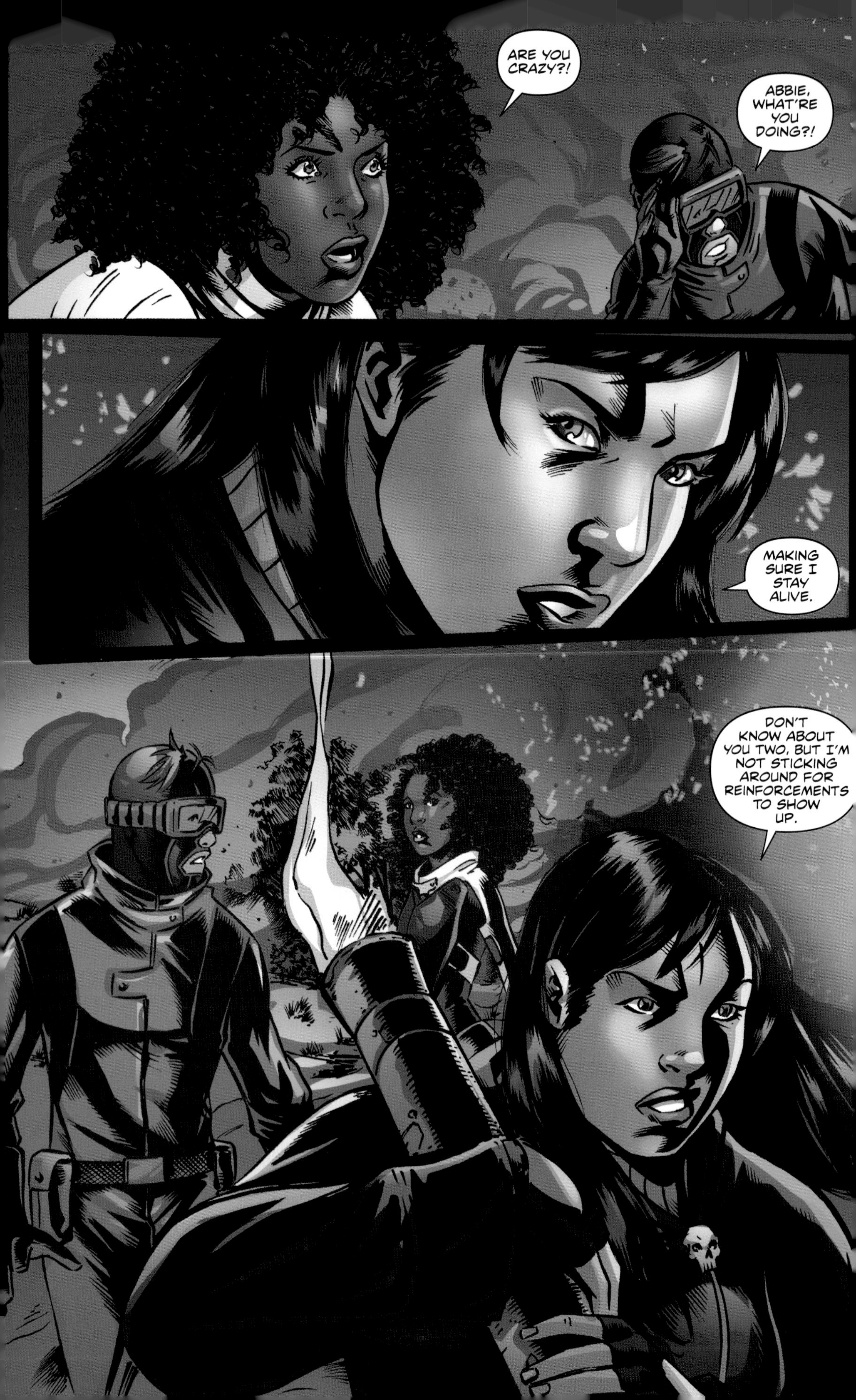
ARE YOU CRAZY?!
ABBIE, WHAT'RE YOU DOING?!
MAKING SURE I STAY ALIVE.
DON'T KNOW ABOUT YOU TWO, BUT I'M NOT STICKING AROUND FOR REINFORCEMENTS TO SHOW UP.

CHAPTER FIVE

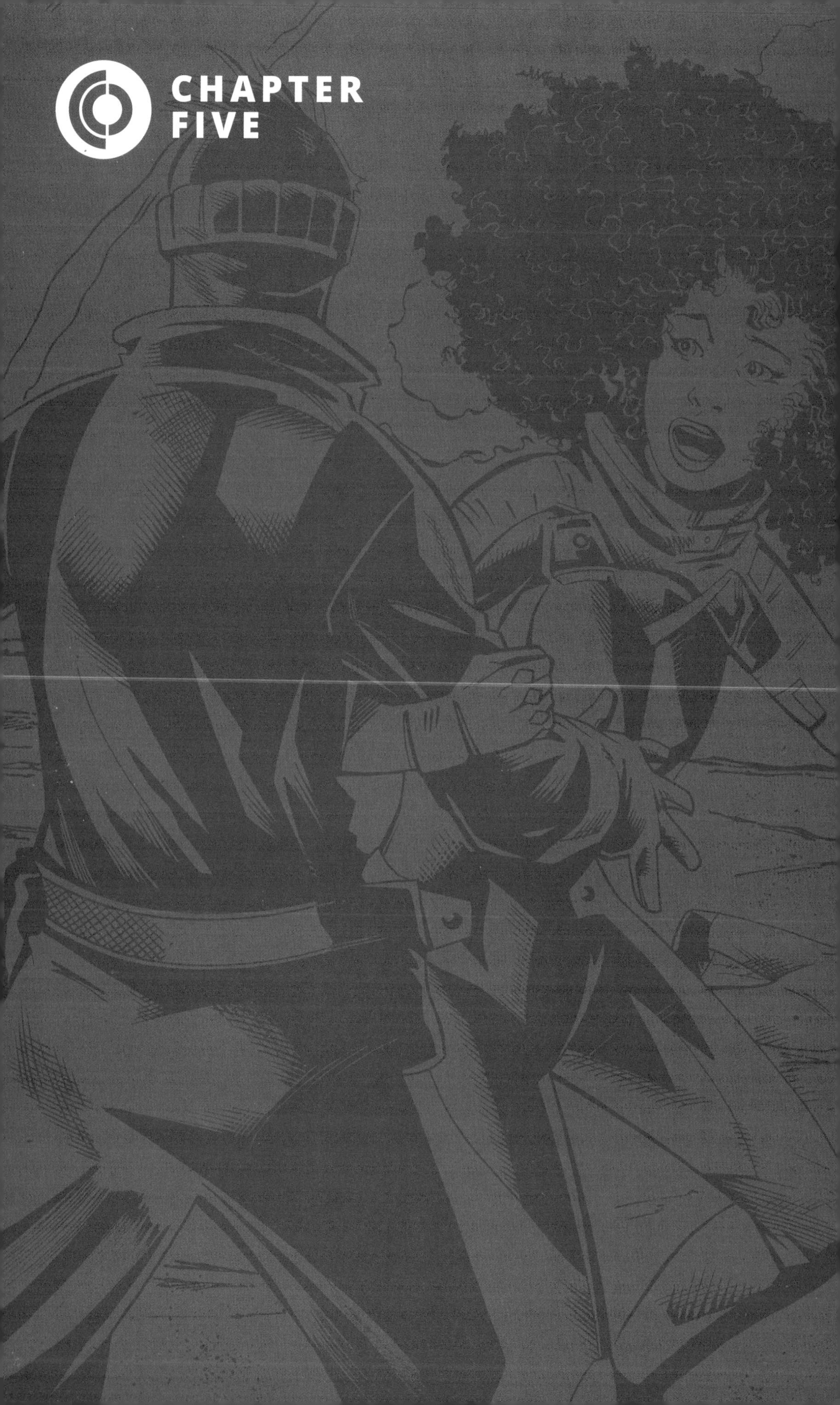

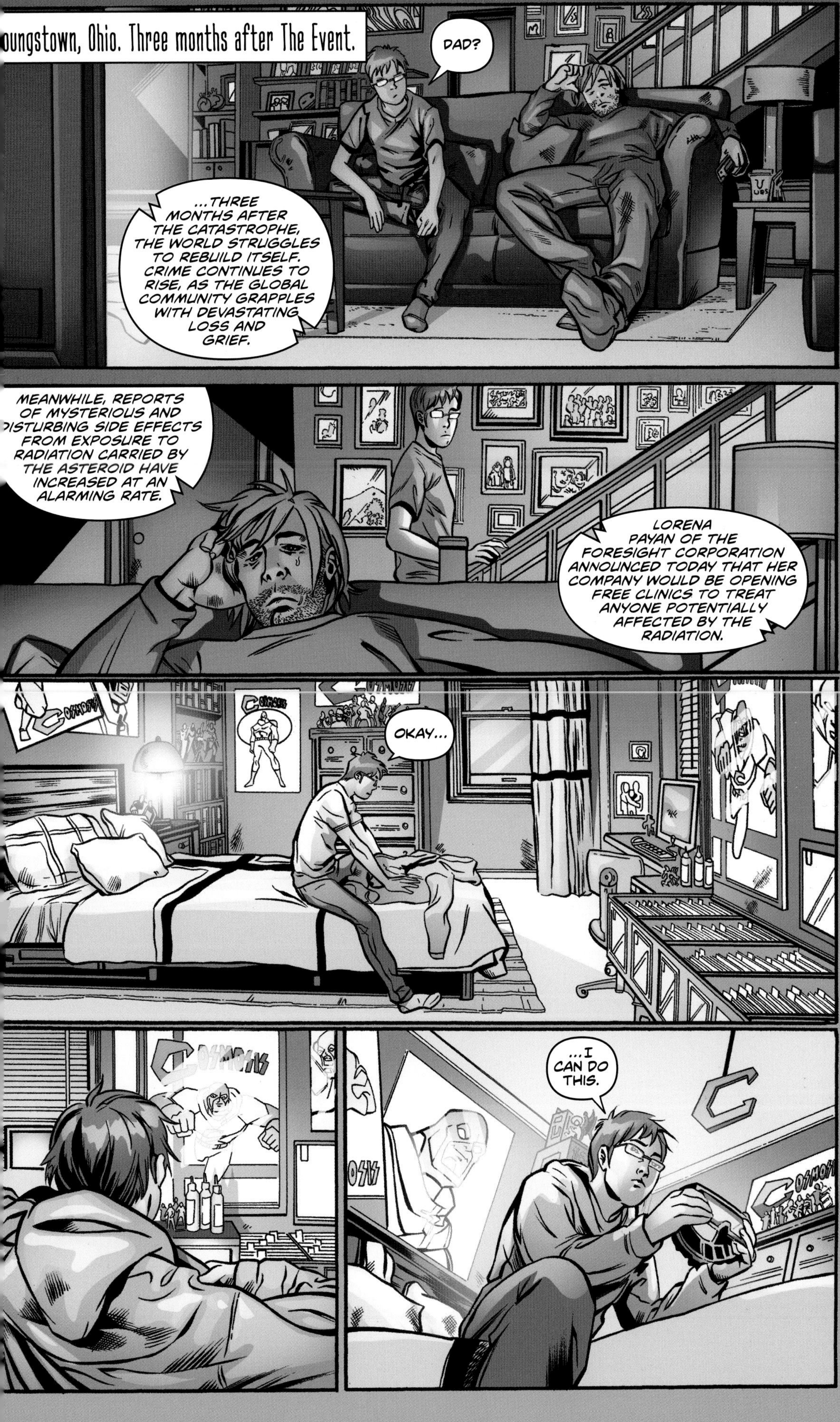
oungstown, Ohio. Three months after The Event.
DAD?
...THREE MONTHS AFTER THE CATASTROPHE, THE WORLD STRUGGLES TO REBUILD ITSELF. CRIME CONTINUES TO RISE, AS THE GLOBAL COMMUNITY GRAPPLES WITH DEVASTATING LOSS AND GRIEF.
MEANWHILE, REPORTS OF MYSTERIOUS AND DISTURBING SIDE EFFECTS FROM EXPOSURE TO RADIATION CARRIED BY THE ASTEROID HAVE INCREASED AT AN ALARMING RATE.
LORENA PAYAN OF THE FORESIGHT CORPORATION ANNOUNCED TODAY THAT HER COMPANY WOULD BE OPENING FREE CLINICS TO TREAT ANYONE POTENTIALLY AFFECTED BY THE RADIATION.
OKAY...
...I CAN DO THIS.

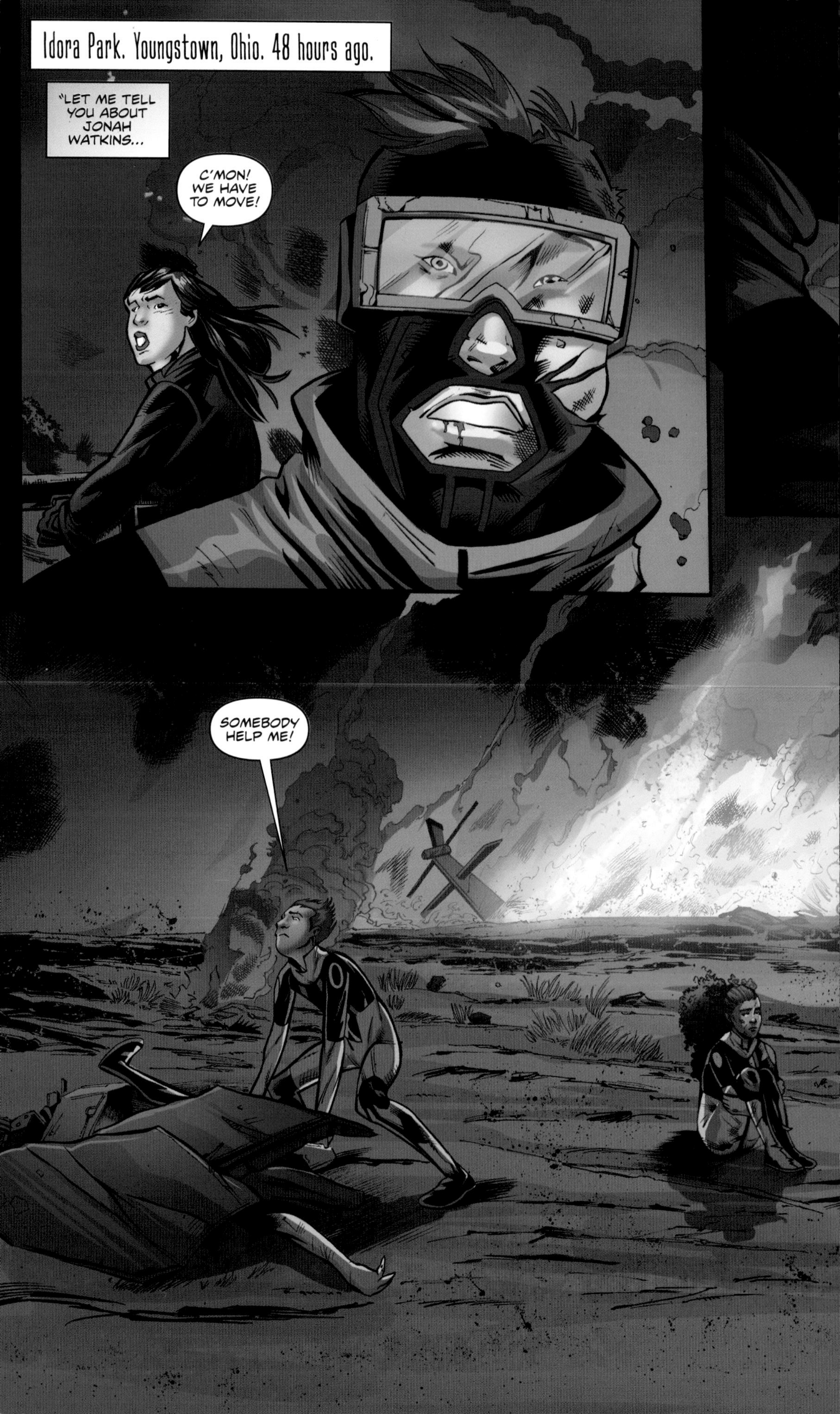
Idora Park. Youngstown, Ohio. 48 hours ago.
"LET ME TELL YOU ABOUT JONAH WATKINS...
C'MON! WE HAVE TO MOVE!
SOMEBODY HELP ME!

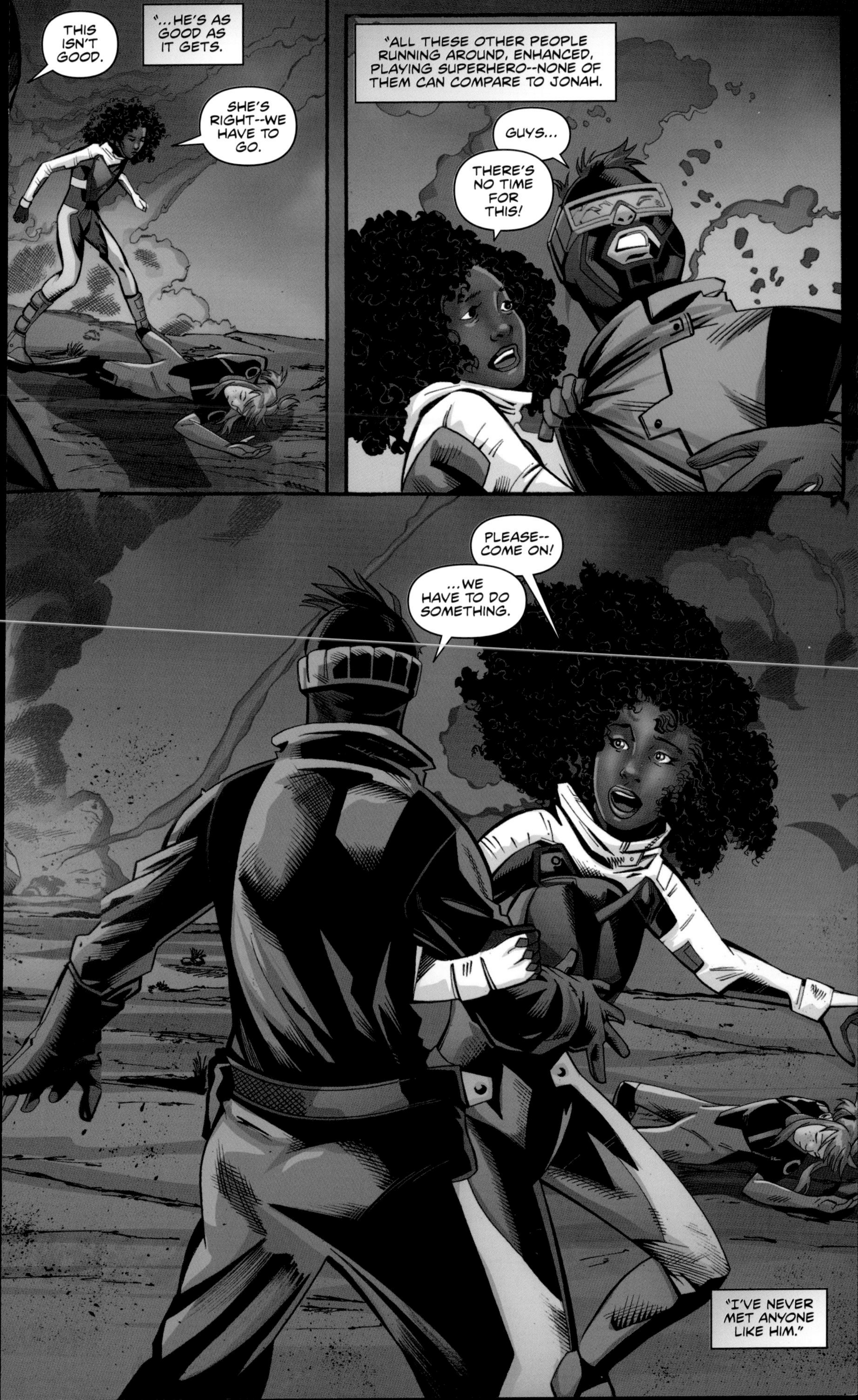

THIS ISN'T GOOD.
"...HE'S AS GOOD AS IT GETS.
SHE'S RIGHT--WE HAVE TO GO.
"ALL THESE OTHER PEOPLE RUNNING AROUND, ENHANCED, PLAYING SUPERHERO--NONE OF THEM CAN COMPARE TO JONAH.
GUYS...
THERE'S NO TIME FOR THIS!
PLEASE--COME ON!
...WE HAVE TO DO SOMETHING.
"I'VE NEVER MET ANYONE LIKE HIM."

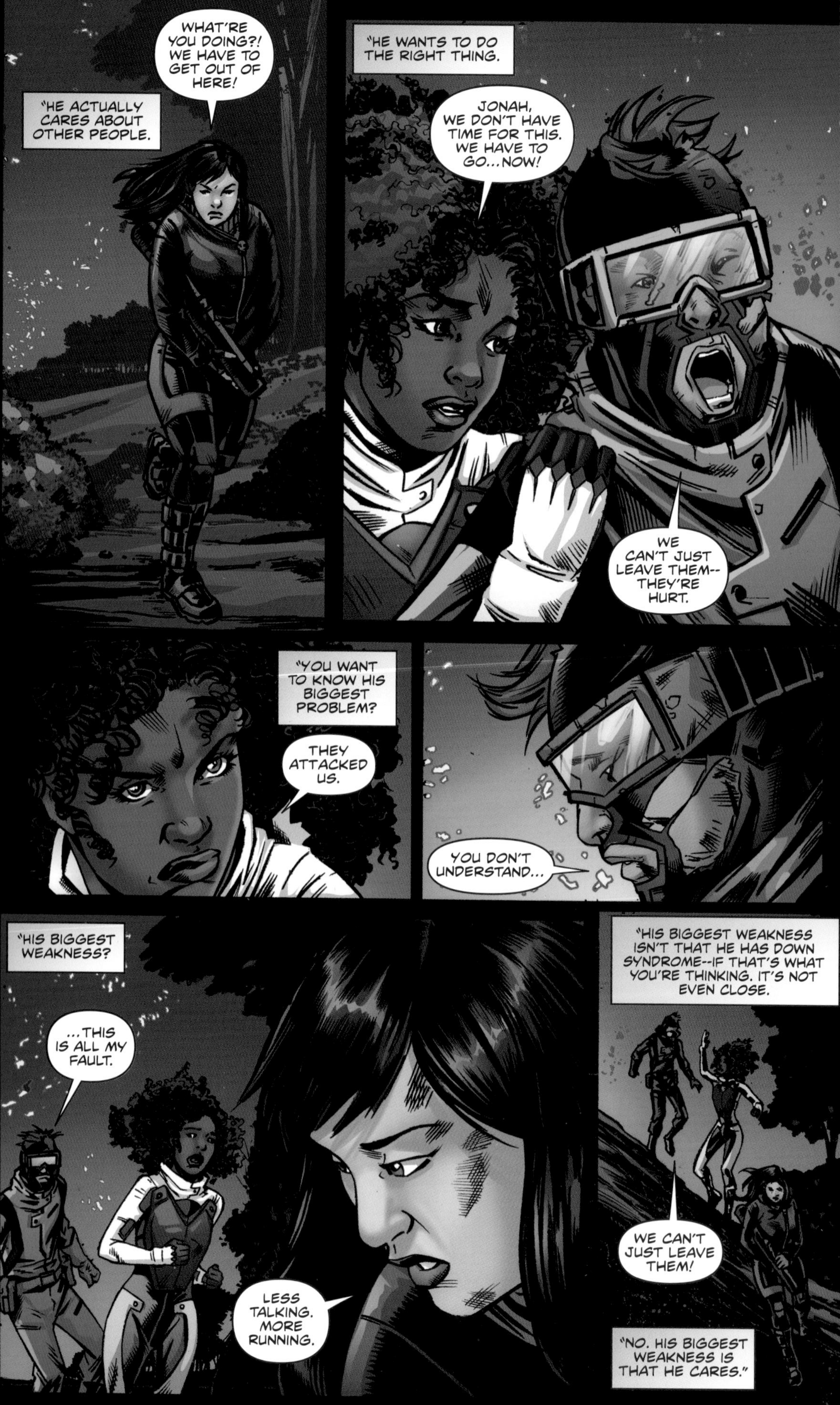
"HE ACTUALLY CARES ABOUT OTHER PEOPLE.
WHAT'RE YOU DOING?! WE HAVE TO GET OUT OF HERE!
"HE WANTS TO DO THE RIGHT THING.
JONAH, WE DON'T HAVE TIME FOR THIS. WE HAVE TO GO...NOW!
WE CAN'T JUST LEAVE THEM--THEY'RE HURT.
"YOU WANT TO KNOW HIS BIGGEST PROBLEM?
THEY ATTACKED US.
YOU DON'T UNDERSTAND...
"HIS BIGGEST WEAKNESS?
...THIS IS ALL MY FAULT.
LESS TALKING. MORE RUNNING.
"HIS BIGGEST WEAKNESS ISN'T THAT HE HAS DOWN SYNDROME--IF THAT'S WHAT YOU'RE THINKING. IT'S NOT EVEN CLOSE.
WE CAN'T JUST LEAVE THEM!
"NO. HIS BIGGEST WEAKNESS IS THAT HE CARES."

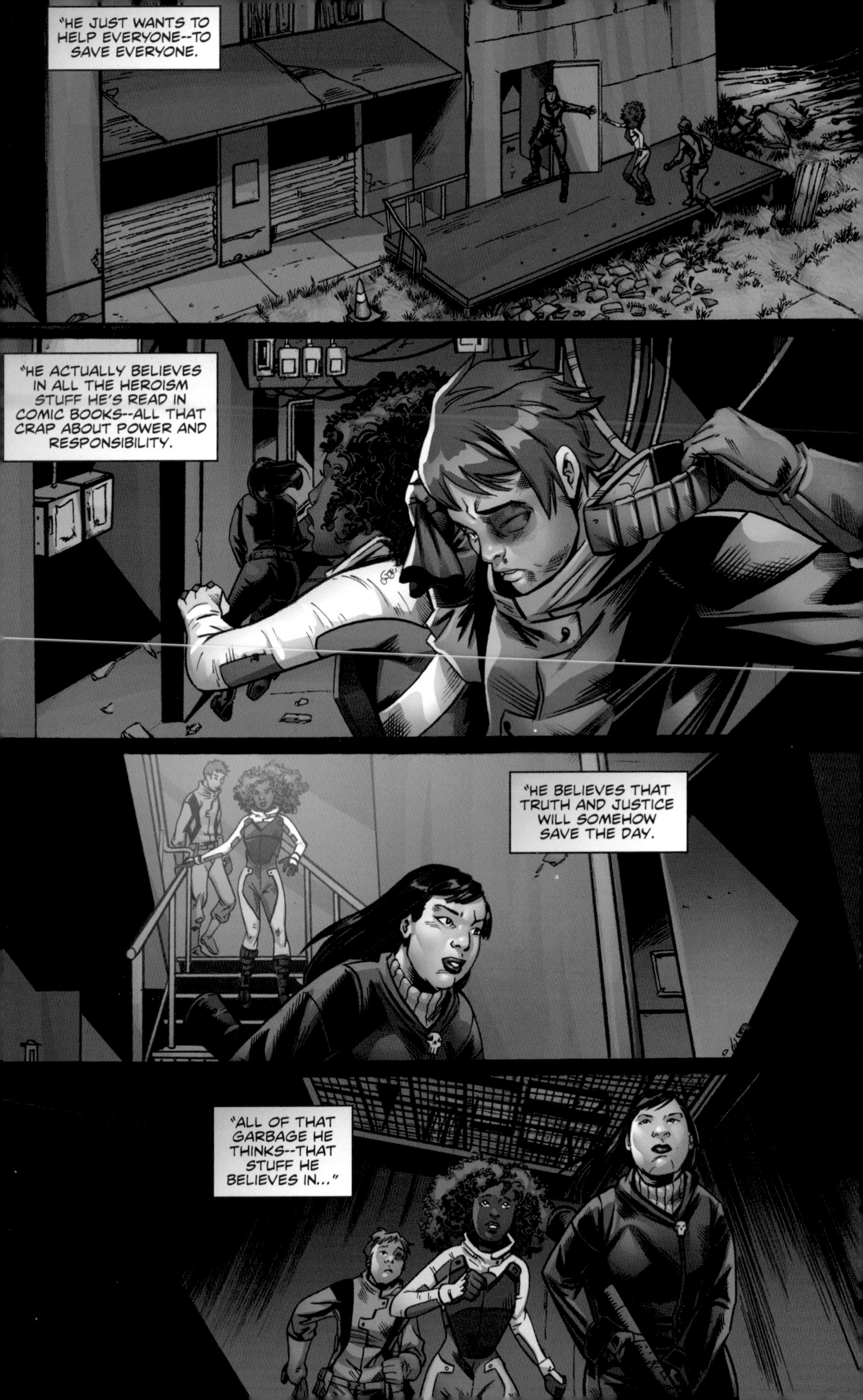
"HE JUST WANTS TO HELP EVERYONE--TO SAVE EVERYONE.
"HE ACTUALLY BELIEVES IN ALL THE HEROISM STUFF HE'S READ IN COMIC BOOKS--ALL THAT CRAP ABOUT POWER AND RESPONSIBILITY.
"HE BELIEVES THAT TRUTH AND JUSTICE WILL SOMEHOW SAVE THE DAY.
"ALL OF THAT GARBAGE HE THINKS--THAT STUFF HE BELIEVES IN..."

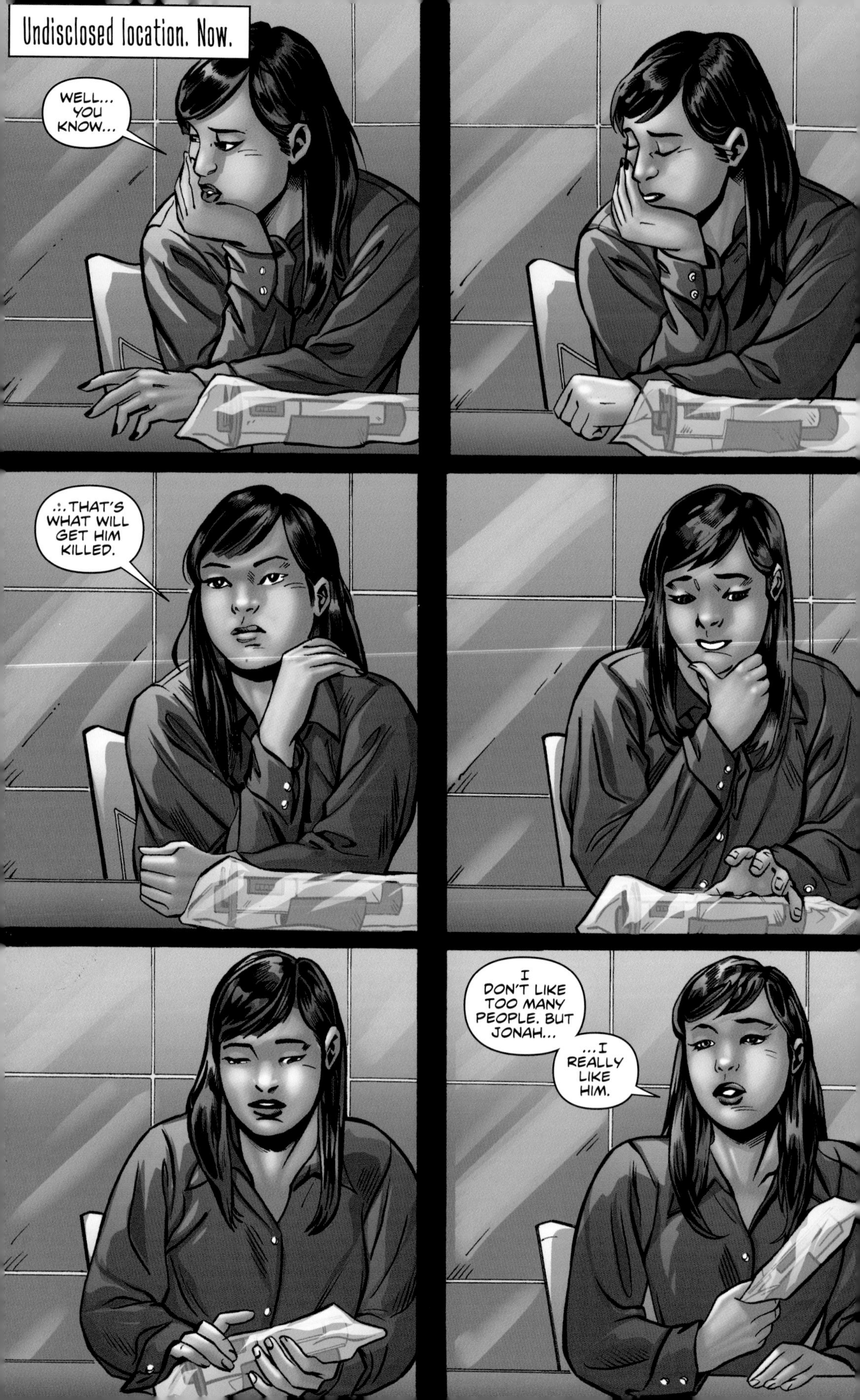
Undisclosed location. Now.
WELL... YOU KNOW...
...THAT'S WHAT WILL GET HIM KILLED.
I DON'T LIKE TOO MANY PEOPLE. BUT JONAH...
...I REALLY LIKE HIM.

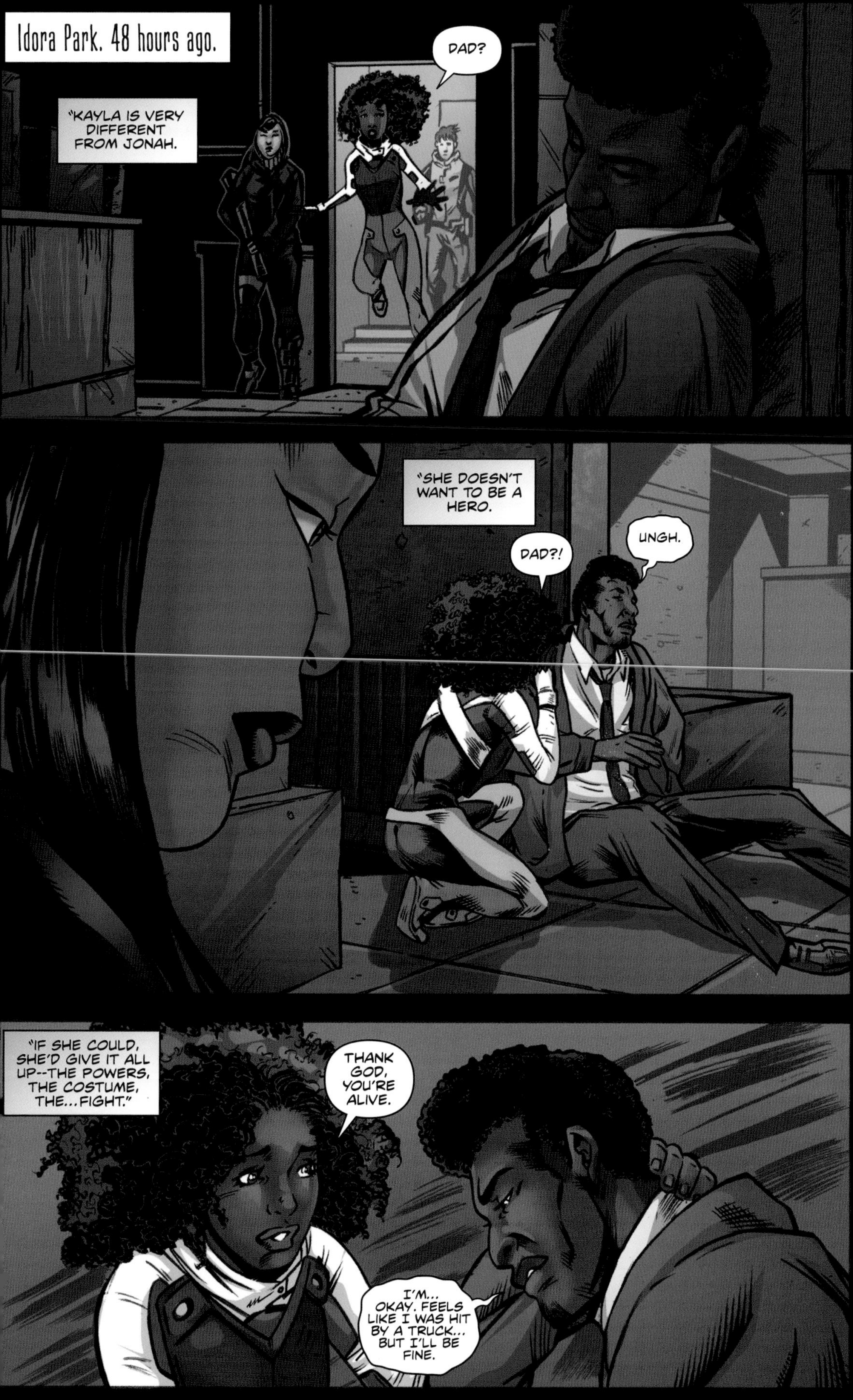
Idora Park. 48 hours ago.
"KAYLA IS VERY DIFFERENT FROM JONAH.
DAD?
"SHE DOESN'T WANT TO BE A HERO.
DAD?!
UNGH.
"IF SHE COULD, SHE'D GIVE IT ALL UP--THE POWERS, THE COSTUME, THE...FIGHT."
THANK GOD, YOU'RE ALIVE.
I'M... OKAY. FEELS LIKE I WAS HIT BY A TRUCK... BUT I'LL BE FINE.

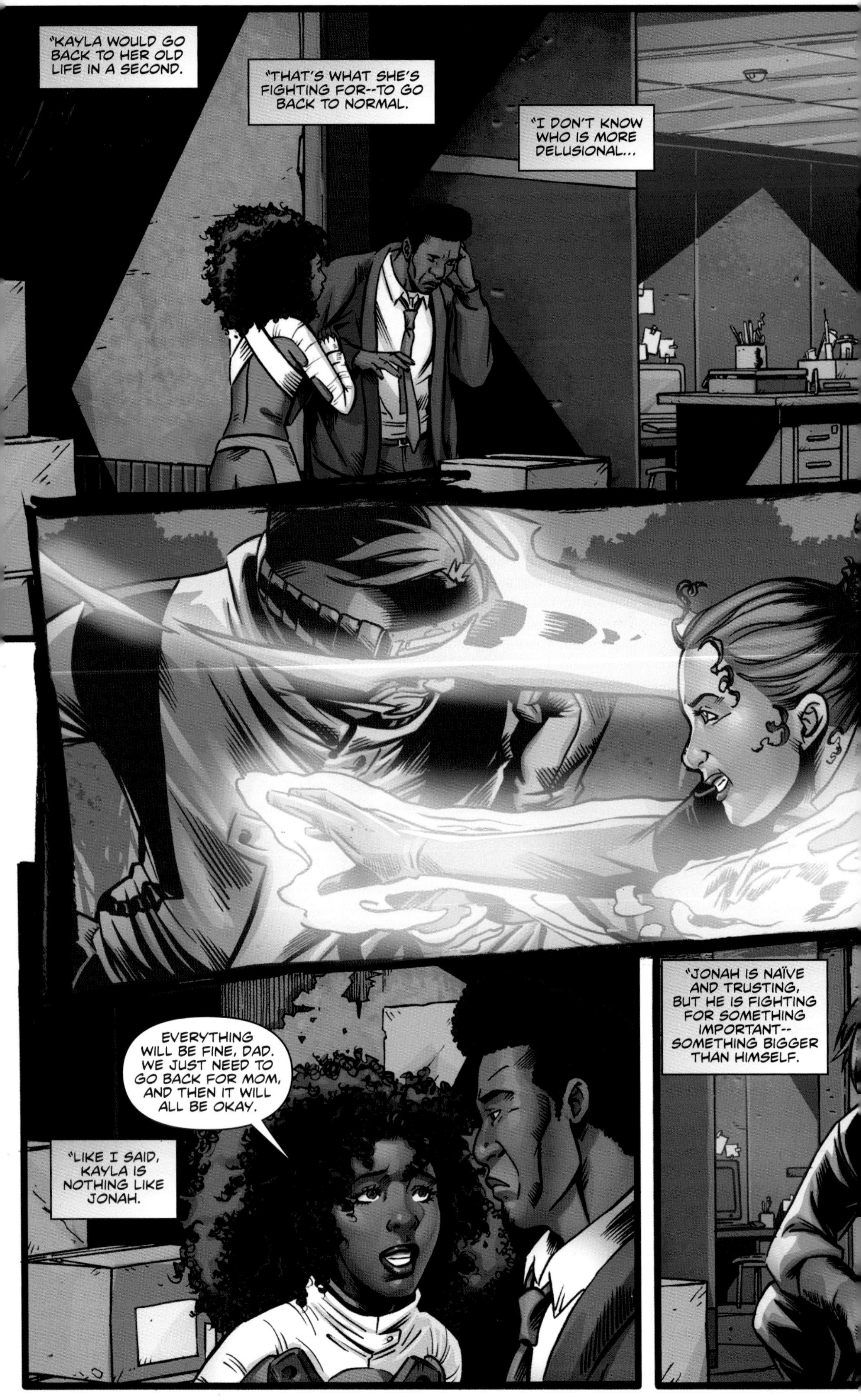
"KAYLA WOULD GO BACK TO HER OLD LIFE IN A SECOND.
"THAT'S WHAT SHE'S FIGHTING FOR--TO GO BACK TO NORMAL.
"I DON'T KNOW WHO IS MORE DELUSIONAL...
EVERYTHING WILL BE FINE, DAD. WE JUST NEED TO GO BACK FOR MOM, AND THEN IT WILL ALL BE OKAY.
"LIKE I SAID, KAYLA IS NOTHING LIKE JONAH.
"JONAH IS NAÏVE AND TRUSTING, BUT HE IS FIGHTING FOR SOMETHING IMPORTANT-- SOMETHING BIGGER THAN HIMSELF.

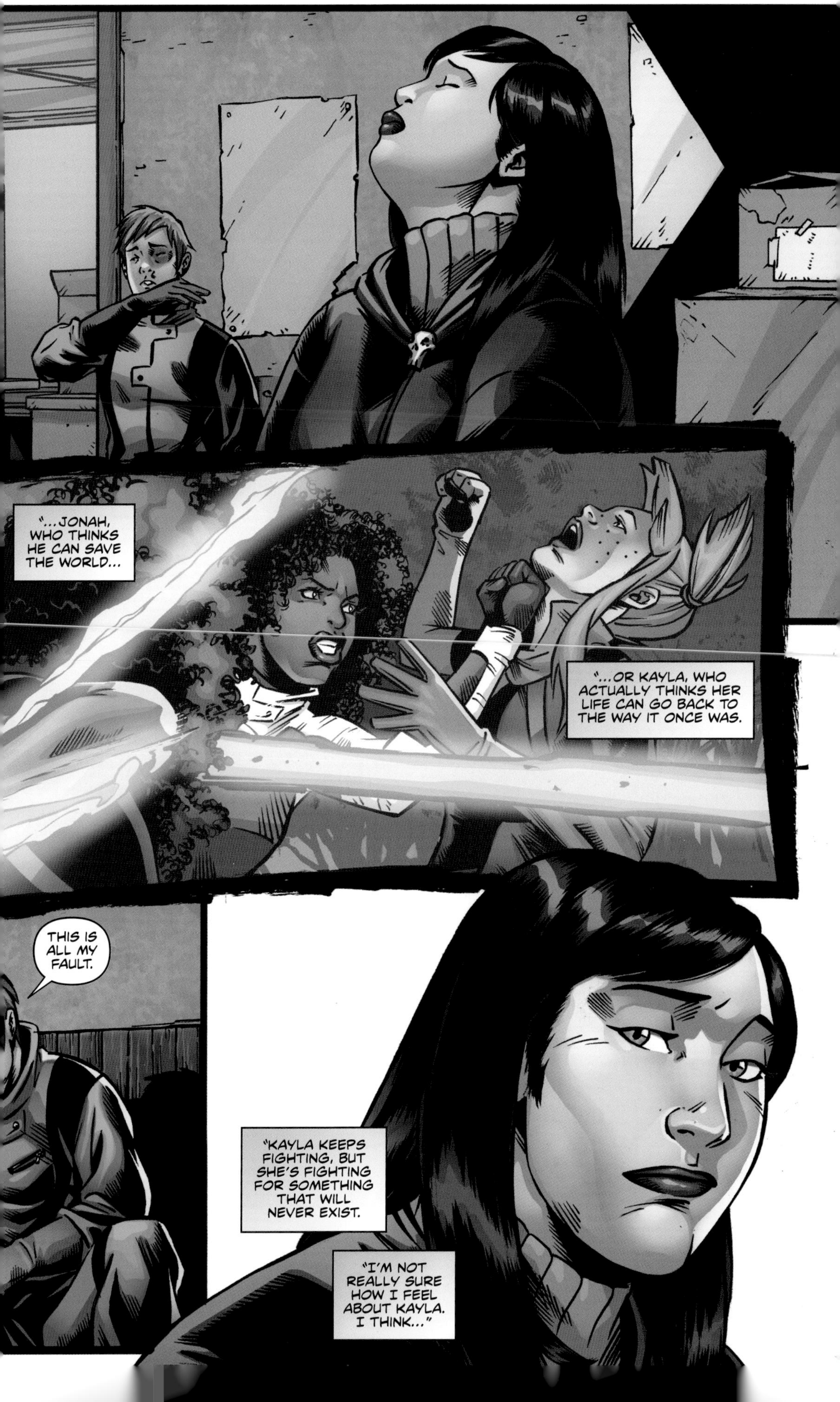
"...JONAH, WHO THINKS HE CAN SAVE THE WORLD...
"...OR KAYLA, WHO ACTUALLY THINKS HER LIFE CAN GO BACK TO THE WAY IT ONCE WAS.
THIS IS ALL MY FAULT.
"KAYLA KEEPS FIGHTING, BUT SHE'S FIGHTING FOR SOMETHING THAT WILL NEVER EXIST.
"I'M NOT REALLY SURE HOW I FEEL ABOUT KAYLA. I THINK..."

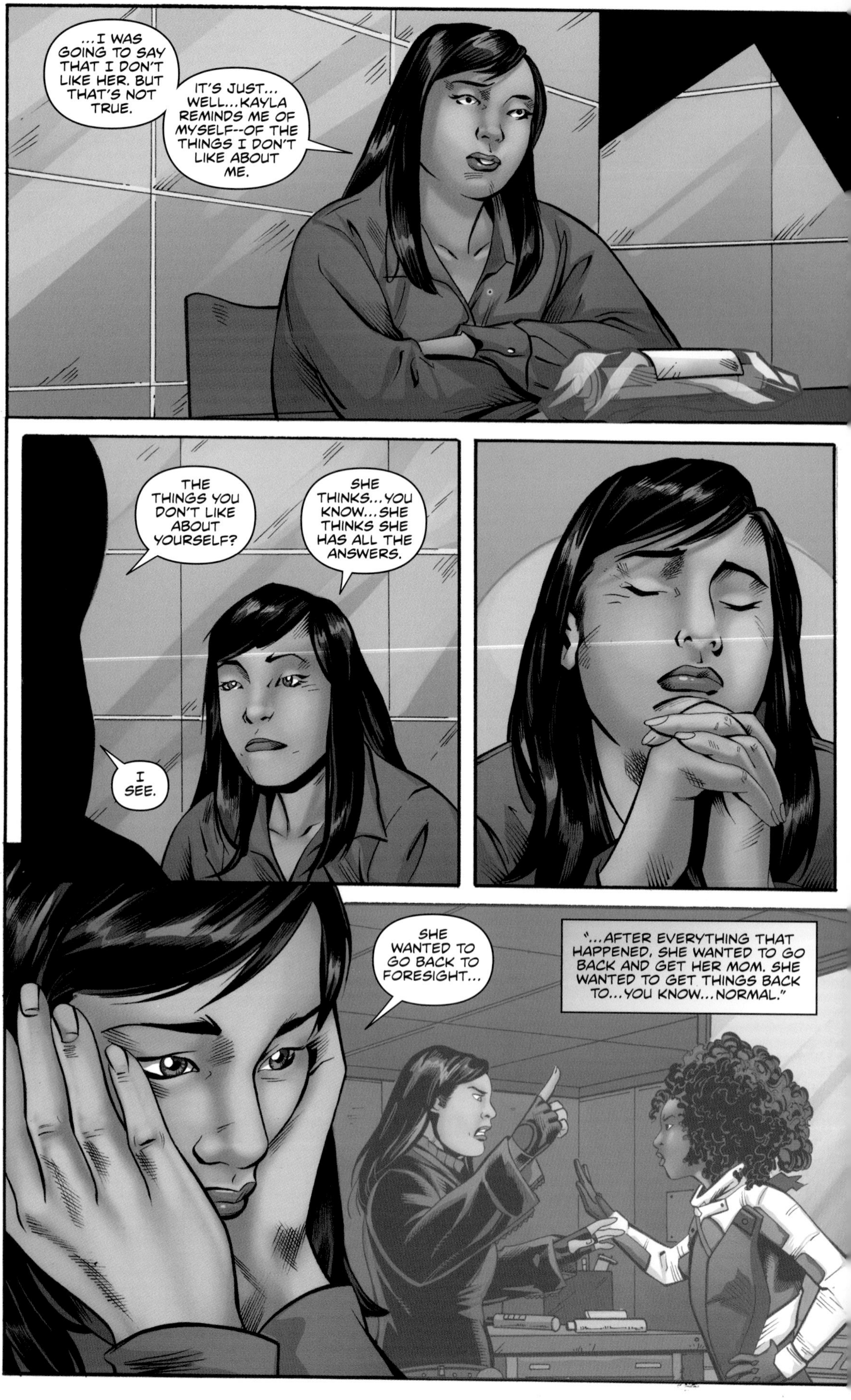
...I WAS GOING TO SAY THAT I DON'T LIKE HER. BUT THAT'S NOT TRUE.
IT'S JUST... WELL...KAYLA REMINDS ME OF MYSELF--OF THE THINGS I DON'T LIKE ABOUT ME.
THE THINGS YOU DON'T LIKE ABOUT YOURSELF?
SHE THINKS...YOU KNOW...SHE THINKS SHE HAS ALL THE ANSWERS.
I SEE.
SHE WANTED TO GO BACK TO FORESIGHT...
"...AFTER EVERYTHING THAT HAPPENED, SHE WANTED TO GO BACK AND GET HER MOM. SHE WANTED TO GET THINGS BACK TO...YOU KNOW...NORMAL."

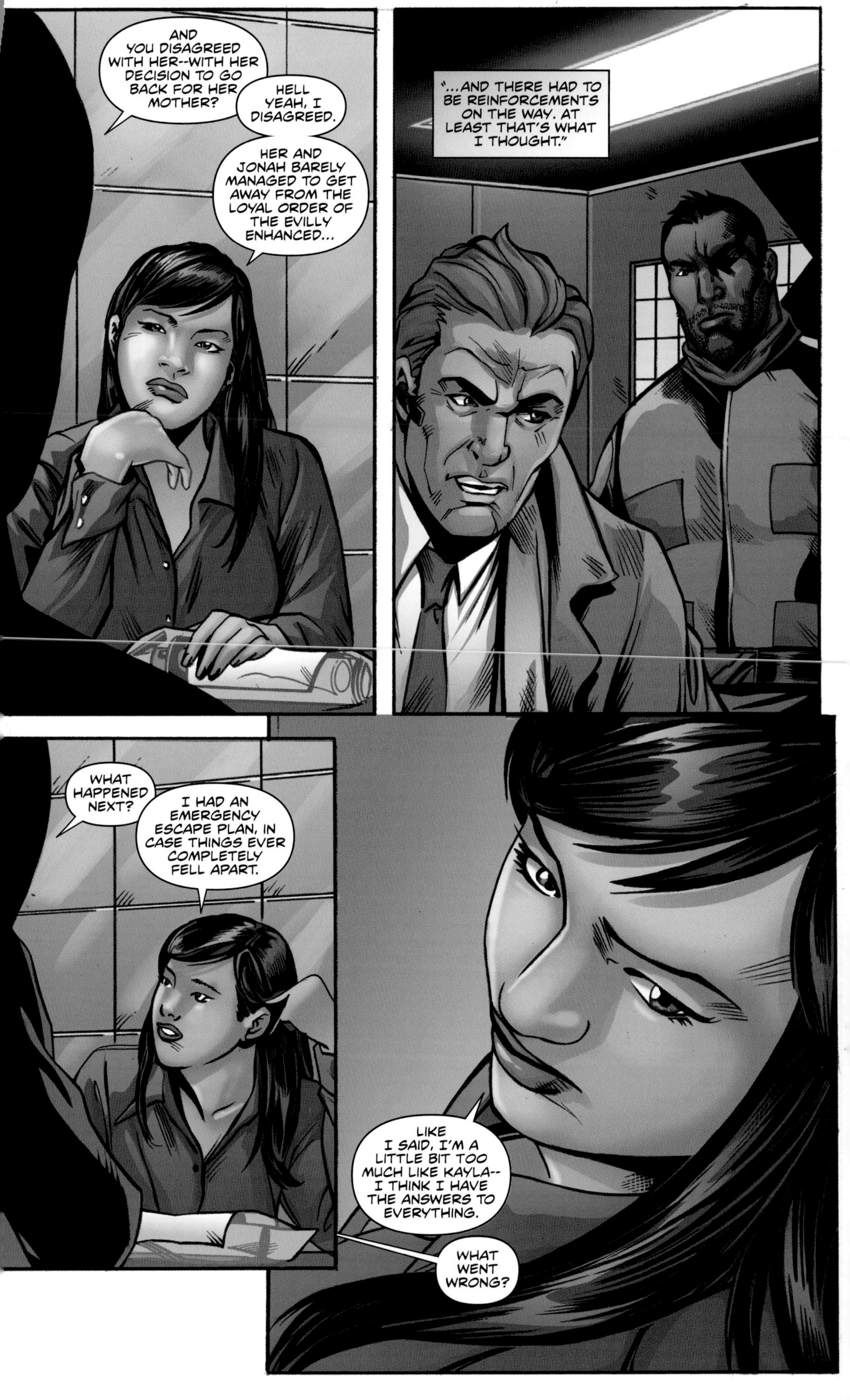
AND YOU DISAGREED WITH HER--WITH HER DECISION TO GO BACK FOR HER MOTHER?
HELL YEAH, I DISAGREED.
HER AND JONAH BARELY MANAGED TO GET AWAY FROM THE LOYAL ORDER OF THE EVILLY ENHANCED...
"...AND THERE HAD TO BE REINFORCEMENTS ON THE WAY. AT LEAST THAT'S WHAT I THOUGHT."
WHAT HAPPENED NEXT?
I HAD AN EMERGENCY ESCAPE PLAN, IN CASE THINGS EVER COMPLETELY FELL APART.
LIKE I SAID, I'M A LITTLE BIT TOO MUCH LIKE KAYLA-- I THINK I HAVE THE ANSWERS TO EVERYTHING.
WHAT WENT WRONG?

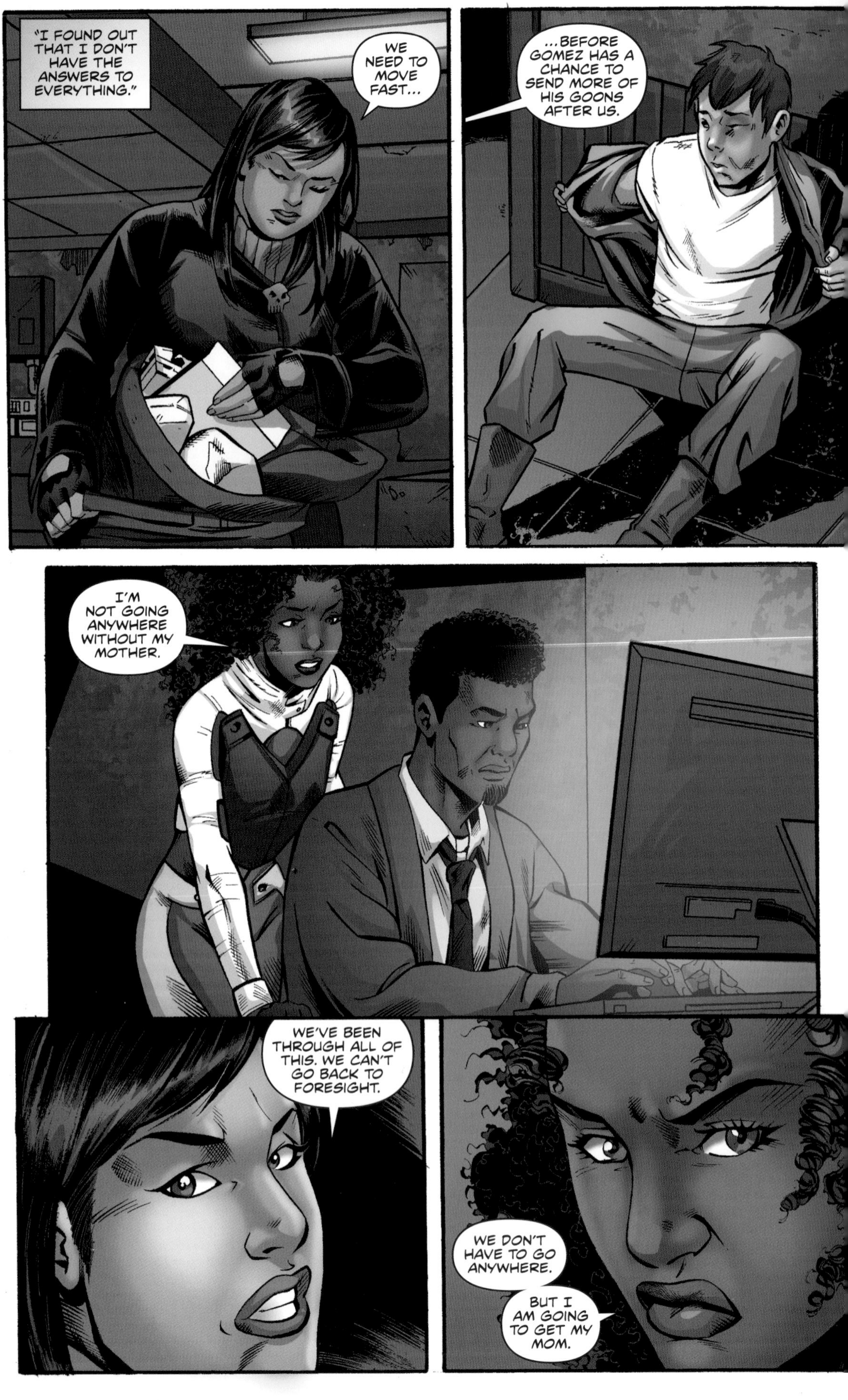
"I FOUND OUT THAT I DON'T HAVE THE ANSWERS TO EVERYTHING."
WE NEED TO MOVE FAST...
...BEFORE GOMEZ HAS A CHANCE TO SEND MORE OF HIS GOONS AFTER US.
I'M NOT GOING ANYWHERE WITHOUT MY MOTHER.
WE'VE BEEN THROUGH ALL OF THIS. WE CAN'T GO BACK TO FORESIGHT.
WE DON'T HAVE TO GO ANYWHERE.
BUT I AM GOING TO GET MY MOM.

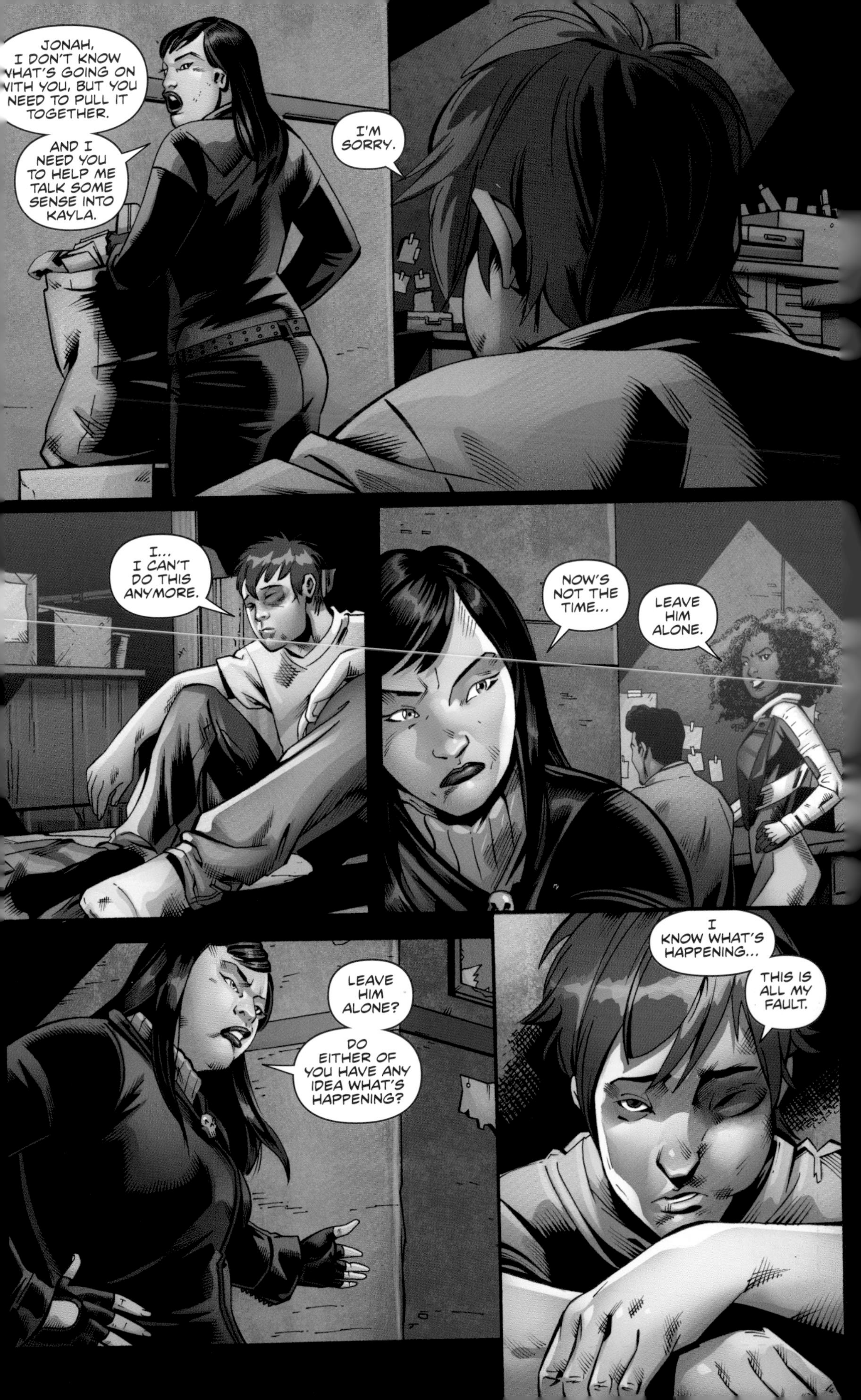
JONAH, I DON'T KNOW WHAT'S GOING ON WITH YOU, BUT YOU NEED TO PULL IT TOGETHER.
AND I NEED YOU TO HELP ME TALK SOME SENSE INTO KAYLA.
I'M SORRY.
I... I CAN'T DO THIS ANYMORE.
NOW'S NOT THE TIME...
LEAVE HIM ALONE.
LEAVE HIM ALONE?
DO EITHER OF YOU HAVE ANY IDEA WHAT'S HAPPENING?
I KNOW WHAT'S HAPPENING...
THIS IS ALL MY FAULT.

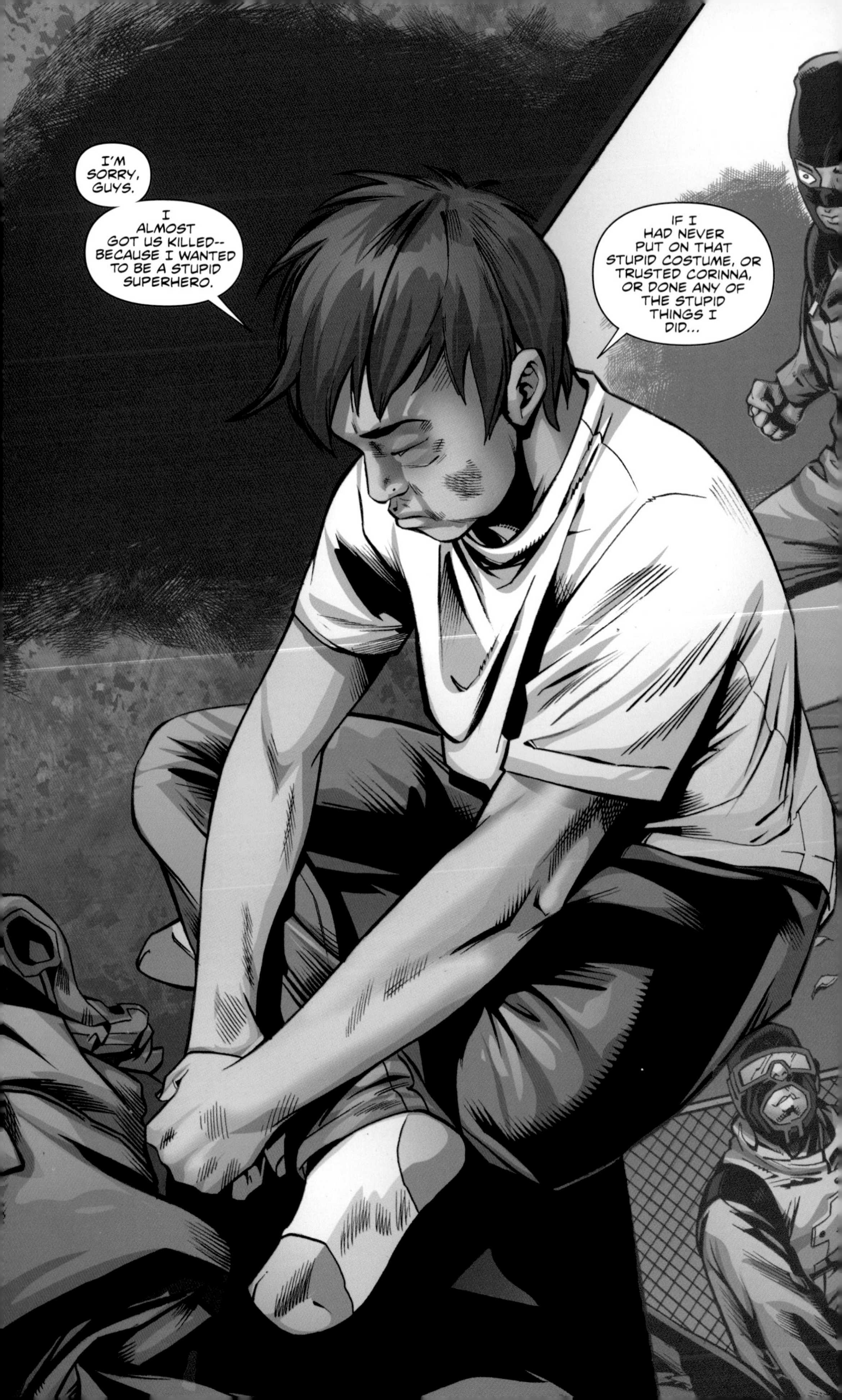
I'M SORRY, GUYS.
I ALMOST GOT US KILLED-- BECAUSE I WANTED TO BE A STUPID SUPERHERO.
IF I HAD NEVER PUT ON THAT STUPID COSTUME, OR TRUSTED CORINNA, OR DONE ANY OF THE STUPID THINGS I DID...

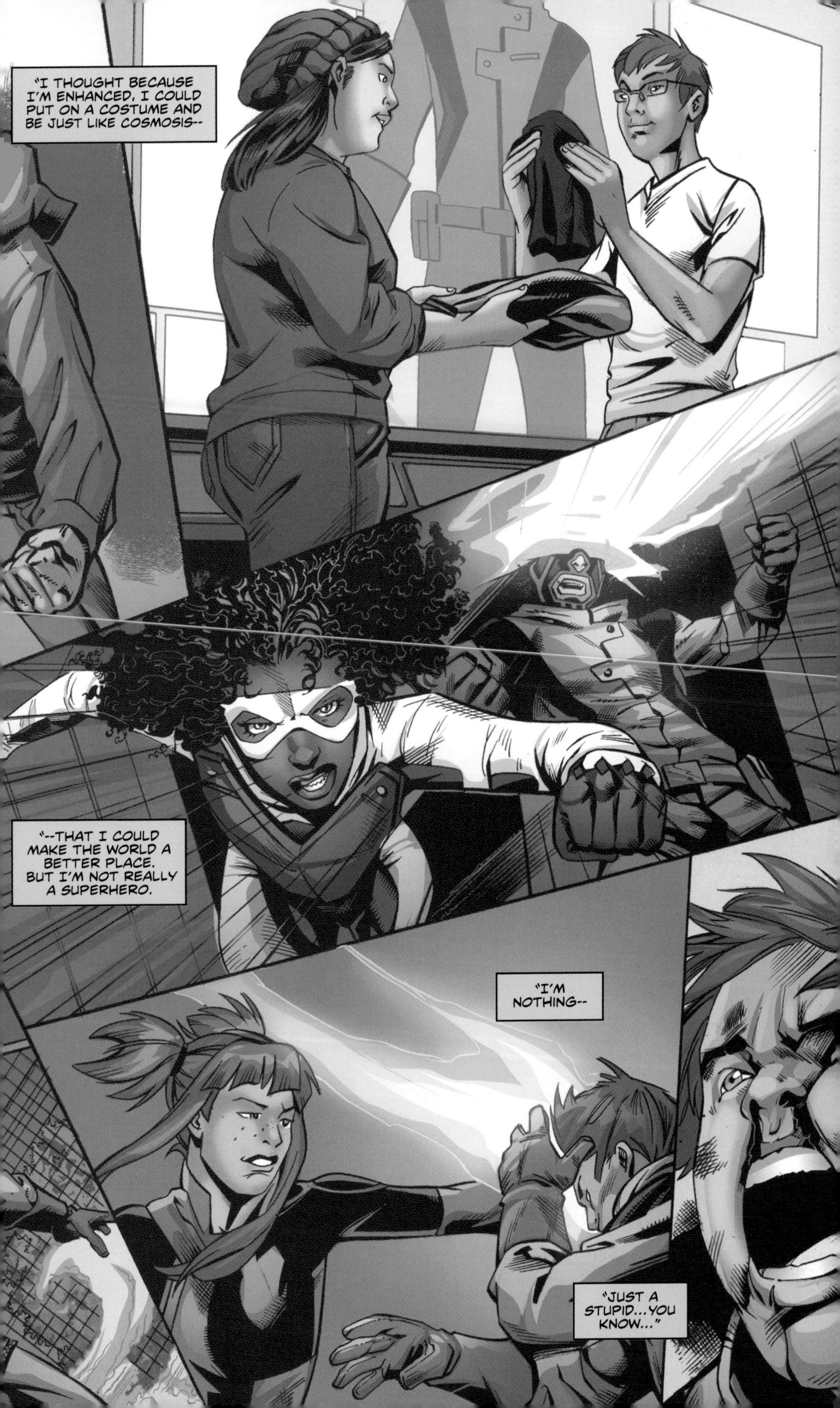
"I THOUGHT BECAUSE I'M ENHANCED, I COULD PUT ON A COSTUME AND BE JUST LIKE COSMOSIS--
"--THAT I COULD MAKE THE WORLD A BETTER PLACE. BUT I'M NOT REALLY A SUPERHERO.
"I'M NOTHING--
"JUST A STUPID...YOU KNOW..."

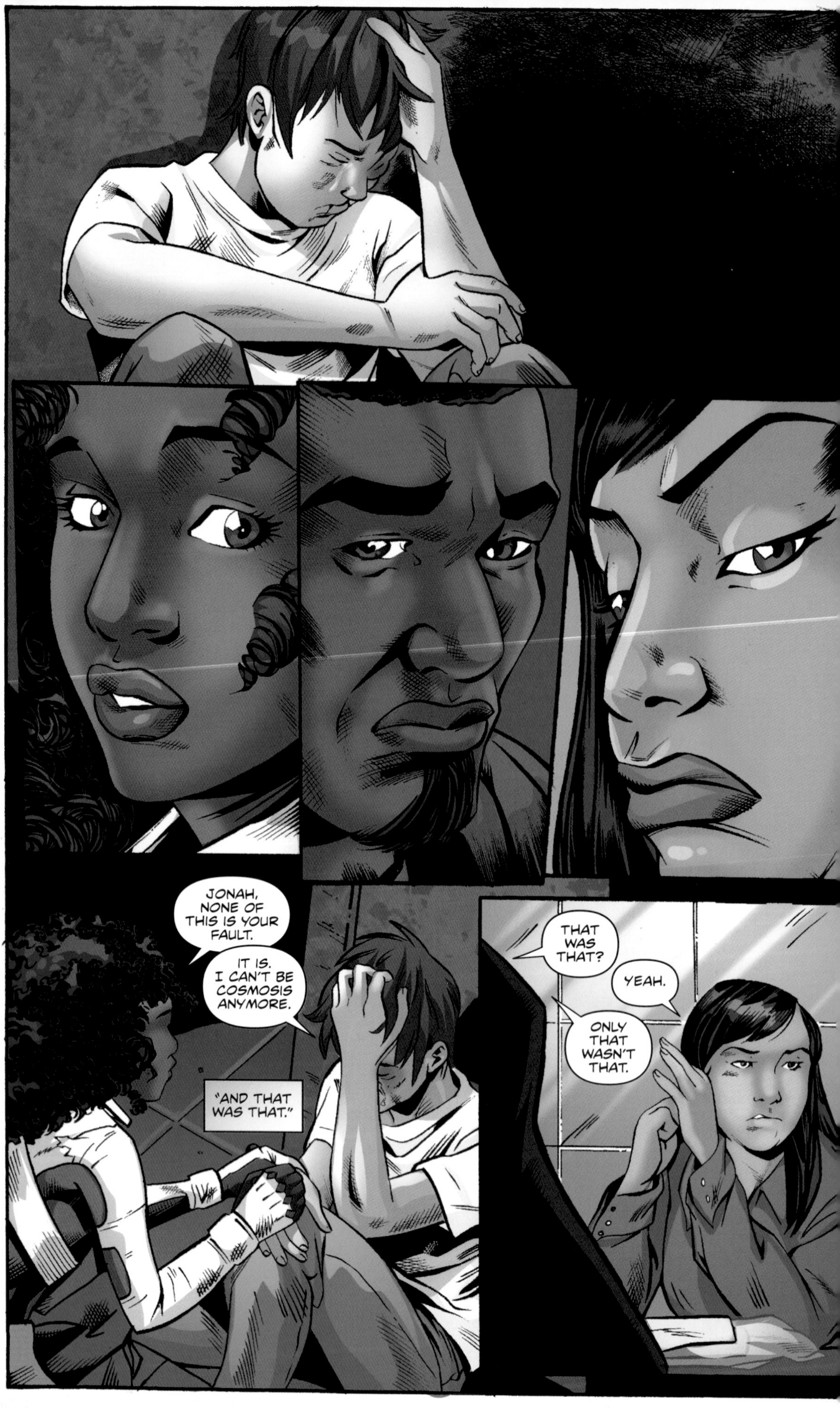

JONAH, NONE OF THIS IS YOUR FAULT.
IT IS. I CAN'T BE COSMOSIS ANYMORE.
"AND THAT WAS THAT."
THAT WAS THAT?
YEAH.
ONLY THAT WASN'T THAT.

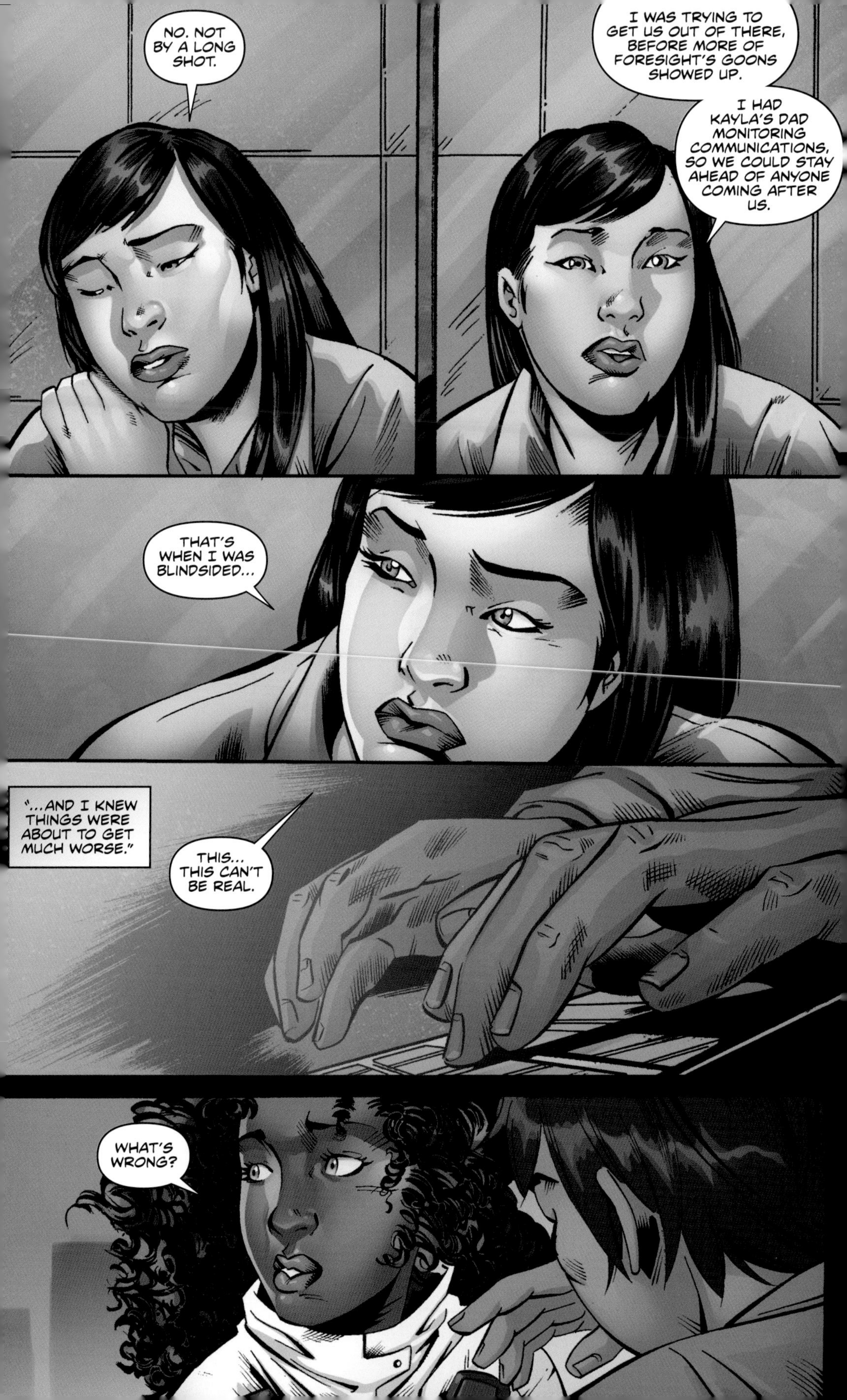
NO. NOT BY A LONG SHOT.
I WAS TRYING TO GET US OUT OF THERE, BEFORE MORE OF FORESIGHT'S GOONS SHOWED UP.
I HAD KAYLA'S DAD MONITORING COMMUNICATIONS, SO WE COULD STAY AHEAD OF ANYONE COMING AFTER US.
THAT'S WHEN I WAS BLINDSIDED...
"...AND I KNEW THINGS WERE ABOUT TO GET MUCH WORSE."
THIS... THIS CAN'T BE REAL.
WHAT'S WRONG?

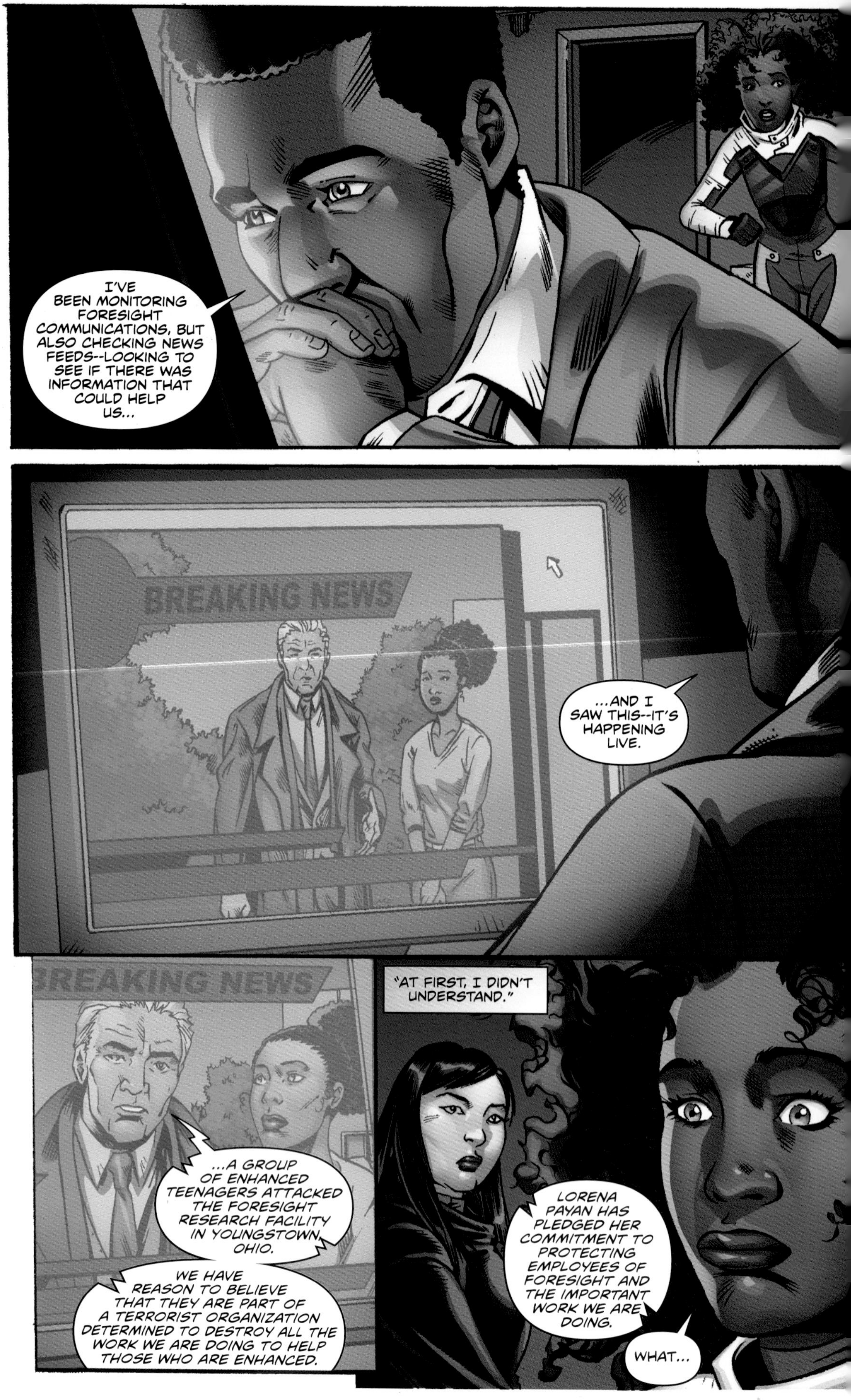
I'VE BEEN MONITORING FORESIGHT COMMUNICATIONS, BUT ALSO CHECKING NEWS FEEDS--LOOKING TO SEE IF THERE WAS INFORMATION THAT COULD HELP US...
BREAKING NEWS
...AND I SAW THIS--IT'S HAPPENING LIVE.
BREAKING NEWS
...A GROUP OF ENHANCED TEENAGERS ATTACKED THE FORESIGHT RESEARCH FACILITY IN YOUNGSTOWN, OHIO.
WE HAVE REASON TO BELIEVE THAT THEY ARE PART OF A TERRORIST ORGANIZATION DETERMINED TO DESTROY ALL THE WORK WE ARE DOING TO HELP THOSE WHO ARE ENHANCED.
"AT FIRST, I DIDN'T UNDERSTAND."
LORENA PAYAN HAS PLEDGED HER COMMITMENT TO PROTECTING EMPLOYEES OF FORESIGHT AND THE IMPORTANT WORK WE ARE DOING.
WHAT...

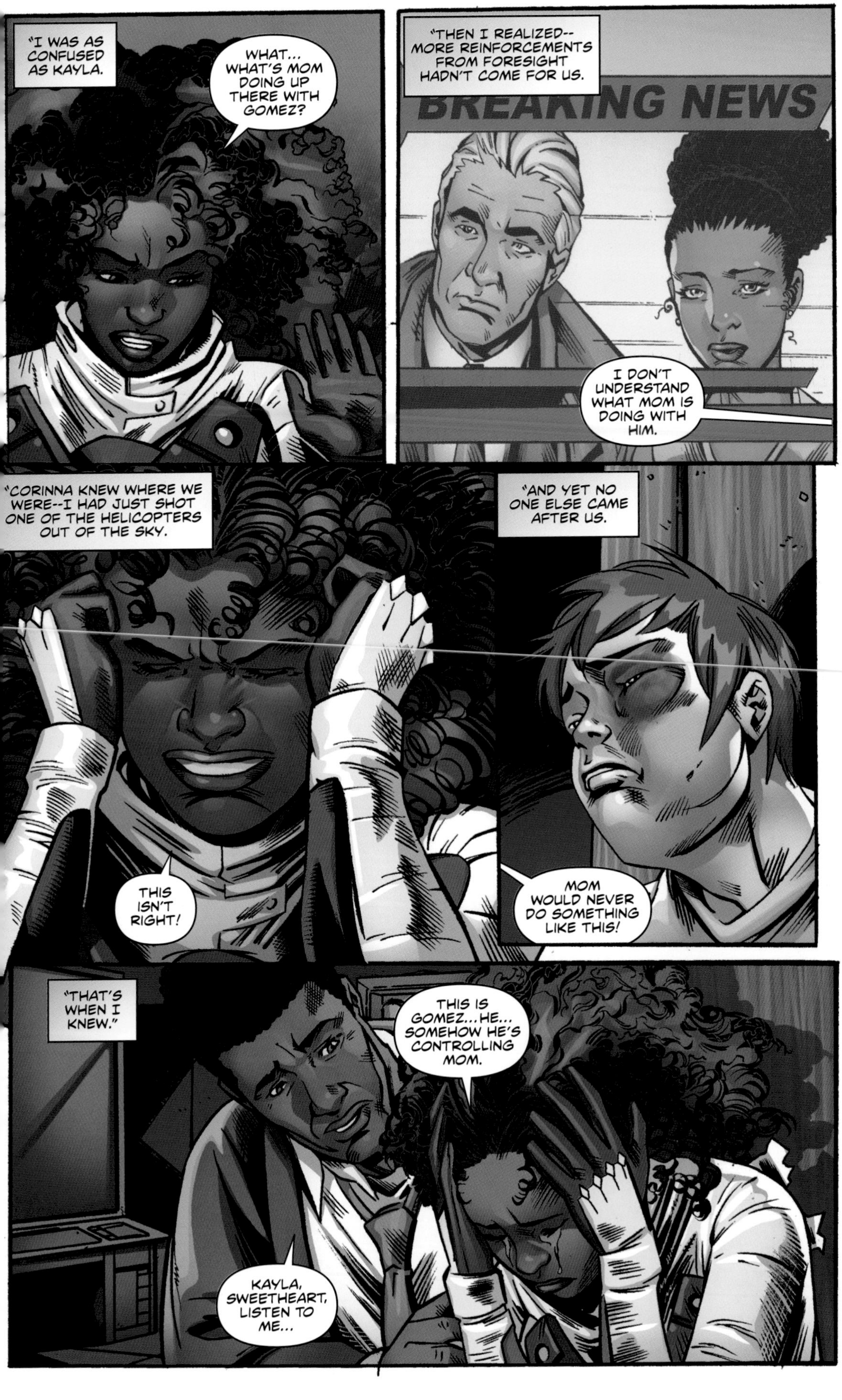
"I WAS AS CONFUSED AS KAYLA.
WHAT... WHAT'S MOM DOING UP THERE WITH GOMEZ?
"THEN I REALIZED--MORE REINFORCEMENTS FROM FORESIGHT HADN'T COME FOR US.
BREAKING NEWS
I DON'T UNDERSTAND WHAT MOM IS DOING WITH HIM.
"CORINNA KNEW WHERE WE WERE--I HAD JUST SHOT ONE OF THE HELICOPTERS OUT OF THE SKY.
THIS ISN'T RIGHT!
"AND YET NO ONE ELSE CAME AFTER US.
MOM WOULD NEVER DO SOMETHING LIKE THIS!
"THAT'S WHEN I KNEW."
THIS IS GOMEZ... HE... SOMEHOW HE'S CONTROLLING MOM.
KAYLA, SWEETHEART, LISTEN TO ME...

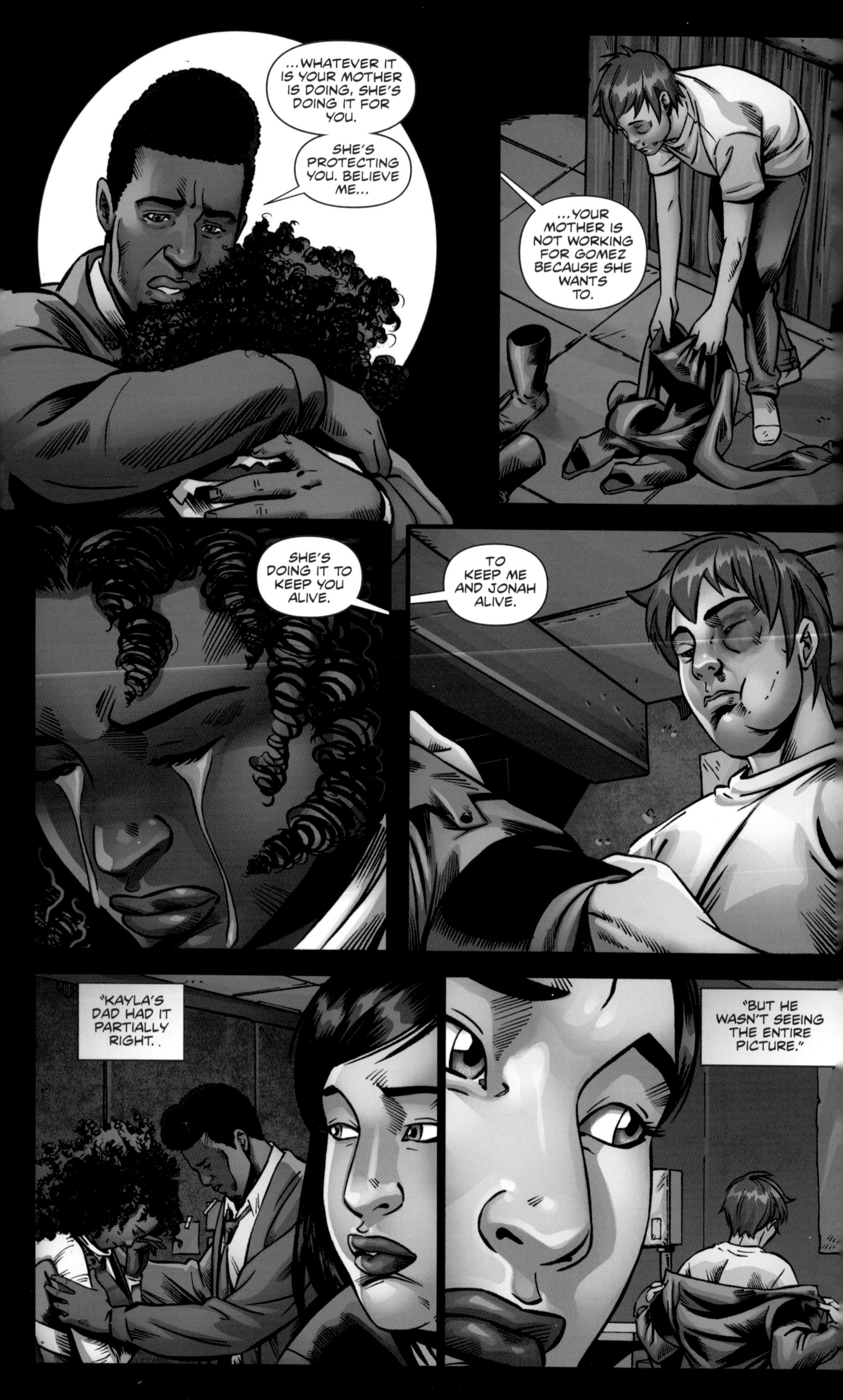
...WHATEVER IT IS YOUR MOTHER IS DOING, SHE'S DOING IT FOR YOU.
SHE'S PROTECTING YOU. BELIEVE ME...
...YOUR MOTHER IS NOT WORKING FOR GOMEZ BECAUSE SHE WANTS TO.
SHE'S DOING IT TO KEEP YOU ALIVE.
TO KEEP ME AND JONAH ALIVE.
"KAYLA'S DAD HAD IT PARTIALLY RIGHT. .
"BUT HE WASN'T SEEING THE ENTIRE PICTURE."

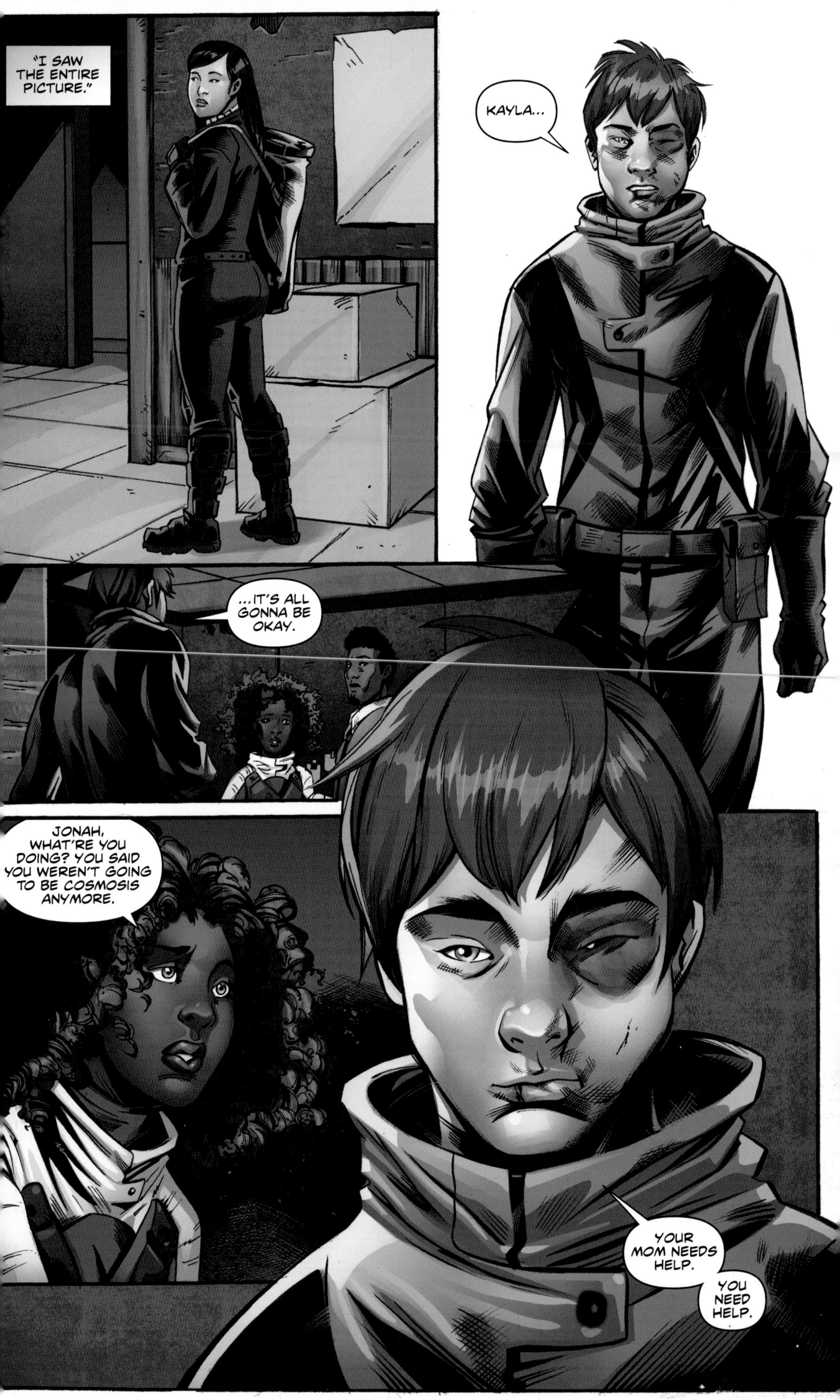
"I SAW THE ENTIRE PICTURE."
KAYLA...
...IT'S ALL GONNA BE OKAY.
JONAH, WHAT'RE YOU DOING? YOU SAID YOU WEREN'T GOING TO BE COSMOSIS ANYMORE.
YOUR MOM NEEDS HELP.
YOU NEED HELP.

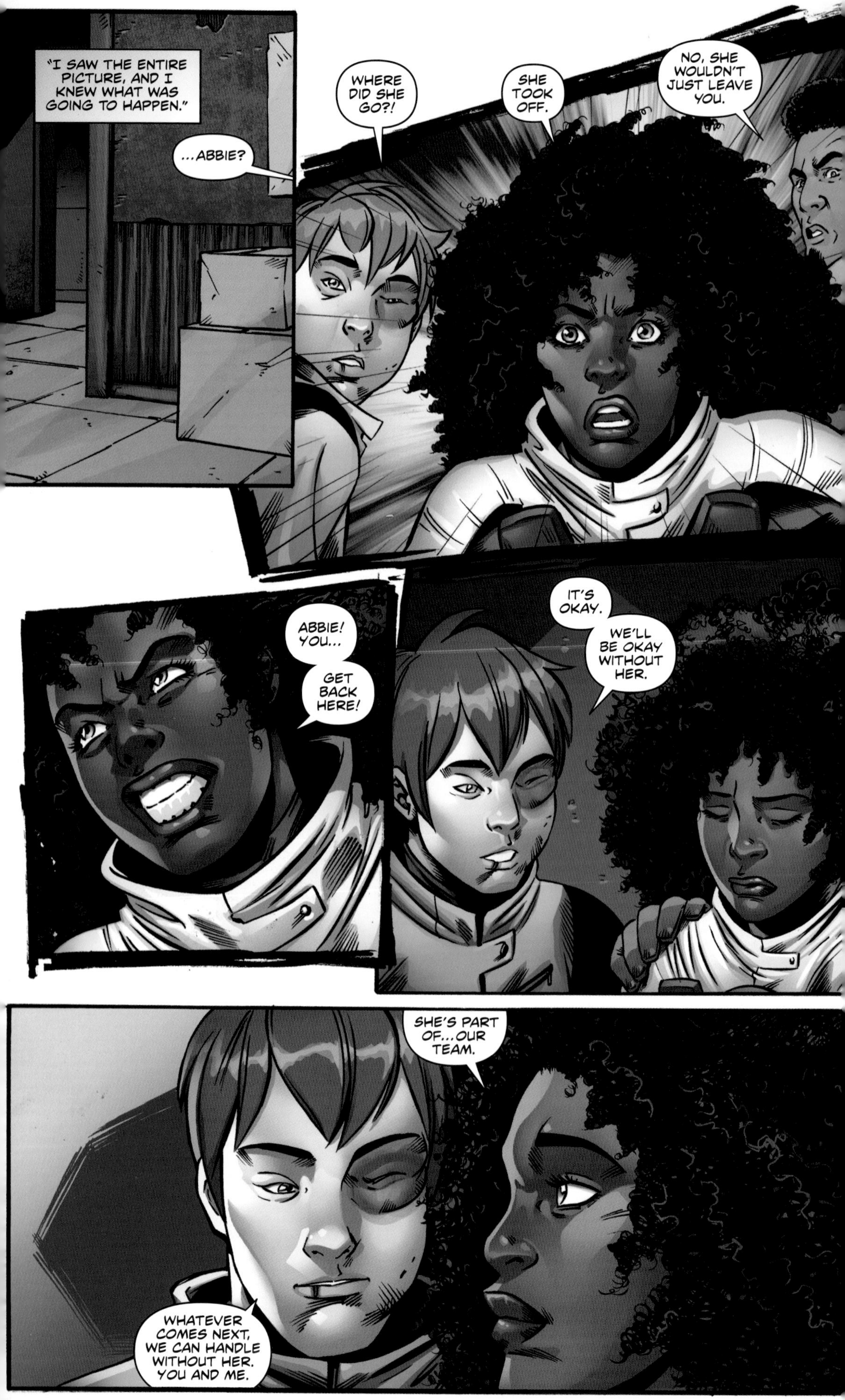
"I SAW THE ENTIRE PICTURE, AND I KNEW WHAT WAS GOING TO HAPPEN."
...ABBIE?
WHERE DID SHE GO?!
SHE TOOK OFF.
NO, SHE WOULDN'T JUST LEAVE YOU.
ABBIE! YOU...
GET BACK HERE!
IT'S OKAY.
WE'LL BE OKAY WITHOUT HER.
SHE'S PART OF...OUR TEAM.
WHATEVER COMES NEXT, WE CAN HANDLE WITHOUT HER. YOU AND ME.

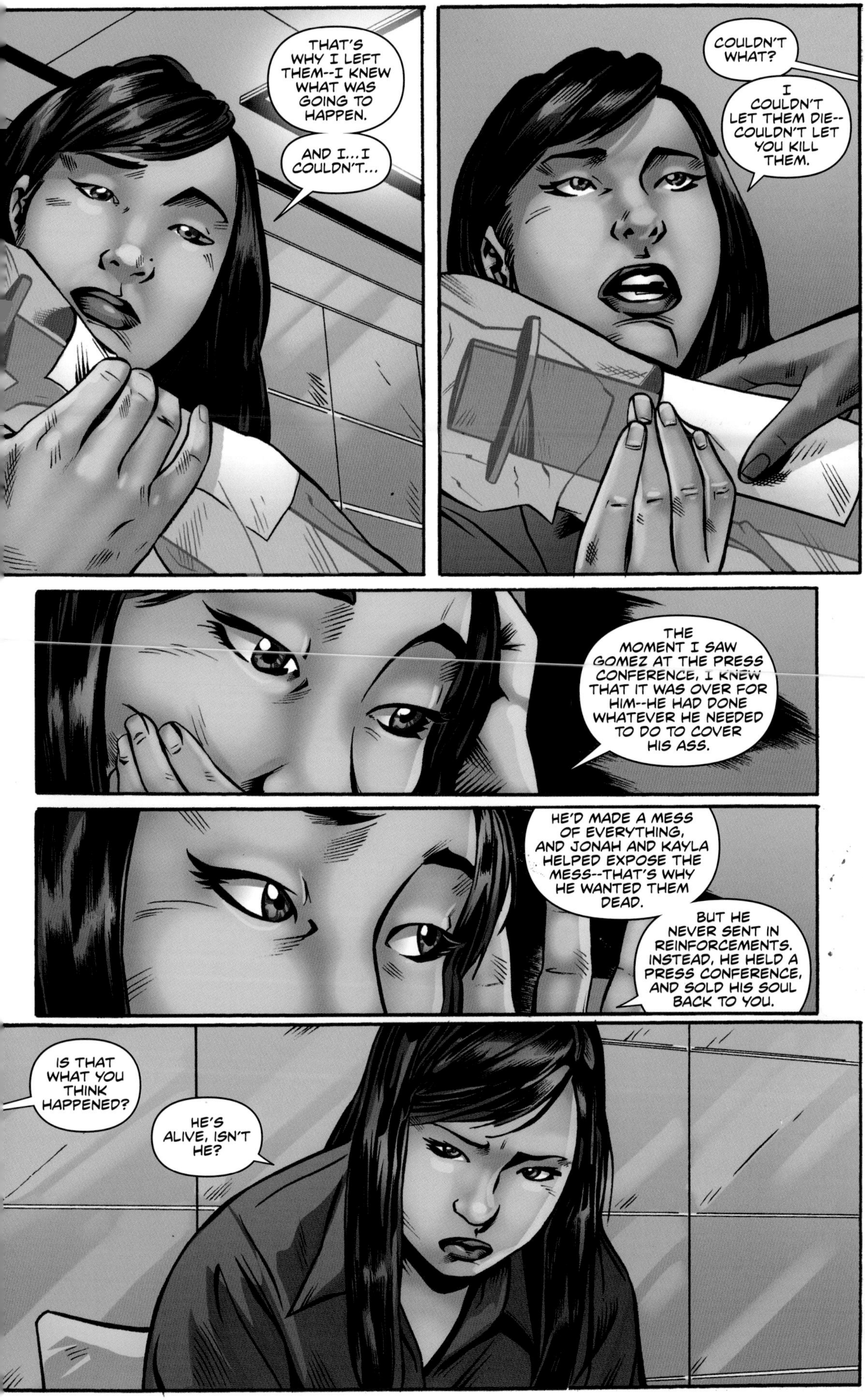
THAT'S WHY I LEFT THEM--I KNEW WHAT WAS GOING TO HAPPEN.
AND I...I COULDN'T...
COULDN'T WHAT?
I COULDN'T LET THEM DIE--COULDN'T LET YOU KILL THEM.
THE MOMENT I SAW GOMEZ AT THE PRESS CONFERENCE, I KNEW THAT IT WAS OVER FOR HIM--HE HAD DONE WHATEVER HE NEEDED TO DO TO COVER HIS ASS.
HE'D MADE A MESS OF EVERYTHING, AND JONAH AND KAYLA HELPED EXPOSE THE MESS--THAT'S WHY HE WANTED THEM DEAD.
BUT HE NEVER SENT IN REINFORCEMENTS. INSTEAD, HE HELD A PRESS CONFERENCE, AND SOLD HIS SOUL BACK TO YOU.
IS THAT WHAT YOU THINK HAPPENED?
HE'S ALIVE, ISN'T HE?

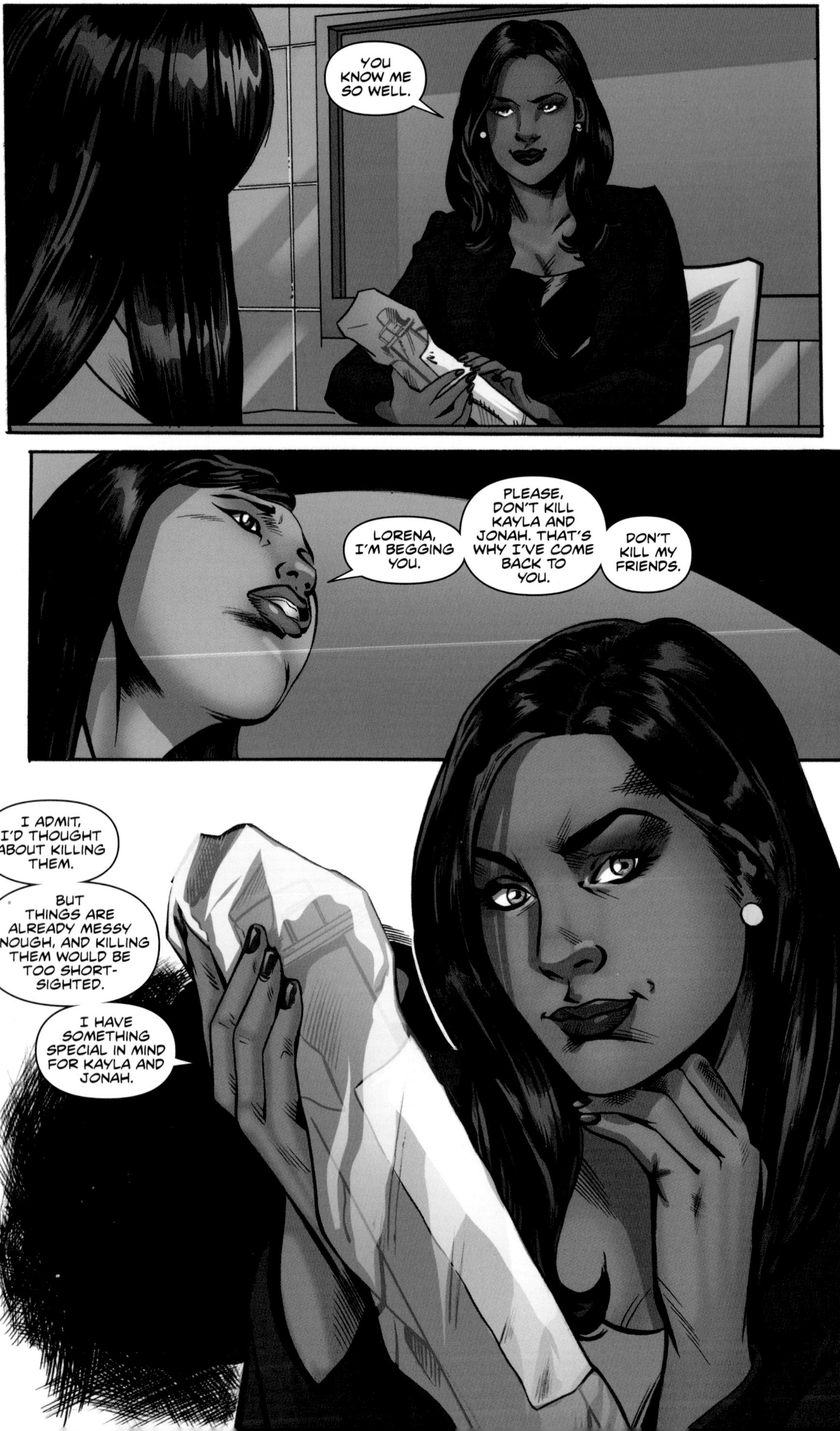
YOU KNOW ME SO WELL.
LORENA, I'M BEGGING YOU.
PLEASE, DON'T KILL KAYLA AND JONAH. THAT'S WHY I'VE COME BACK TO YOU.
DON'T KILL MY FRIENDS.
I ADMIT, I'D THOUGHT ABOUT KILLING THEM.
BUT THINGS ARE ALREADY MESSY ENOUGH, AND KILLING THEM WOULD BE TOO SHORT-SIGHTED.
I HAVE SOMETHING SPECIAL IN MIND FOR KAYLA AND JONAH.

COVER GALLERY

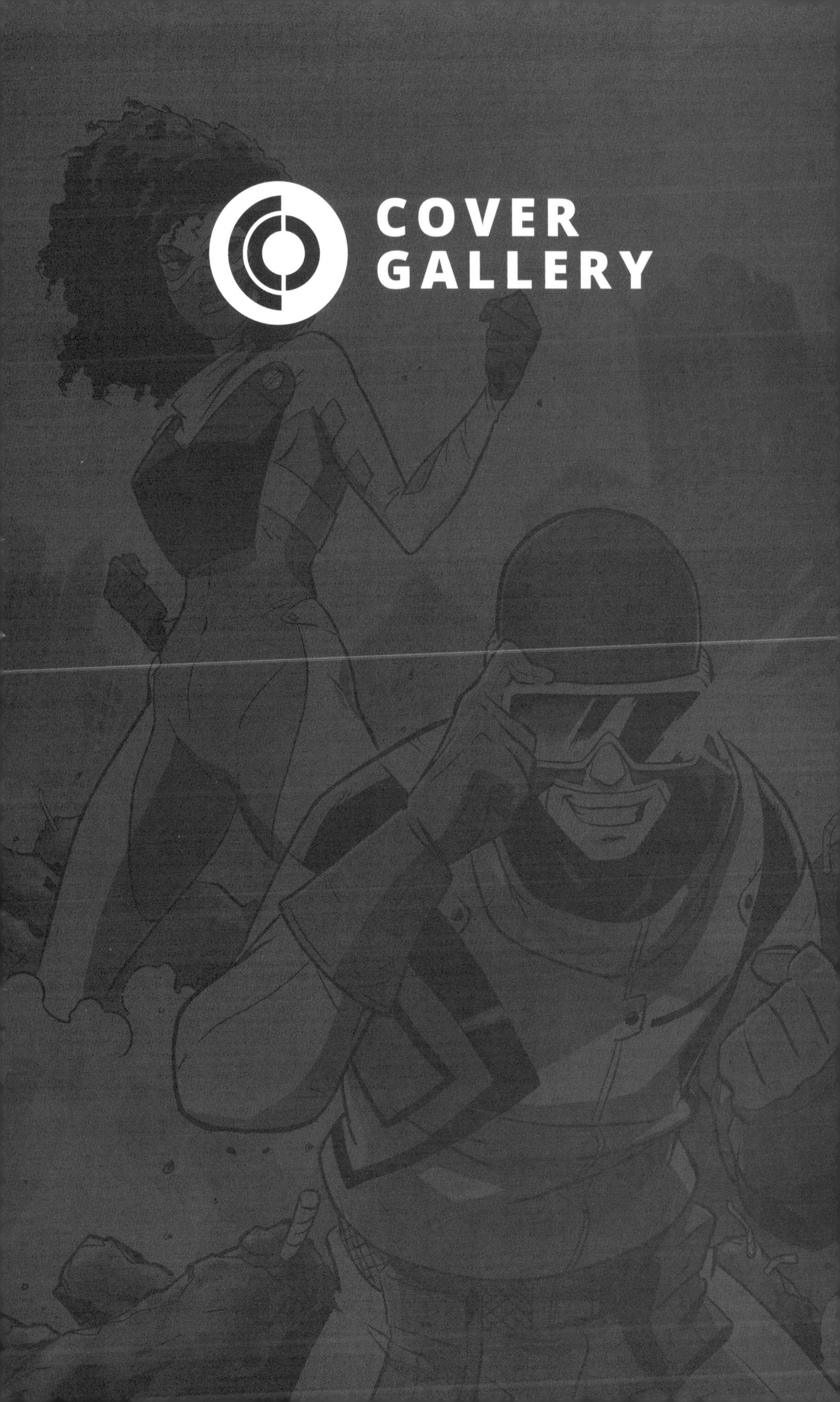

Art by **NILAH MAGRUDER**

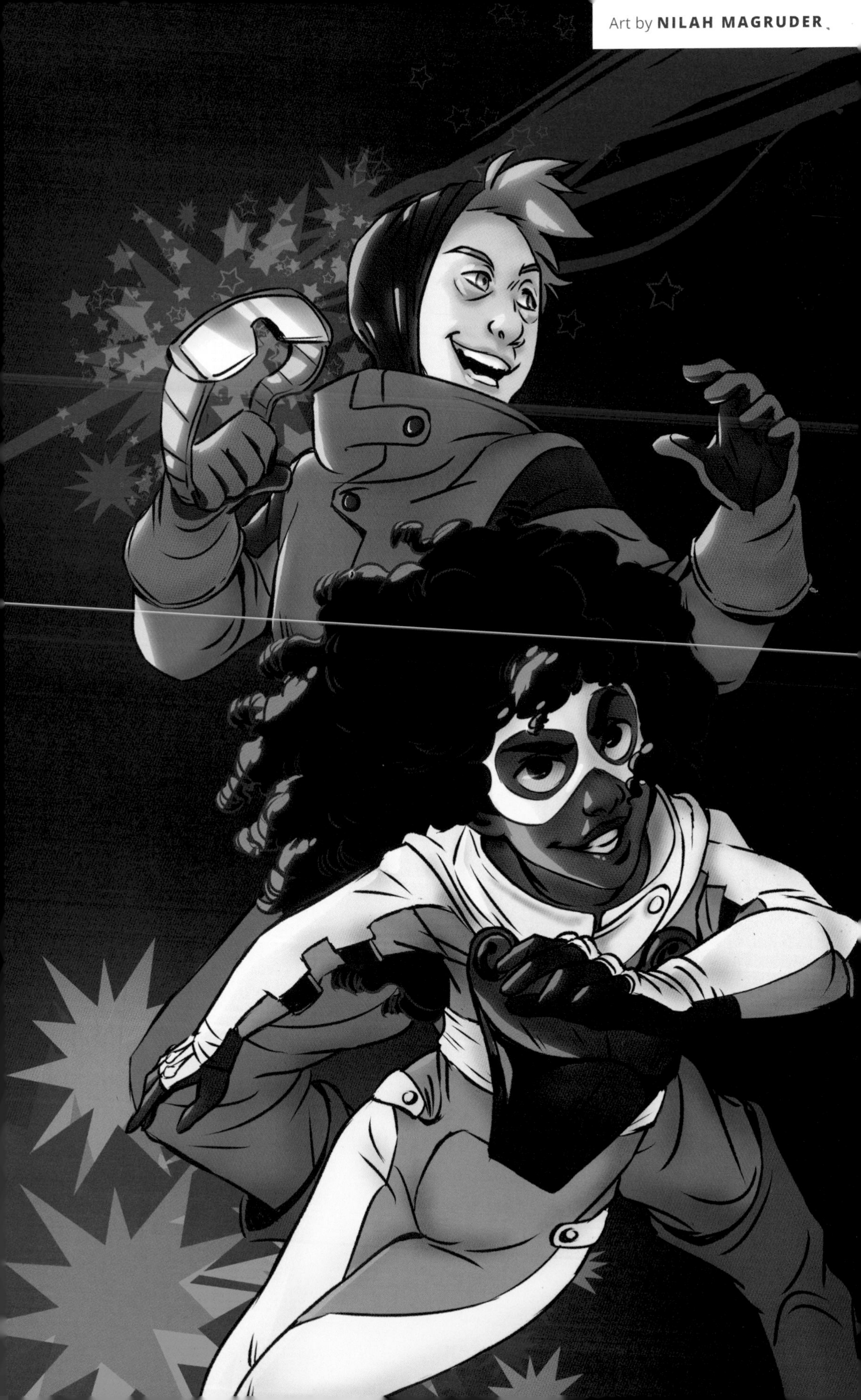

Art by **NILAH MAGRUDER**

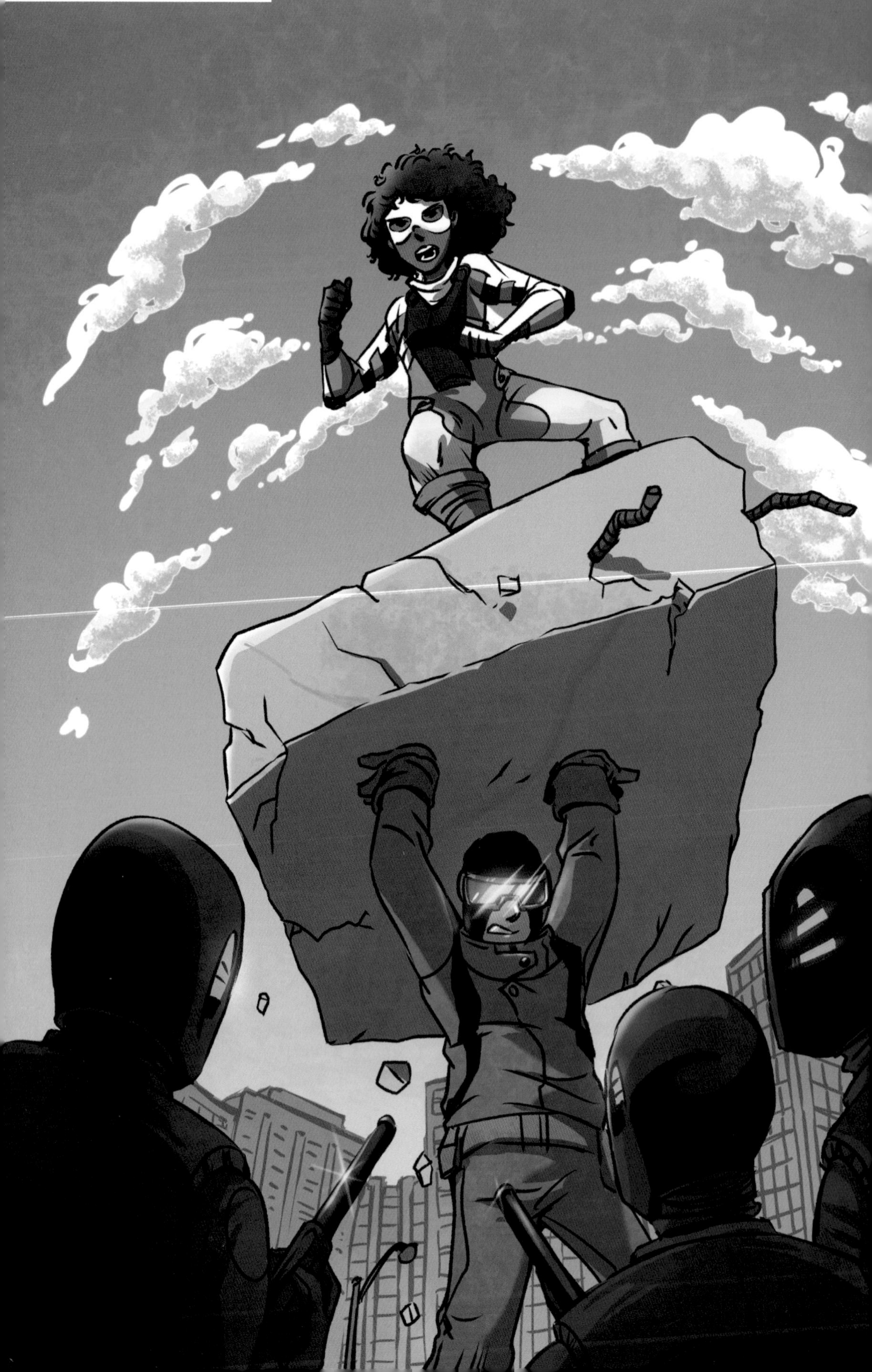

Art by **NILAH MAGRUDER**

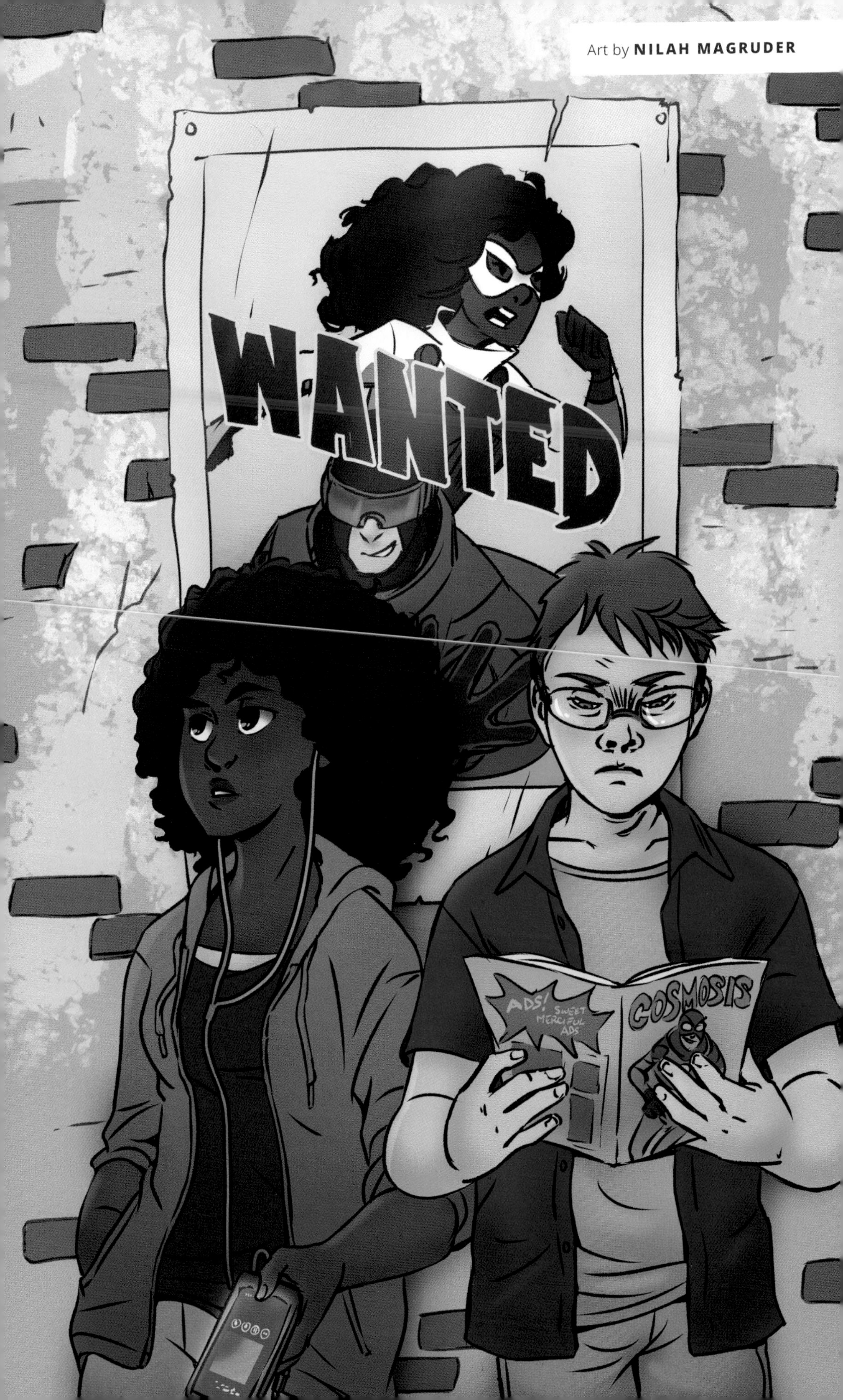
WANTED
ADS! SWEET MERCIFUL ADS
COSMOSIS

Art by **ANTHONY PIPER**

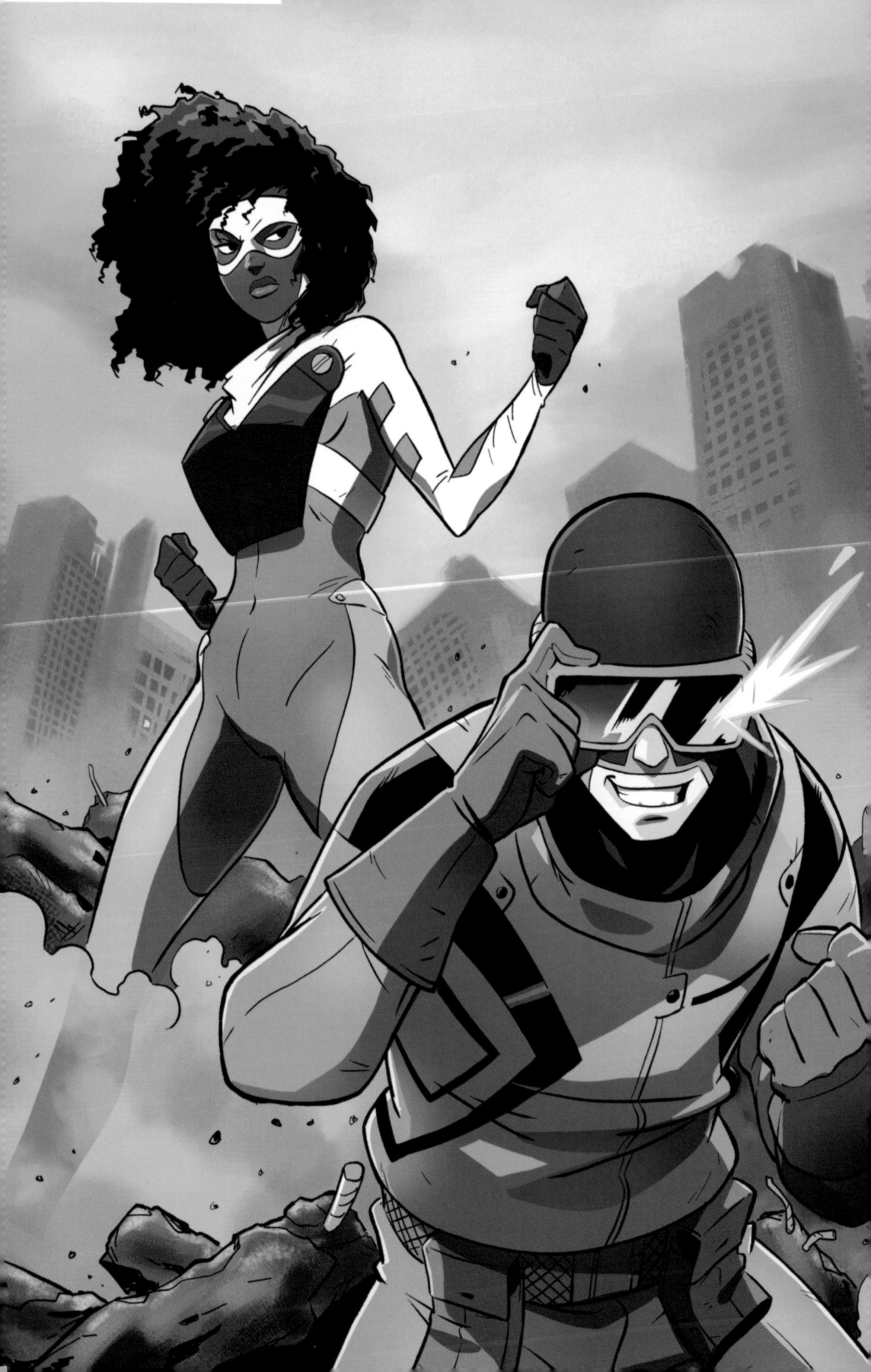

Art by **ANTHONY PIPER**

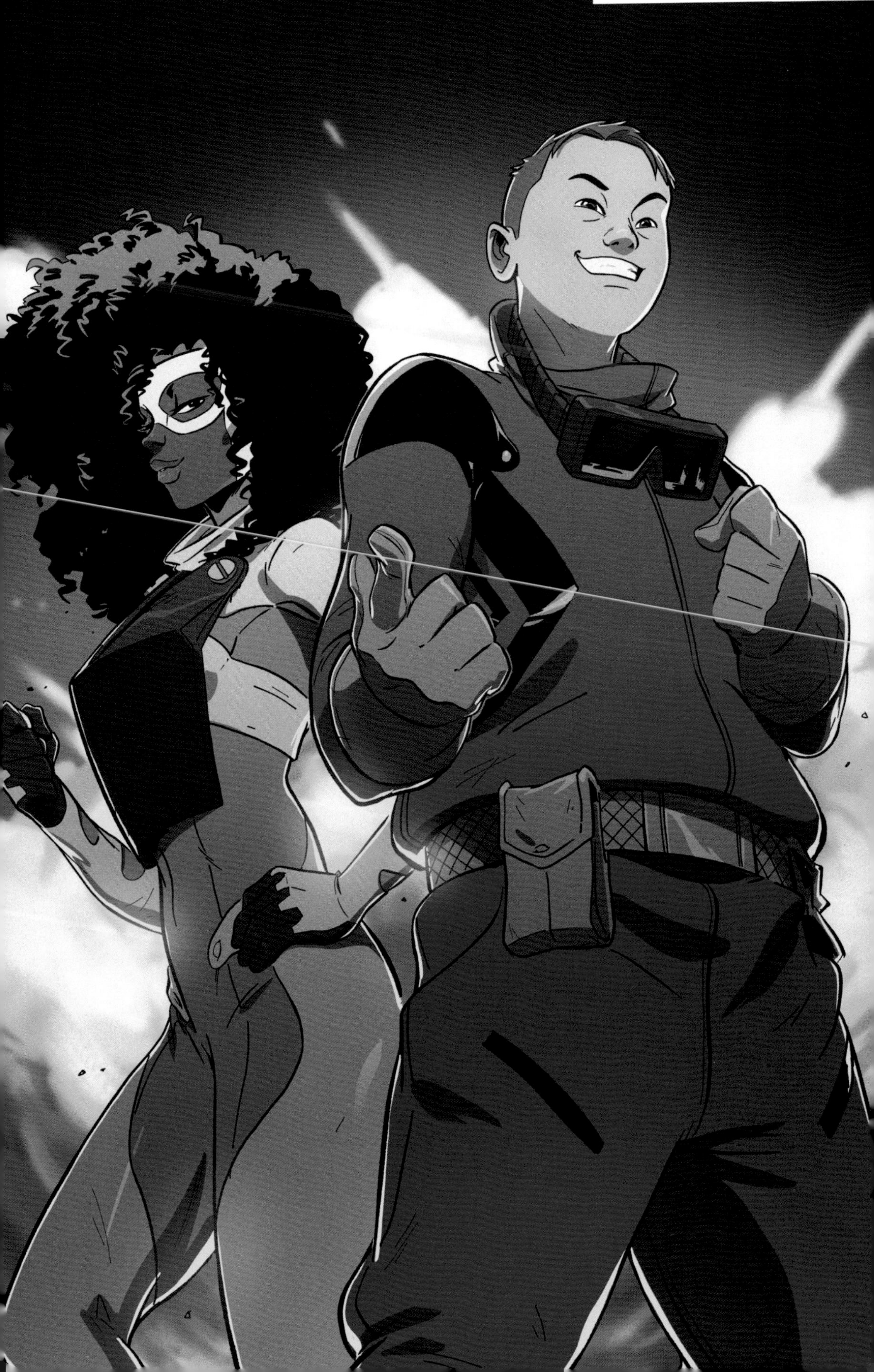

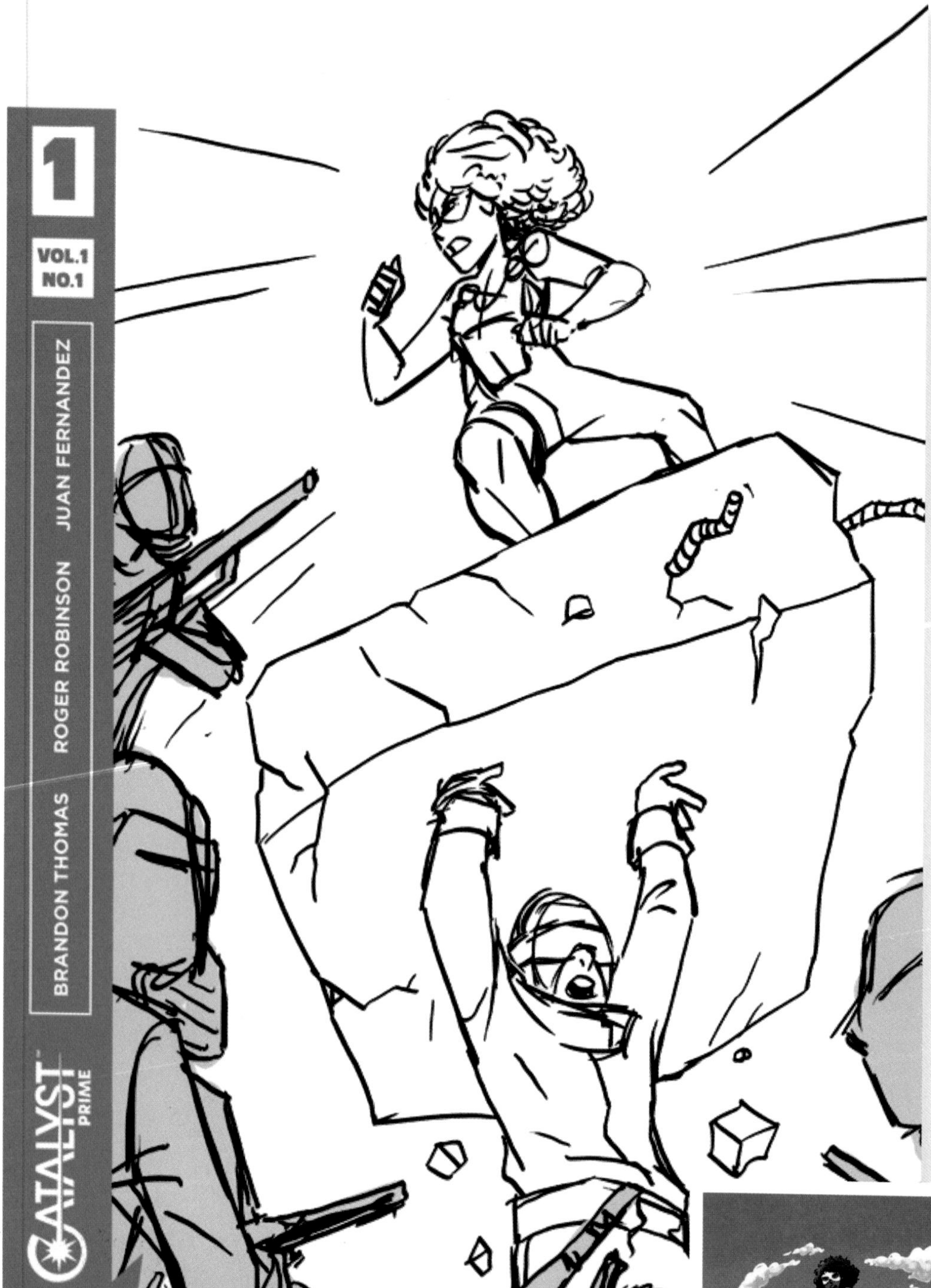
1
VOL.1
NO.1
BRANDON THOMAS
ROGER ROBINSON
JUAN FERNANDEZ
CATALYST
PRIME

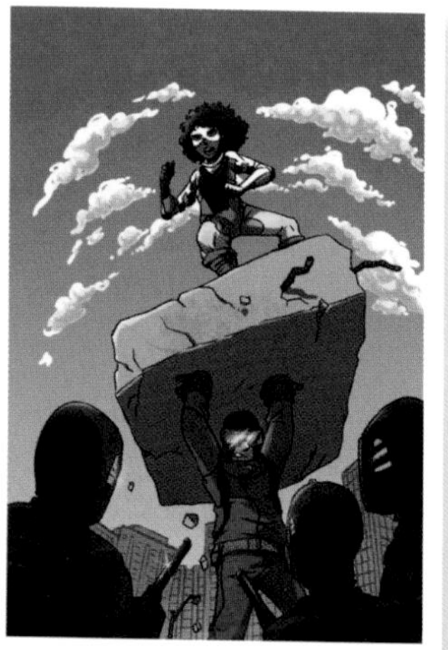

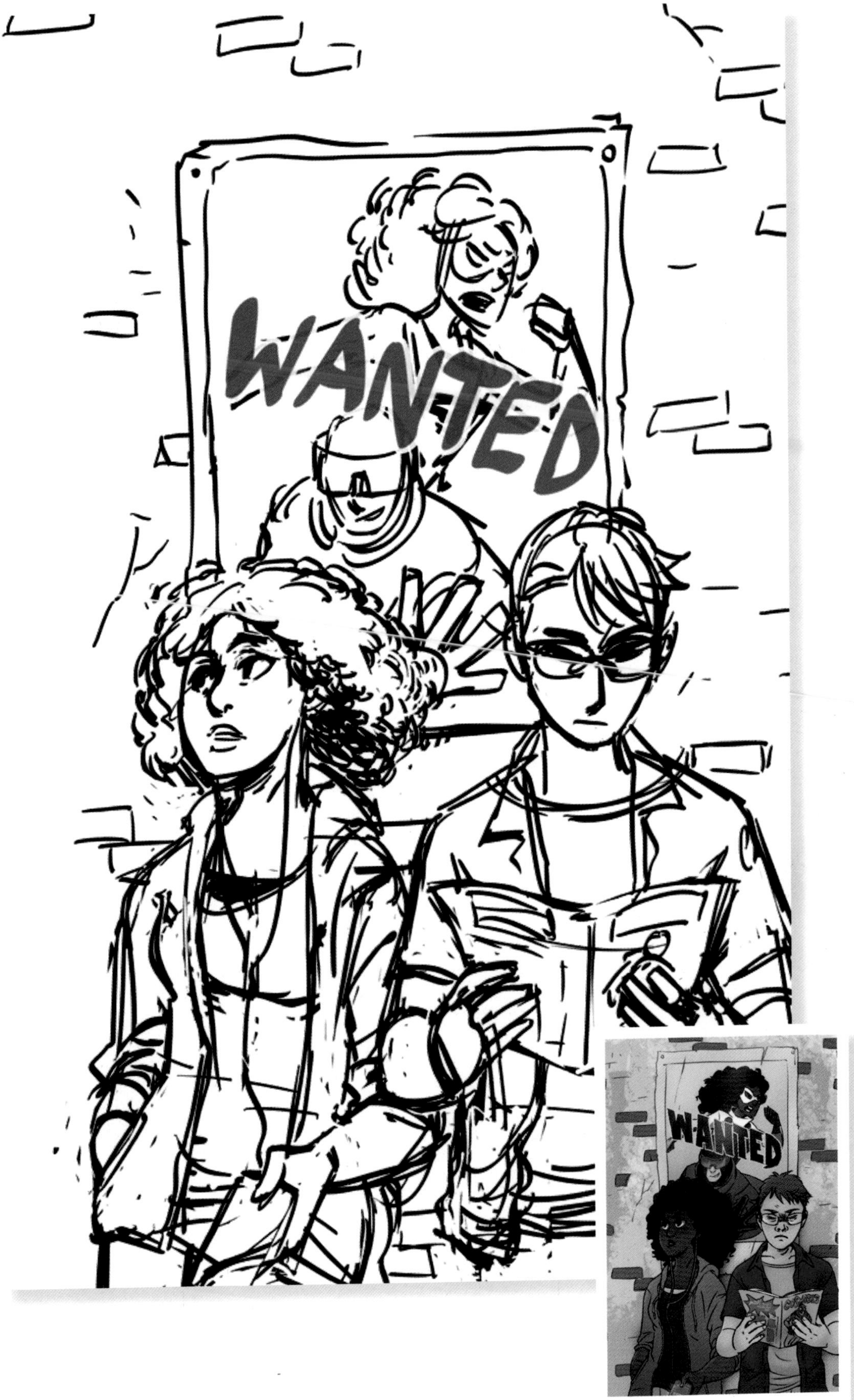
WANTED

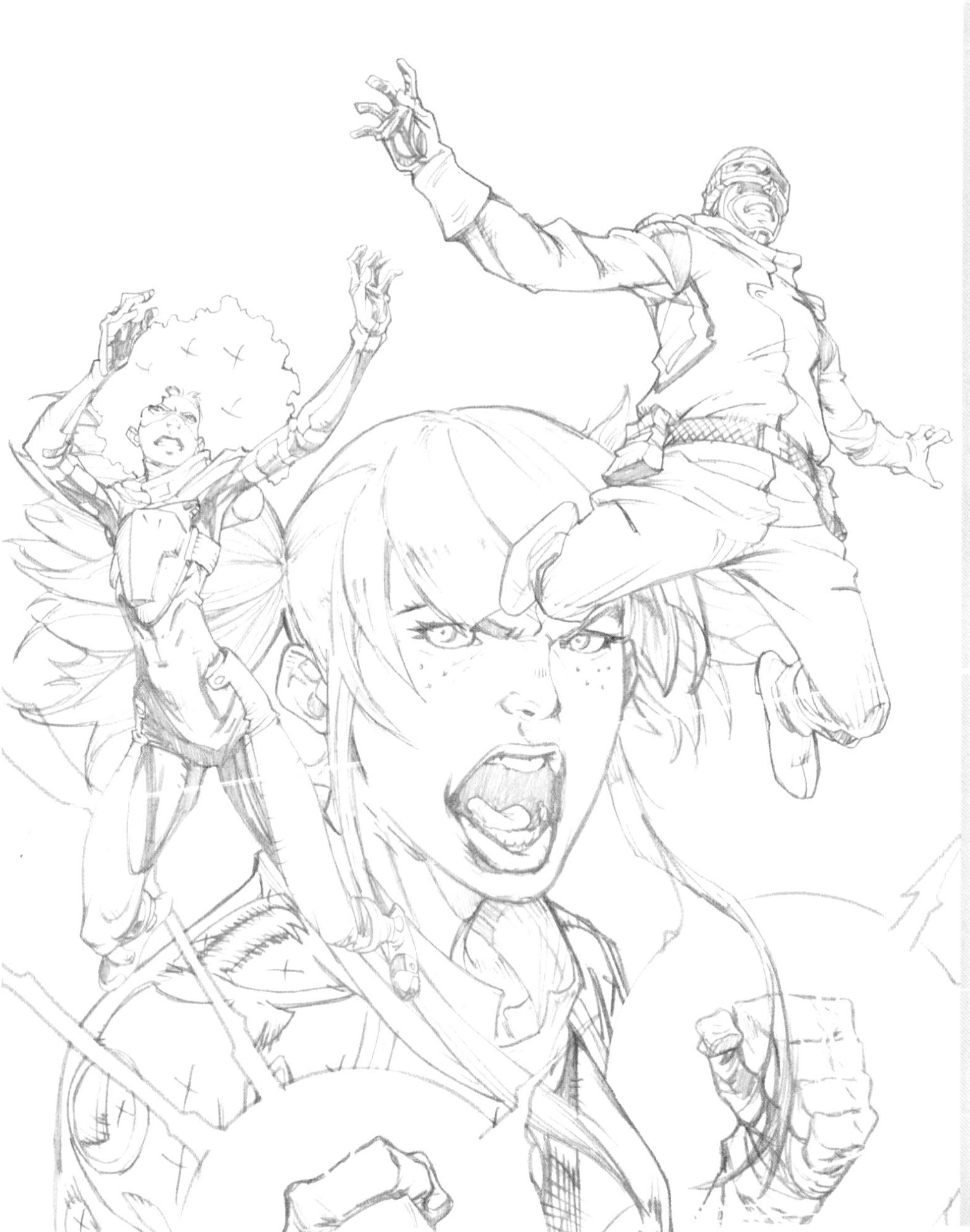

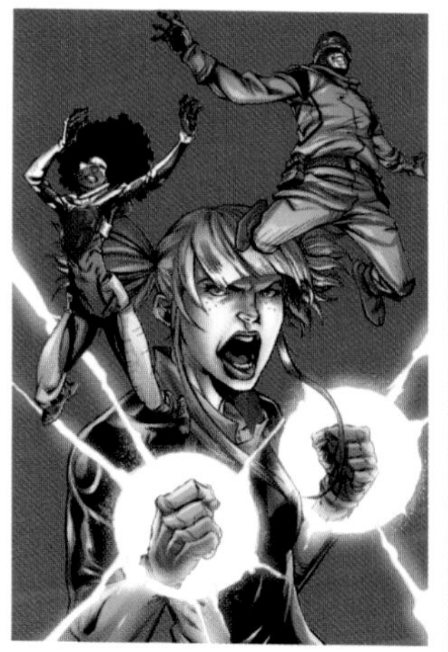

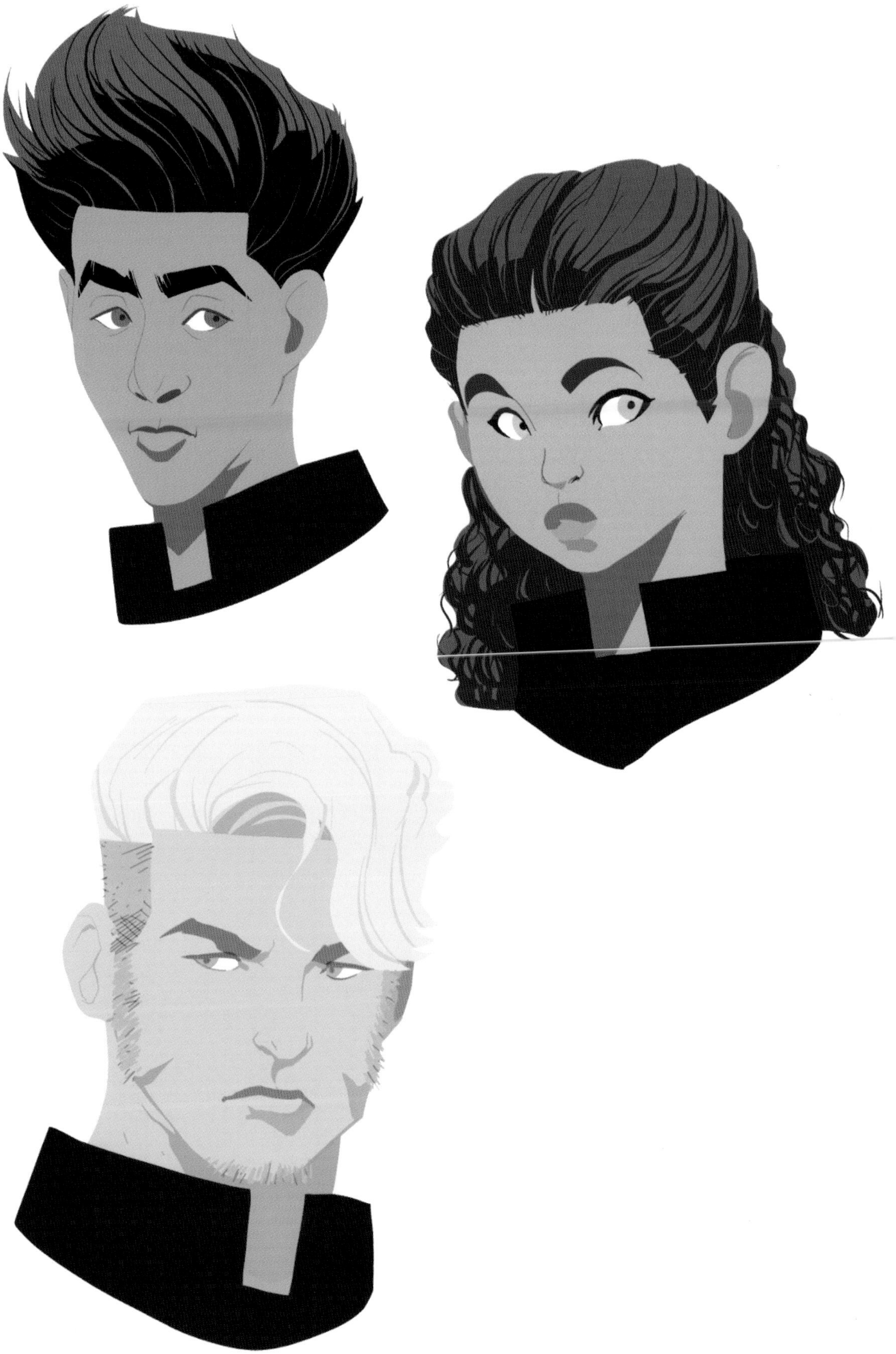

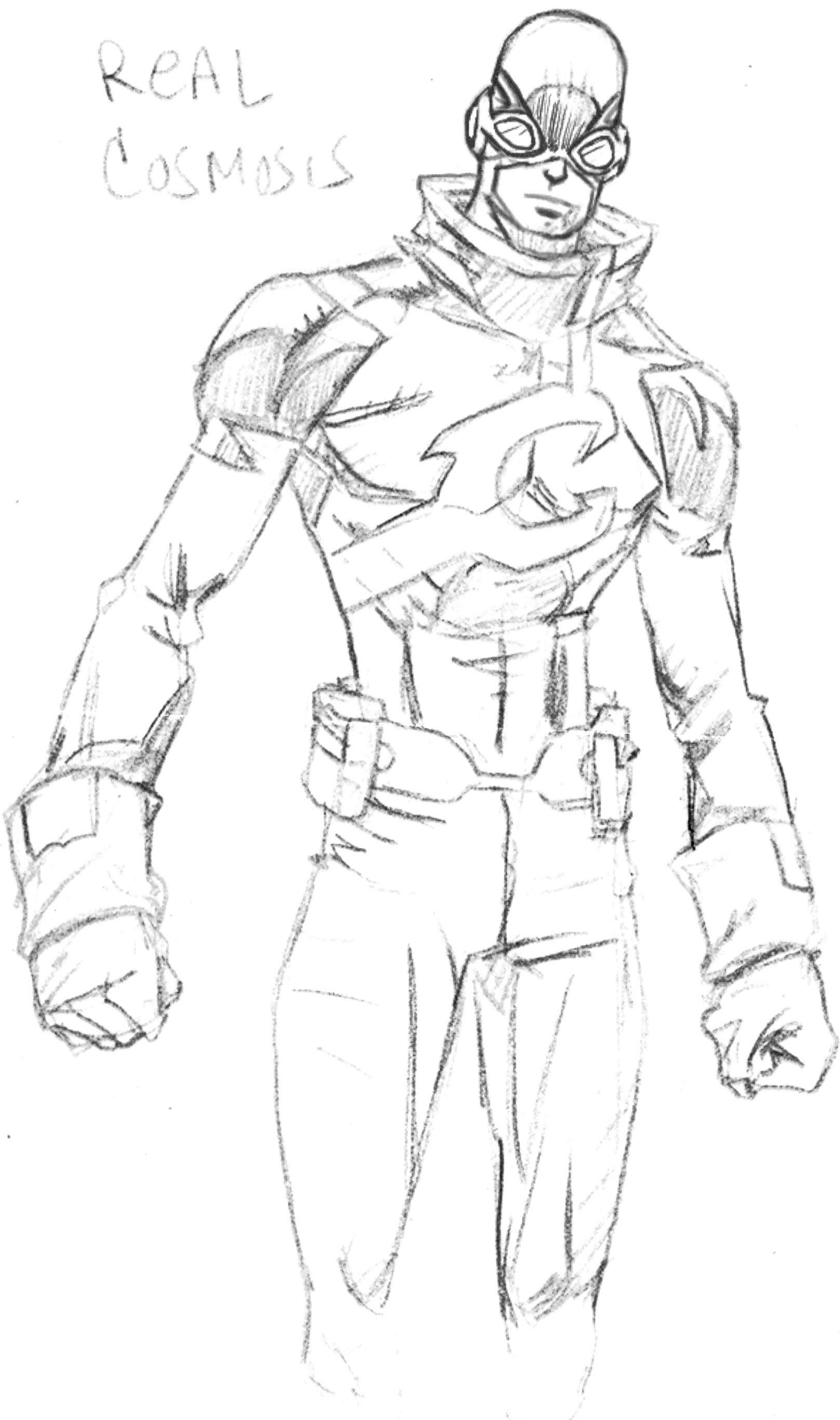
REAL
COSMOSIS